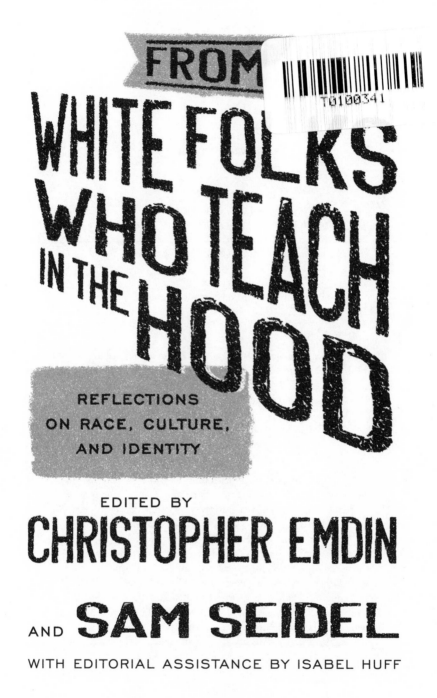

FROM WHITE FOLKS WHO TEACH IN THE HOOD

REFLECTIONS ON RACE, CULTURE, AND IDENTITY

EDITED BY

CHRISTOPHER EMDIN

AND **SAM SEIDEL**

WITH EDITORIAL ASSISTANCE BY ISABEL HUFF

BEACON PRESS
BOSTON

BEACON PRESS
Boston, Massachusetts
www.beacon.org

Beacon Press books
are published under the auspices of
the Unitarian Universalist Association of Congregations.

27 26 25 24   8 7 6 5 4 3 2 1

This book is printed on acid-free paper that meets the uncoated paper
ANSI/NISO specifications for permanence as revised in 1992.

Text design and composition by Kim Arney

With additional assistance by Isabel Huff

Library of Congress Cataloging-in-Publication Data

Names: Emdin, Christopher, editor. |
Seidel, Samuel Steinberg, editor.
Title: From white folks who teach in the hood : reflections on race,
culture, and identity / edited by Christopher Emdin and Sam Seidel.
Description: Boston : Beacon Press, 2024. | Includes bibliographical
references. | Summary: "Progressive white educators on the challenges
and reimaginings of anti-racist education, cultural responsiveness, and
sustained liberatory learning practices" — Provided by publisher.
Identifiers: LCCN 2024001533 (print) | LCCN 2024001534 (ebook) |
ISBN 9780807006733 (paperback) | ISBN 9780807006740 (ebook)
Subjects: LCSH: Culturally-relevant pedagogy—United States. |
African Americans—Education—Social aspects. | Teachers,
White—United States. | Anti-racism—United States.
Classification: LCC LC1099.3 .F78 2024 (print) | LCC LC1099.3 (ebook) |
DDC 370.1170973—dc23/eng/20240228
LC record available at https://lccn.loc.gov/2024001533
LC ebook record available at https://lccn.loc.gov/2024001534

For Sydney, Malcolm, and Solamae

CONTENTS

WELCOMING

We do this work [to get ourselves] out of a sense of hopelessness,
sort of a desperation. Through that desperation we become addicted
[to the ways things have always been]. . . .

We feel we have nothing to lose. Everything to gain. So, we
offer you [these words, these stories.] What do you bring to the table?

—An educator's take on Jay-Z's "Can I Live"

Notice your impulses as you read this book. Perhaps there's an impulse to judge the authors, the actions they did or did not take in the stories they share, or their views of the world. Or perhaps your instinct is to excuse their decisions and perspectives. Or just to close the book and think about something else—anything else.

Whatever the impulse, we invite you to interrogate it: Why do I need to find fault in these contributors? Why am I rushing to make excuses for someone I don't even know? Why don't I want to engage with this text?

You may have been drawn to this book for a diverse set of reasons. As the personal statements on the following pages share, the two of us had specific reasons for wanting to create it. But whatever brought you to these pages, we are glad you are here.

Addressing the impacts of racism on urban students is a complex knot of work that may never be completely untangled. But it absolutely needs to be removed. If we accept that we all have some part in it—however different those parts might look—then we each have some crucial strand of work to do. What's yours?

FROM CHRIS

When I wrote *For White Folks Who Teach in the Hood . . . and the Rest of Y'all Too*, I received hundreds of letters and emails. Many of them came from people in the field of education who were inspired by the book and found value in the stories, techniques, and critiques that I shared from my work in the US school system. Some came from teachers who saw themselves in the book and were motivated to transform their teaching. Most came from people (who mostly had not read the full book) that accused me of being racist. The more mild communications carried a sentiment captured in one of the emails I received that asked, "How dare you, as a Black man who may have experienced racism, attack white teachers who are teaching kids that no one else wants to teach?" Others included personal insults and attempts to undermine my (extensive) academic credentials and teaching expertise. They threw around terms like "reverse racism" and "race baiting." The most intriguing messages were around my use of the words "white folks." I had no idea that calling white teachers "white" would conjure up such anger. I was simply naming something any mirror could tell a white person and offering some insight and perspective on teaching that white teachers had been shielded from in teacher-prep programs or in life in general. What that book was doing, and what I continue to do, is offer a critique of a system that has robbed the majority of teachers in our country of the opportunity to reflect on their whiteness and how it impacts the children they are charged with teaching. As the title of the book reflected, my work is as much for white folks as it is for "the rest of y'all too." Everybody holds gradients of white supremacist ideologies and problematic pedagogies in their psyche. We live in a world that demonizes Black bodies and frames other people's children like wards of the state who are under the care/protection/ instruction of teachers who are grossly underprepared for the task at hand. If these children have black or brown skin, the likelihood of their mistreatment under the supervision of the state's employees is high. Endless statistics related to miseducation, suspension, and incarceration tell us this. I am simply saying that if a majority of the teachers so happen to be white and the majority of those harmed by these teachers so happen to be Black, there is something worth exploring here. Inequity is not coincidence, and consistent harm is not accidental. We need to explore what is going wrong and name what is going right. I think most folks who send me letters understand the necessity of identifying what is working and what isn't. What they have an issue with is the honesty with which that message is being conveyed and who is saying it. Any scholar calling out the reality that teachers have been generally ineffective in reaching young people in urban schools is generally acceptable. A Black scholar calling out white teachers as underprepared for teaching in urban schools is seen as offensive. Any scholar naming research-based techniques for improving teaching in urban settings is acceptable. A Black scholar naming research-based techniques for improving teaching in urban settings that are rooted in culture and community knowledge that most white teachers do not naturally have is offensive. So, because it has been framed as problematic when I share the truth about where we need to go to transform urban education, I offer you *From White Folks Who Teach in the Hood*, a collection of essays from white teachers who have worked in urban America and who offer insights, perspectives, and truths about what they have seen and experienced in urban education. They write about their unpreparedness, challenges and experiences with how to successfully teach Black and Brown children.

This is not a celebration of white saviors or heroes. This is not a propping up of white bodies who claim to have devoted themselves to the greater cause of making urban youth "be better." It is a highlighting of those who may not share the same cultural and ethnic backgrounds as their students but come to this work recognizing that. It is a constellation of stories and experiences from people owning their privilege while recognizing that we can only approach this work of making schools better with humility and radical truth.

FROM SAM

When I was a high school student, there was a full-length mirror directly outside the door of my bedroom. Every morning, I'd step out of my room and immediately wrench my neck to the left to avoid seeing my reflection. Like so many adolescents, I was self-conscious about my appearance. I had found that when I looked in the mirror, I'd notice things I thought were ugly, like my crooked front tooth. Hours later at school, someone would say something funny in class, and I'd do this awkward closed-mouth grin. When I skipped studying my reflection for a few days, I'd ease up during the day and let myself genuinely laugh with a relaxed face. In a weird way, not looking at myself too much allowed me to be more fully myself. But when does that teenage mirror-dodging shift from a healthy adolescent action into an unhealthy adult avoidance?

Like the contributors to this volume, I am a white educator who has taught in what many call "the hood." And I don't know how to talk about it fully. I can tell stories, I can offer systemic critiques, and I can shine a light on promising practices. But when it comes time to turn that light around and shine it on myself, opaque shadows abound.

While working on this volume, I had video conversations with all the contributors. The most common piece of feedback I gave was actually a question: *Where are you in this piece?* By and large, our contributors knew (how) to talk about race and racism, knew (how) to challenge systems of oppression, and knew (how) to recognize and celebrate their Black and Brown students' brilliance . . . but still didn't know how to talk about themselves.

I'm saying "them" here, but including myself would be more accurate. We still don't know how to put words to the ways our whiteness shows up when we are with our students, and we still don't know how to put words to the ways our whiteness shows up when they are not around.

Twelve years ago, I wrote *Hip Hop Genius*, a book about hip-hop culture and education, which talked extensively about Black culture and extensively about racism, and only in the closing note right before the index did I even mention my whiteness. I was intentionally not centering it because I believed there were enough coming-of-rage stories by white authors about the violence enacted on Black and Brown young people by our country's education system, and I believed my whiteness should not get in the way of the important story of a Black-led school. But I was also avoiding it because I didn't know how to do it.

After *Hip Hop Genius* came out, I spent several years giving keynotes and facilitating professional development sessions with educators. I started to notice a pattern: Black administrators in districts that primarily served Black and Brown students were inviting me to talk to their teachers and school leaders who were primarily white. Through prep calls and dinners at local restaurants after long days of facilitation, I learned that while they were interested in me sharing ideas about hip-hop pedagogy and project-based learning, they were also hungry for me to talk with their educators about building authentic relationships across racial and cultural divides. They were keen for me to model how to be a white educator who is comfortable thinking and talking about race. Mind you, this was not what I thought I'd been writing and talking about, but I came to understand that it was one of the things these readers and listeners were finding most relevant and necessary.

This realization led to several years of relative quiet for me. I knew that before I picked up the mic again, I had work to do—interrogating my own racial identity and how it shows up in my work and writing, and trying to figure out how to talk critically and productively (and not-too-annoyingly!) about (my) whiteness. If that's what was most needed, I wanted to figure out how to do it well before taking up any more airspace.

When I would point out to our contributors on this volume that they had dissected racism in their school with surgical precision or described their work with Black and Brown students in vivid detail *without ever mentioning their own whiteness* (which was a central goal of this project), they would apologize and confess that they did not quite know how to do it. My response would always be that this is the exact reason we are creating this book: to learn how to do this, *together*. Unfortunately, even among those of us who work explicitly on issues related to race, most of us have not exercised these muscles; and it shows and slows progress.

As someone who has deliberately tried to build those muscles—through things like racial justice courses, trainings specifically for "white allies," and one-on-one equity-leadership coaching—working on this book has been an essential puzzle piece in seeing how my whiteness shows up in my work as an educator. I can guarantee that neither I nor any of the contributors have any aspect of this fully figured out. But I know that we will move through the world with distorted images of ourselves and awkward closed-mouth smiles unless we build up our ability to look in the mirror.

PART ONE

REFLECTING ON EARLY-CAREER EXPERIENCES

We begin this book with a series of essays from white teachers reflecting on how they began their careers: From their upbringings to interactions with BIPOC students and colleagues to diversity, equity, and inclusion (DEI) trainings. From reading books to help them make sense of their whiteness to engaging in self-reflection practices. Each of these educators shares stories of how they learned about race, racism, and teaching in the context of identity and cultural differences from their students. These stories of learning raise many important questions: How are white people who come from racist and unsupportive families supposed to learn about these things? How do white educators learn valuable lessons not at the expense or "invisible labor" of Black and Brown students and educators? What are the potential benefits and limitations of DEI trainings for (white) educators? These are not questions that the chapters answer per se. They are the questions the authors provoke, and their writings may offer some path toward your discovery of answers to these questions in your own work.

The contributors represent different types of schools, different geographies, different durations of experience in the classroom, and different depths of experience in interrogating their whiteness. We believe it is important to hear and engage with all these voices.

As they have gotten deeper into their careers, the contributors in this section have found multiple ways to bang on the education system: They are engaging in self-change work, classroom-change work, and institutional-change work. They are taking themselves out of the school and into the surrounding communities, and they are inviting members of the surrounding communities into their classrooms.

Ultimately, they all return to *care* and *listening* as the baseline of good teaching. This orientation resonates deeply with us, *and* we find ourselves questioning how this sits with the necessity of not just being what Zaretta Hammond and Judith Kleinfeld would call "sentimentalists" who prioritize caring for students, but being what they would call "warm demanders" who are willing and able to push through discomfort to make sure our babies are learning.

CAN WE WATER OUR STUDENTS
AND OURSELVES AT THE SAME TIME?

– Maya Park –

"In watering my students," says Cliff Alexander, "I am watering myself."

Cliff is a twenty-five-year-old Black man from Detroit. He is beginning his fourth year teaching at a Brooklyn charter middle school. He is known to carry a foot-high stack of student packets topped with Styrofoam plates of cafeteria chicken nuggets down the hallway. Despite his load, he almost always pauses to look you in the eye and ask, "Are you okay?"

It is August of 2018, my third year teaching, and our school's whole staff sits in professional development. The podcast we've just listened to dispels the dominant (and racist) narrative that *Brown v. Board of Education* had predominantly positive impacts on Black students and educators. Before integration, the podcast explains, Black schools were havens of celebrating Blackness, where teachers saw themselves in their students and students saw themselves in their teachers. The call for integration presumed white schools to be supreme, for whiteness was supreme. Black educators who had been loving and growing Black students for decades lost their jobs in droves as Black students walked into school buildings where teachers did not look like them. White teachers did not see themselves in Black students and often failed to love Black students and foster their growth in the ways they did with students they empathized with. Hearing this story, Cliff Alexander promised to remember that as a Black educator, his work to heal himself and his students are intertwined.

People breathe audibly around the room, *mm*-ing and snapping to affirm his words and join his dedication. But there is a tension, a wondering, lingering in the white bodies in the room.

Is *our* healing, we wonder, intertwined with that of our students? Could we water ourselves and our students at the same time? Or might our investment in caring for ourselves exacerbate the divide between the privilege we represent and the oppression we aim to obliterate? Perhaps we are obstacles to our school growing into a haven for Black joy, learning, and liberation. If so, wouldn't it be best to drain ourselves into our students and then disappear? If we water our students with all the water we have and have none left for ourselves, does that make us the best kind of white people? The kind who achieve perfection through a commitment to depleting ourselves?

Why did we fear that our place as white educators of Black students did not include healing but rather centered on the perfection of our craft? And how did the craving for perfection lead us to view ourselves through a deficit lens in which we search for the problems with ourselves and our classrooms that we need to fix, rather than through an asset lens in which we delight in the strengths of ourselves and our students?

I came into teaching wary of the white-savior dynamic perpetuated by teacher-preparation programs around the country that presume that white people—particularly those who had graduated from elite universities—would be an automatic asset in predominantly Black schools where poverty was prevalent. This notion both fails to see the strengths students in those schools possess and implies that the problem is teachers who have been there for years, rather than a broad scale divestment from Black life and learning. I knew from the beginning that I was not automatically an asset to my students; I was barely ten years older than them and I didn't yet know what love looked like in the classroom. I knew that my flaws and failures as I learned would hurt children, and I worked hard to reduce that harm by trying to be as flawless as possible.

Exhaustion swelled the pressure I felt toward perfection. As did adages like "Get this done before Friday so you can really enjoy your weekend!" for they made pouring into my students and pouring into myself sound mutually exclusive rather than mutually constitutive. For white educators of Black and Brown students, I find this false competition between meeting students' needs and meeting your own needs can feel especially true. School leaders may ask for extra work from staff with the rationale "It's for the kids," leveraging our white guilt in service of our consensual exploitation. I and many other white teachers I know have thus—perhaps unconsciously—created equations that pit the energy we pour into our students against the energy we pour into ourselves as if it is a zero-sum game.

"What our students are seeing," says Melika Butcher, "is the triumph of white mediocrity."

In November of my first year teaching, our staff sits in a circle in a bar where our principal has convened us in order to process the day after the 2016 election. Melika is a Black educator and school leader who grew up in East New York. She turns every moment in a classroom into an opportunity to affirm young people, whether they are looking at another student in order to actively listen or simply passing in their exit ticket. Students and teachers alike straighten up when Melika walks in their room because they want her to know they are exactly as brilliant as she believes them to be.

Just as our students see white mediocrity in the highest office of the United States, Melika says, they see it in our school building with white staff who are not doing their jobs effectively. As our BIPOC colleagues either work constantly to maintain a reliable reputation or are disciplined for their imperfections, Melika points out, white people in our school and everywhere can be mediocre with impunity. While I had already known that my poor teaching was harmful, from that night on, I saw my imperfections as a teacher as inseparable from my racism. Perfectionism would become my tool against racism.

I make twenty-five family contacts per week. On self-evaluation rubrics, I grade myself low so that I won't face the humiliation of thinking more highly of myself than someone else does of me. I invite more experienced teachers to my class to give me feedback. I visit the assistant principal to plan and practice my questioning sequences. I give "packet perfection grades" in which I skim through each student packet and spot-check ten distinct parts I expected to be complete. If I must fail, at least I might build a reputation as tirelessly dedicated to growing and learning and trying.

No matter how hard I worked though, when I looked at my classroom in those early years, all I could see was its distance from perfection. When two students out of thirty-two were disengaged, their faces lingered in my mind as I walked out of class. Even the students who did everything I expected of them provided evidence of my deficiencies. When Aaliyah Hernandez[1] tried desperately to make every single different kind of annotation I had instructed students to make on a standardized exam in the hope that it would help them all earn proficient scores, she ran out of time without finishing the test. I clung to my students' proficiency as if it would demonstrate that I was not white mediocrity. Meanwhile, Aaliyah was near tears.

In an exasperated attempt to create firmness for Deiondre Williams, whom I feared I had failed by being too soft, I once kneeled down next to him, looked him in the eye, and told him it was pathetic that he had not written anything on his paper. It wasn't until I told my friend I had done this and saw the shock on my friend's face that I registered how deeply confused I had become about imperfection. As I tried desperately to evade perpetuating racism by overworking myself, I was deteriorating internally in ways I wouldn't acknowledge, for I told myself a story that my self-deprivation was what my students deserved. What I missed was that when I am depleted, I find it is incredibly challenging to protect students from being infected with that depletion.

My imperfection was my humanity. So was Deiondre's. To pursue perfection was to dehumanize us both.

"Whether you like it or not," warns my graduate professor Steve Mahoney, "teaching is going to be a lot like therapy."

I could never have fathomed that one day I would refer to a student's work as pathetic. This was a version of me that I didn't recognize. In July 2016, I stand in a closing circle at the end of my first summer-teaching assignment. My graduate school cohort of eighteen listens expectantly to our professors as we prepare to embark on our first full year of teaching in different cities. With his bowtie slightly crooked, one professor warns us that, like therapy, teaching will reveal to us things that we'd managed hitherto to hide—from ourselves as well as others. Whether or not we intended, our classrooms would become reflections of our internal world.

Because of this, white teachers' self-loathing is one of our most dangerous weapons. As a cis white woman, I tend to apologize for existing even though most of the world welcomes me. I expertly find a way to make anything bad that happens my fault. Both of these characteristics have gotten me into trouble as a teacher. While it is imperative for me to analyze the ways that my students' challenges reveal my own gaps as an educator, overestimating my own responsibility perpetuates white supremacy by denying my students the agency of their own choices.

Further, the notion that I can take responsibility for my classroom in a way that absolves my students of responsibility tends to backfire. I've found that when I am in a place of self-blame, I'm in a place of blaming everybody rather than thinking clearly. *How could I have . . .* quickly turns into *Well, because they . . .* , and *It's all my fault . . .* sits right next to *But actually I wouldn't have had to do that if they hadn't . . .* in the eternal shame-blame spiral.

I want to model owning my power in the process of dismantling oppressive structures to encourage students to own theirs. And yet, if I tell myself a story that I'm the one shield standing between students and the ubiquitous forces of oppression, not only am I blowing my significance out of proportion, but I am also guaranteed to feel like I'm falling short. And as long as I feel like I'm always falling short, my classroom will be a space in which *always falling short* is in the air for students to inhale. My continued mistake was to believe I could separate myself from my students. I overestimated my ability to protect them from the self-cruelty, critique, and apology that I allowed to infect me. In believing I could create and use my perfection to set my students free, I rendered myself a glorified and guilty white savior.

"I'm not trying to silence any of my people," Dioni Daley says. "But Black people have been the only ones speaking, and I'd like to hear from some of the white staff."

March 2020. Zoom. Ahmaud Arbery has been murdered, but Breonna Taylor and George Floyd have not yet been. We sit in a virtual staff meeting from our homes, and Dioni, a Black teacher with a love for cartwheels in the Teacher Work Room, once again takes responsibility for naming the tension of whiteness and white silence about Blackness in a space for Black children. Our fear of saying the wrong thing is miles beside the point when juxtaposed with the Black death that results from white fear and ignorance daily. Weeks later, when another Black woman invites BIPOC staff to a processing space about Breonna Taylor and George Floyd, she adds a line at the end, "For Non-POCs, I invite you to utilize this resource to start your own conversation," and linked a database of anti-racism resources.

Within an hour of receiving that message, a white colleague replies to all recipients: "Today at 5PM my Zoom room will be open for the white staff to process the recent events and begin some anti-racist work." Those of us who show up that evening pick an afternoon a week later when we will meet again. And again. What begins is disorganized. We know we have an aim but can't put our finger on exactly what it is. We are groundless. Sitting in the reality. Fumbling, we are tempted to see our presence at our school as inherently problematic, as an obstacle to the liberation of our students. But we can't go back to hiding behind problematizing ourselves. Our Black colleagues are tired of our silence. We need to buck up.

We decide the most concrete thing we can do is continue to show up. Not just to our jobs but to a space dedicated specifically to white people collaborating to uproot our racism, together. We agree that all white staff will meet each week over the summer. We have a lot of unlearning to do. As we work, we find that our racism is tethered to myriad learned behaviors installed within us, the way necklaces are tethered to others in a tangled pile of jewelry; you can't extricate one necklace without coaxing each individual chain and hook. We can't just unlearn our whiteness. We have to unlearn our supremacy.

"I'm curious why no one is speaking," I say, attempting to sound more curious than anxious.

"Because we have no direction," replies Cooper Davis.

On a Tuesday morning in June 2020, I stand in the sun on my roof as I co-facilitate our first mandatory white staff meeting of the summer. The perfectionist in me panics. How could I have asked a question that gave people no direction? Well, because they're supposed to be taking initiative to not be silent anymore and actively create and commit to moving in a new direction. It's all my fault, though. I took responsibility for planning this session, and now I've asked a vague question and people are confused. But actually I wouldn't have had to do that if they hadn't been silent in all the other staff meetings in the first place such that our colleagues of color don't trust us.

And suddenly, it is clear that so much of the harm I've caused children with my perfectionism doesn't even require children's presence to be activated. All I need is one other human to seemingly feel anything other than absolute delight with me or to not be impressed with what I'm producing to launch me into my shame-blame spiral. It begins to dawn on each of us that a lot of the work we need to do together actually isn't in what needs to be produced but in the way that we engage with that production. As we notice things happening in our bodies, hearts, and minds when faced with tension in this nascent classroom we've created, we learn about our tendencies in the classrooms we co-create with children. In a sense, we do have "no direction." We need to be still for a spell and notice all the movement and noise within us when there is nowhere to go.

As we notice that noise, we also read about tenets of white supremacy culture like perfectionism, urgency, either/or thinking, only-one-right-way thinking, and power hoarding. We start to recognize the movement and noise that arises in stillness as pieces of white supremacy culture come alive within us.

Me? I notice myself constantly craving affirmation for what I say or write during the group meeting. I have to confront that I'm waiting for people to tell me I am enough. Which means that I'm often looking to my students to affirm my worth, and I'm implicitly positioning myself as an arbiter of theirs. I notice that white supremacy has installed in me the sense that I am destined for some kind of zenith, that I always have the potential to be as high up as possible. I begin to track every time that a part of me feels better than someone else because I've written more, or referenced books I've read outside our required readings, or because the idea I proposed becomes the plan for the session. I register how quick the comedown is when I hear one word that makes me feel unseen or misunderstood.

We move at the speed of trust. We spend two extra weeks co-creating guiding principles. We close each session with time for teachers to write feedback to everyone in the group as well as our gratitude for one another, and then have one person share their gratitude publicly. We open each meeting by sharing some of the prior week's gratitude. We name trends in feedback we received and offer our plan for responding. We reflect on a moment of tension from the prior week. I tell the group that when Cooper said, "We have no direction," I noticed myself feeling attacked and that my perfectionist parts began to freak out. I texted him ahead of time so that he would know my purpose in sharing was not to accuse him of anything but rather to give a window into how I process a situation in which I feel responsible for people's learning.

We write about the ways white supremacy has impacted us. As I see the guilt and cruelty with which my colleagues speak to and about themselves, it becomes increasingly clear to me how intertwined our ability to oppress our students is with our tendencies to deplete ourselves in the name of serving them. Despite the pain people are in, most write about their privilege, at first. We are hesitant to claim the ways that white supremacy harms us too, the way we harm and dehumanize ourselves, too, by being racist. Our instinct is still to atone, to apologize for the ways we have benefitted from an oppressive system.

To apologize for being there. My instinct is to fight them. How could they not realize we can't see ourselves as separate from our BIPOC colleagues even though we are obviously experiencing racism differently? Apply my perfection here. Radiate it.

Instead, I decide not to be sorry to be there. I decide to make "there" a place I want to be. I practice leading the space with gratitude for people bringing all they have to give, with love for the deep care people have for each other and our students and all Black people, and with keen awareness of how smart and full of contribution each person is in their own way. I realize I have never before led a class with unconditional love. I taste my voice in a learning space as someone who sees what people do have to give, and I am someone who celebrates their contributions as a gift to the space, rather than someone who looks around the room at the liabilities that need to be navigated and the problems that need to be fixed.

Together, we enumerate the ways we know we've harmed our students. We stop hiding from the shame that engulfs us. We try to identify the root causes that enabled us to perpetuate that harm. We want to heal from the roots, to yank out the perfectionism that drove us to erase Joshua Brown or silence Kadidiatou Jefferson or shame Diego Wilson. We want to plant something else there instead. To heal from the roots requires sitting with the pain of knowing how much we've hurt students we meant to love. We sit with our failure as we resist the impulse to castigate ourselves, for we know now that the way we talk to ourselves will be the way we talk to children, whether we intend to or not.

We sit with the knowledge that if we are cruel to ourselves, even in an attempt to atone for our racism, our classrooms become spaces of cruelty. Free from the misconception that we can separate ourselves from our students, our fight from theirs, we can no longer wishfully think this cruelty will stop when we are speaking to children instead of ourselves. We begin to embrace that if the roots of the harm we've done are deep in us, we, too, need to heal and free ourselves from our own internalized tenets of white supremacy culture. We need to learn to speak to ourselves in fundamentally different ways.

Come September 2020, I start my seventh-grade history class each day with a slide of three truths to honor in our space: (1) We all matter, and we all deserve to be listened to and loved no matter what we do/don't do. (2) We are already enough, and we are also always capable of growing. (3) When we

CAN WE WATER OUR STUDENTS AND OURSELVES AT THE SAME TIME? / 11

show up together, we will be okay. We need each other's commitment, support, and feedback.

We, white educators of Black students, do need to water ourselves and each other. And we need to trust that by doing so, we are also watering our students. We grow together.

HOW TO DRAW A PENIS AND OTHER LESSONS FROM A SPECIAL EDUCATION CLASSROOM

– Jamie Wilber –

There were penises everywhere. I'd turn on the projector and find no less than nine penciled penises on the back of the stand. There were penises on the desks. Microscopic penises on the faded yellow walls. Our only source of natural light came from the tiny window in the door where penises crept up the frame, threatening a blackout. If I left a dry-erase marker unattended, I'd find a giant penis on the whiteboard. It seemed these teenage boys were obsessed with their genitalia.

One day the breaking point came—two giant penises on the board. I picked up a marker and started drawing. The first penis became a freckled face with thick-framed glasses, a curly red fro, and a big toothy grin. The second became a rocket taking off, red and orange flames at the base.

Some days later, two students approached the whiteboard and grabbed a marker, each drawing a giant penis, but they didn't stop there; they kept adding until the penises were no longer penises. It was a phallic re-envisioning—artistic growth on full display. America's future architects were hard at work in my class. Clown faces and rocket ships were followed by skyscrapers, airplanes, and historical monuments. This was the beginning of the end of your average penis drawings.

We were operating in a school where anatomical drawings were a punishable offense. Most teachers would have written the students up, sent them to the dean, called their homes, or even suspended them for a doodle on a desk. I had done some of this (even when it didn't feel right) because it was expected and I didn't know what else to do. I was seen as weak or enabling if I handled things in any way that wasn't punitive. That was the school culture.

If I deescalated a conflict, the deans would arrive flustered to find "Wilber broke it up," shrugging their shoulders in bemusement, not knowing what to do now that there was no one to punish.

If, on the other hand, I kicked a student out of class, I'd be in the deans' office right after to talk to that student. Eventually, the day came when the deans decided I'd overstayed my welcome in the office. I had gone to speak with a student I'd sent to the office and was kicked out, told I couldn't talk to the student as the door closed in my face. The deans believed this kid needed to be punished, and my approach went against the school culture.

When a staff member's purse was taken, two of my students were blamed. I was shown blurry surveillance photos of dark figures. "It was them," one of the deans said. "Can't you tell?" said the other dean. No. I could not possibly identify those two shadowy blobs. Despite my reply, they were suspended and arrested.

I was in a school-culture nightmare—your classic example of a school centered on white supremacy funneling BIPOC students through the school-to-prison pipeline. It was a school of mostly white teachers and mostly Black and Brown students. It was a school of metal detectors, mandated school uniforms, and a predominately white administration with a "gotcha" mentality toward teachers and students. There were two choices: be obedient or be punished. This was true for students and for staff. Any sign of noncompliance or non-conformity was seen as an infraction. It was all punitive discipline and never anything close to restorative justice.

There were days I sat in an almost empty-arse classroom because most of my students had been suspended for some minor infraction. My students had targets on their backs. It didn't matter that they had Individualized Education Plans (IEPs) noting their personal struggles in following the school's "rules," or that parents could sue the Department of Education for not taking these legal documents into consideration when determining a student's fate. These Black and Brown students had been stigmatized and labeled troublemakers—the predominantly white administration was unable or unwilling to see them as anything else.

I quickly learned not to involve outsiders in my classroom. If one student was "wilding" out, I'd move the rest of the class to the hallway so we could go on with the lesson, until some authority figure would come by and say, "You can't do that."

It seemed anytime I tried something outside the box, I was told I wasn't allowed to do that. When some students were repeating a derogatory slur, I wanted to show a scene from *American History X* demonstrating the inherent harm of that slur but was told, "I think you know deep down it's not okay to show that" because it dropped a few F-bombs. Why was hearing the F-word worse than addressing racism and anti-Semitism? At first, I relented and did what I was told, but the slurs continued, so I closed the door and showed the clip anyway. The students' jaws dropped as they watched. When it was over, a student said, "I'm never going to say that word again." I learned to stop asking permission and follow my gut.

In the weeks that followed, after the rest of the school's staff and students went home, my students and I stayed late in our classroom, which wasn't really a classroom but rather was a larger computer lab now divided into two micro-classrooms, tucked away where no one could see us but the security cameras. We practiced spelling and vocabulary, read books aloud, worked on homework, and drew penis drawings that were no longer penis drawings.

Well, that's what I thought happened anyway until I revisited my journals and notebooks from that time. My memory of what had happened and what I found in those writings didn't match up. This story I concocted was all part of a white-savior fantasy—a narrative I created. I was revising my history. And why wouldn't I? It felt good to believe that in my first two years of teaching I was doing the best I could and killing it, that my heart was always in the right place. In my revisionist recollection I cast myself as some sort of *great white hope* (ol' Jim Jeffries would've been proud), a magical beacon of light in the darkest corners of the school. Together, my students and I were all trying to survive the bureaucracy of a system built on power and inequity. As much as I wanted to believe this is how the story went, this idolized portrait of myself was not entirely accurate. I thought I was an alternative to these systems of discipline and obedience education, but I, too, was part of the problem.

The idea that one day, out of nowhere, I had instinctively transformed my students' drawings into something more was a fallacy. In fact, this afternoon of artistic evolution had all started with a punitive disciplinary measure I was attempting to enforce:

April 10, 2010. I gave two students, Angel and Martin, detention for drawing penises and writing "dick" on the desks. . . . They kept goofing around and arguing and trying to play music on the computer. I told them,

"This isn't fun time, it's detention." They were staying after because their behavior was inappropriate. . . . I had to have them sit on opposite sides of the room so they wouldn't touch each other. Martin asked if he could clean my room so I had him clean all the desks and the whiteboard. Of course Angel wanted to joke around and try to spray the desks and make Martin's job harder. Eventually they both calmed down enough that they were able to work on their essays.

The world of detention is so far from my teaching practice now that I don't even remember it being a part of my practice then. Looking back at my notebooks, I see how much my teaching has changed over the last twelve years. I hardly recognize the teacher I was back then. What was I thinking by prescribing this punishment? How was detention meant to teach them what "appropriate behavior" looked like? And what did I mean by "they calmed down enough"—they stopped playing? They stopped having fun while cleaning? Martin, in an act of generosity and playfulness, was volunteering to clean desks covered with his erotic art. *He* was showing *me* what a restorative approach looked like, but I didn't see it. Why was I describing a bit of playful ingenuity as misbehavior? I see now that it was their guiding impulse to transcend systems of "good and bad" and "right and wrong"—in spite of my succumbing to these very systems—that opened up a possibility for our extended time together to become something more.

The following day both students voluntarily stayed after school to finish their essays. . . . After working for a while, they joined me on a walk to the deans' office. When we walked in, the deans asked how Martin and Angel were doing, and I let them know the boys were having a good day and got a lot done. The two deans complimented them on their progress and said, "Isn't it nice to have teachers ask you how your day is and you can say it was good? Doesn't it feel good to have people be proud of you when you get your work done?" Martin and Angel nodded and smiled. I was happy to see the deans give them positive encouragement. It's important for them to see that they can get just as much attention for doing the right thing.

What was I deeming "the right thing"? This supposed harmony with the deans was all part of the same disciplinary framework: my students can choose to conform and behave like good little boys or they can rebel, be bad boys, and face the consequences. Why didn't I see the harm in this messaging? We were telling Martin and Angel that they were willfully bad. We were tangled up in obedience education. "Good" and "bad" were defined by whether the students were subordinate and followed the "rules" no matter how oppressive those "rules" were.

In retrospect, I wonder how much student behavior was influenced by the small physical space we were stuck in. Of course there was stigma associated with this half-sized classroom that everyone knew was the special ed room. Bright-yellow laminated signs on the doors announced it. Was I so caught up in my mission to get them to be "good" that I couldn't see their rebellion against the shame and embarrassment of being confined to this tiny room?

When other staff members saw my class rosters from those first two years, the response they gave was always the same: "You got set up." But that response only motivated the white savior in me. All of my classes were on the school's "lowest track"—most received special education or ESL services. The rest were considered the "lowest performing" general ed students. This school administration loved tracking—a highly criticized practice of grouping together the kids who struggled the most academically. My rosters included an overwhelming number of Black and Brown students, mostly boys, many with disability classifications. I can't help but wonder about the legitimacy of those classifications.

Nationally, BIPOC students are disproportionately overrepresented among children with disabilities. It's possible that most of my students had disability classifications because of their race—because they weren't conforming to white standards. They didn't properly assimilate. Once classified, these students were more likely to receive harsher punishments, all feeding into the school-to-prison pipeline. They benefited from additional academic support and counseling services, but ultimately, they were isolated, punished, and pushed out of school.

Reflecting on my role in perpetuating my former school's culture is also a reckoning of how I participate in and enable, consciously or not, the broader society's systems of inequity and white supremacy. My former school (like most American schools) was a microcosm of American society, where whiteness was prioritized and uplifted and Blackness was punished. I'd been complicit in the school system's treatment of students who didn't fall in line: excluding them from activities, acting surprised or disappointed when nothing changed after they were punished, then labeling them as bad or dumb and hiding them away from the rest of the community. Then, as educators, we wonder why they struggle in school, why they act out, why they aren't passing their classes, why they drop out. We send a message that we don't want them to be seen. We shame them into conformity, and when that doesn't work, we push them out of school. We don't consider their socioemotional health or development. We don't try to help them learn and grow from their mistakes. We don't prioritize conflict resolution or healing. We don't uplift their humanity. We act like they are broken and can't be fixed.

But my students were showing us another way, a more liberatory path. I just didn't see it at the time. That same day on our way to the deans' office, we paused for a moment of play:

> In the hallway, construction workers had left unguarded ladders set up. Martin and Angel, after performing cartwheels for me, climbed up two side-by-side ladders. When I asked them to come down, they told me, "We just want to touch the ceiling." So they climbed to the top, touched the ceiling, and climbed back down.

Perhaps the view from the top of this ladder was not all they hoped it would be. Touching the ceiling was fun for a short moment but nothing to keep their interest up. At the time, their "self-control" (as I described it) surprised me. After our visit to the deans' office, Martin and Angel climbed those ladders again. On their second ascent, a dean was there observing nervously. When they returned to the floor, the dean muttered, "Well, okay. They went up, they came right back down. Alright. Okay. Fine." This playful behavior couldn't be easily classified in our binary systems of compliance or resistance. Were they doing something wrong? Sure, it was risky for students to just climb up some ladders, but were they harming anyone? There wasn't anything written in the discipline code about what to do when a student climbs a ladder. Were Martin and Angel performing for their larger audience of two now? Or did they think confusing authority was the best method to fight it? Or maybe they just thought it would be fun to climb high enough to touch the ceiling (twice!).

> When we returned back to the classroom, they started drawing penises and breasts on the board. I picked up a marker and turned the penis into a rocket launching and the breasts into a person's face with crazy red hair

and a goofy smile with crooked teeth. I said, "Look how much more fun this is to draw."

So it wasn't all penises all the time. Breasts also made an appearance—easily transformed into googly eyes bordered by thick glasses. My artistic revisions began with a misguided "detention" that Angel and Martin developed into informal, voluntary after-school tutoring sessions. It wasn't simply my role in the school's counterculture that led us to this anatomical-art creation process. In actuality, it was my attempt at a punitive discipline measure melding with my student's sense of play that brought us to a place of deeper inspiration and understanding. Shortly after that first detention, our afternoons together became more frequent. They came for tutoring and extra help and stayed for conversation, fun, and games. We were building a community.

It was only a matter of time before our little community was disrupted. In my second year at the school, Martin got a thirty-day suspension after throwing cherry tomatoes at some students in the cafeteria who retaliated with milk cartons. This was the last straw for Martin, and after his suspension, he was sent to Job Corps. As another student, Josh, left the scene of the tomato incident, a school safety officer repeatedly grabbed at his shirt. He asked her not to touch him, and when she didn't listen, he smacked her hand away. Surveillance cameras showed the school safety officer was out of line, yet Josh received a thirty-day suspension. When Josh returned, many of his friends, like Martin, were already gone:

JOSH: Don't you miss Martin? Your best student. (*Laughs*)
ME: Have you talked to him?
JOSH: No. He ain't never coming back.
ME: I know, he went to Job Corps.
JOSH: (*Pauses*) Could he come back if he wanted to?
ME: Maybe?
JOSH: I bet he wishes he didn't get suspended.
ME: I'm sure he does. Don't you wish that?
JOSH: I didn't—I didn't (*stutters*) have to go to Job Corps.
ME: Right, but still don't you wish you didn't get suspended?
JOSH: Yeah, but if I had to go to Job Corps then I'd really wish
    I didn't get suspended.

ME: Okay, but now you still could end up going to a different school.
That's still a possibility so do you wish you didn't get suspended
because of that?

JOSH: Yeah, [the dean] is an ass.

ME: What does that have to do with [the dean]?

JOSH: He's just an ass.

The administration had decided enough was enough. It was time for *these kids* to go. When the special education department started showing up en masse to IEP meetings, advocating for these students, fighting to keep them in the school, we were pushed out too.

Looking back, I realize how hard it was to think outside this punitive framework while I was in it. My reflections, now, come because I have some distance from the time and place—and, of course, because of my journals. Back then, I was fortunate in that I knew other models of education existed; I had experienced them as a student. So I did my research and found a school I love being at. And, I started to become the teacher I want to be.

I still dream about my old school—sporadic nightmares in which I'm back inside that building, haunted by my participation in what that school was and what's still in me. I'm left wondering how I come to terms with the ghosts of who I've been, who I was as a twenty-four-year-old white teacher in a room full of BIPOC students, and who I am now, fourteen years later; I wonder at the intersectionality of it all. In my waking hours, I struggle to forgive my younger self's mistakes, the harm I caused, and, at the same time, I recognize teaching as a continuous journey of self-reflection, learning, and growth. I can show up differently today than I did yesterday in how I see and treat young people. I can move beyond how things have traditionally been done, acknowledge and challenge my own biases, hold myself accountable when I mess up, and throw out harmful teaching practices. I can collaborate with my students to create more equitable and humanizing learning environments. Like the students doing penis drawings that evolved into structures and artistic renderings, I'm doing my own artistic reimagining of who I want to be.

THE PATH TO FORMING MY IDENTITY

— Jim Bentley —

Our identities form at a young age but change over time. When I was young, I listened to my maternal grandfather tell stories about our earliest known ancestor, Ygnacio Cantúa. He had come to California in 1774 as a soldier in the De Anza Expedition. My grandfather was a rancher. Tall, lanky, lantern-jawed, with skin like aged brown leather. He looked like a Spanish conquistador and punctuated the air with his enormous hands when he spoke. He was a serious man not prone to humor, but he would become animated when he talked about our family's history. In 1841, Ygnacio's son, José de Guadalupe Cantúa, received over four thousand acres of land from the Mexican governor of California via the San Luisito Land Grant. Two of Cantúa's sons went on to join the legendary Joaquin Murrieta gang, and a grandson grew up to become the infamous Californio bandido Tiburcio Vasquez. Our family was *Californio*. It was a point of pride for my grandfather. We were *not* Mexican. As a child, I didn't realize my grandfather was showing me his racism when he said this. Instead, he normalized it for me.

And I didn't even realize it.

I began teaching in 1996 in a rural, white, single-school district with just under three hundred students in the foothills of the Sierra Nevada in Northern California. Now, I teach in the fifth-biggest district in the state of California with over 63,000 students speaking 110 languages. Only 21 percent are white.[1] Each of the districts in which I've taught have in turn taught me a great deal about myself. After twenty-seven years as an educator, I've come to realize the stories we hear as children and replay in our minds as adults can effectively inoculate us against critically analyzing our role and impact in educational systems, which have failed both BIPOC students and educators.

I grew up on the Central Coast of California in a rural, predominantly white community east of San Luis Obispo. Throughout my K–12 education, there were two Black families I was aware of in my school community. There were more kids whose parents were Latinx farmworkers, since the dominant industry in the region was agriculture. When most people think of California, they think of a blue state on the "Left Coast." What many fail to understand is this: once you move inland, crossing the coastal mountains, the political landscape tilts red. Bakersfield has more in common with the state of Oklahoma than it does with the city of San Francisco. This circumstance is not unique. A lot of red states have blue urban islands.

The stories of my childhood shaped my view of who I was. I was not simply and anonymously "white." I had a deep history and colorful heritage. I considered myself "of Hispanic descent." I even checked that box on my college application when I applied to Cal Poly, San Luis Obispo. I had been advised to do so by a friend of the family who was white and a history professor at the university and who had interviewed my grandfather for oral histories on the descendants of the Californio families who had occupied San Luis Obispo County since the eighteenth century.

Over the past few years, my awareness of what it means to be white has grown exponentially as I have embarked on a self-guided learning path, aided by books, blogs, social media, online news sources, and nonprofit organizations in which I've served, and by having honest conversations with BIPOC educator friends. From my lived experience, each of the school districts in which I have worked has failed to make racial equity and understanding racism a top priority for white educators, such as myself. I cannot imagine how the handful of BIPOC educators I've worked with have felt over the years as initiatives have continued to roll out that overlook the issues at the top of their minds and that their fellow white educators and education leaders overlook.

When I look in the mirror today, I see a white male staring back. I feel foolish when I realize that for much of my life I had quietly enjoyed replaying stories of my Hispanic past while simultaneously enjoying all the privileges that come with being white.

And I didn't even realize it.

Rewind twenty years. I had just graduated college and had begun teaching first at a small white school, then at a larger, Title I site with a larger number of BIPOC students, and finally at my current district where only 21 percent of students are white. During those years, I served in various leadership capacities. I worked as a peer coach, mentored new teachers, and worked with a civic-education nonprofit focused on engaging youth in civic-action projects. I received many hours of training and facilitated countless professional development sessions focused on best practices for teaching different content areas and specialized skills. I learned about the "achievement gap" through various district and state initiatives and participated in "trainer of trainer" programs to spread pedagogical practices to reach and teach students by way of influencing their teachers' practices.

I took pride in growing as an educator of students and trainer of other educators. Yet, in all the years of training I had received and given, one thing now stands out to me: The trainings were led nearly 100 percent of the time by white experts and were missing the perspectives of BIPOC students and educators.

And I didn't even realize it.

After twenty years in education, I joined the National Faculty of PBLWorks in 2015. I remained a full-time teacher and took on this new role with the hope of promoting high-quality project-based learning and continuing to grow my own skills.

"As a person with Hispanic heritage, how could I be racist?" I thought as I read an email about an upcoming PBLWorks Spring Summit. It announced we were embarking on a new initiative focusing on adding the lenses of justice, racial equity, diversity, and inclusion to our work, which focused on making project-based learning available to all students by delivering training to their teachers. We were told the work we were beginning would likely force us to embrace discomfort as we questioned our own notions of race and complicity with white supremacist systems of oppression.

I was intrigued but not worried. I "knew" about racism, or so I thought. I comforted myself, repeating a phrase many white folks say to themselves when approaching a moment of racial discomfort. I'll share that phrase in just a moment. I'll wager you've heard others repeat it too.

What I had failed to grasp was just how superficial my personal understanding of racism was. It had been conveyed to me heretofore by white K–12 teachers via a unit here or a lesson there on the civil rights movement, often during Black History Month.

In my own educational experience, I've learned not all teachers give equal air time to Black history. And even fewer broach the concept of white "complicity" with systems of oppression.

When the topic of racism was broached, it was often portrayed as something that happened historically involving specific events and characters. It was framed in a tidy narrative with a beginning, middle, and end and with characters who were portrayed as either heroic or tragic.

ROSA PARKS: Heroic. She won. Buses were integrated.
MEDGAR EVERS: Tragic. He died. Racism continued.

Contemporary stories of racist actions often cast perpetrators as "bad apples" and in no way emblematic of white people in general. These narratives fail to account for the longstanding systems of oppression all too familiar for many BIPOC folks yet cleverly concealed for white educators like me who had not experienced their sting or rebuke.

Did I deeply understand the focus of civil rights leaders' work? No. The narrative I'd been taught was they had suffered while fighting for equal rights. Black-and-white photos and movies depicted marches and sit-ins with sensational racist responses from angry mobs or law enforcement. The emphasis had been on the outcomes of racism and not on the invisible mindset or "heartset" that powered those systems of oppression. Redlining? I only learned of that in 2015. I was sixteen years old and a junior in high school when the first Martin Luther King Jr. Day was celebrated in 1986. I was not taught during my K–12 education nor at university that Black history *was* American history. The more I learn today, the more gaps I identify within my learning in the past.

I was white and unaware. I did not think to dig deeper nor was I encouraged by my white teachers and mentors to question and understand race or racism or systems of oppression and how my being white shaped my worldview. I had been thoroughly socialized into a predominantly white culture.

I did not know what I did not know.

It's ironic that I went on to graduate with a bachelor of science in the social sciences with a special emphasis in cross-cultural studies. In all the geography, anthropology, political science, and sociology courses I took during my undergraduate years, not once did I ever do a deep dive into anti-Black racism or systems of oppression. The political science courses came close, but they tended to emphasize the historic nature of the topics and not the current manifestation of racist policies and systems of oppression.

So when that PBLWorks email announced to our then mostly white national faculty we were going to focus on justice, equity, diversity, and inclusion, I thought, "No problem."

Why?

After graduating college and working as an educator for twenty years, I knew one thing about myself. It was encapsulated in that oft-repeated phrase used by white folks to insulate themselves from racial discomfort.

I'm not racist.

THE PATH TO TRANSFORMING MY IDENTITY

Juan Carlos Arauz from E3: Education, Excellence & Equity[2] was the first person to set me on a path of transformation by pushing me to critically evaluate my mindset and heartset as a white educator working with BIPOC students.

At a PBLWorks Summit over the course of a weekend in a hotel meeting room near San Francisco, Arauz led a then predominantly white national faculty through a series of activities. He prompted me to question my understanding of educational and racial equity. He reframed education by centering for me the lived realities, skills, and capacities BIPOC students possess but that are often overlooked by educational systems focused intensely on standards, scores, and outcomes.

And Arauz did something else I had never before experienced.

He brought BIPOC students into our summit space to speak with us, to invite us to work with them, to understand their perspectives, and to help each of us analyze how we must question ourselves and what we as educators do in order to grow in our practices with them.

It was an intense two days. The readings and discussions pushed me to question my educational values and my biases. Arauz explicitly spelled out for me for the first time the concept of asset-based thinking and how to more critically and honestly evaluate and identify the strengths each of my students brings into the classroom.

And the most enduring and lasting gift Arauz gave me was a mantra. It's one I repeat often with my students and in professional development I lead with educators around the country because the ideas it contains apply to both students and educators.

It goes like this: "It's not about what's wrong but what's missing. It's not about improving—which implies a deficit—but growing."

When I work with students or teachers, I dare them to point to a person who has every skill, knowledge, and tool they need and who uses them perfectly 100 percent of the time.

They can't.

And I know this about myself as an educator: I am not done learning or growing. When I see or hear white educators put on an act of invincibility or infallibility in my professional-development sessions as we talk about equity and racial justice, I know I need to give them extra attention.

Because they don't know what they don't know.

Educator and author Shane Safir was the second person to lead me on my path of transformation as a white educator. Her book *The Listening Leader* further refined my understanding of equity and built on it by pushing me to critically evaluate the neuroscience involved with the act of listening and how crucial that is when becoming a warm demander for equity with both students and teachers.

My grandfather, who relayed stories of our ancestral history, would frequently bark at me, "God gave you two ears and one mouth, so listen!"

I've known listening is important. Safir taught me how to do it more effectively. Especially when working with BIPOC students.

After working with Safir, I had a Black female student in my fifth-grade class. I'll fictionalize her name as Jamila. The communication card I received from Jamila's previous teacher was filled with observations focusing on her negative behavior and academic deficits.

I soon learned Jamila was quick to anger and would argue with classmates or myself when she perceived a statement as incorrect, an assigned task as irrational, or an act by myself or a classmate as unjust.

Viewing the assets within these behaviors, Jamila showed she was courageous, detail oriented, logical, and persuasive and possessed an incredibly strong sense of social justice.

When working with Jamila, I focused on being a mindful listener for Jamila's sake as well as my own. "Feed the lizard," I would repeat to myself.[3] From Safir I learned when we feel threatened, an "amygdala hijack" can pump cortisol to our brain and shut off our prefrontal cortex, or the "thinking brain."[4] This activates the limbic system. Meanwhile, the brain stem, or "lizard brain," ratchets up breathing and heart rate in preparation for a fight or flight. Interactions involving the limbic system are based on feelings, impulses, and implicit biases.[5] If I allowed Jamila's behavior to trigger me, I could perceive her as a threat. If I triggered Jamila by not listening to her, she might perceive me as the threat. How could I avoid this?

First, I couldn't take Jamila's behavior personally. Second, I had to control my response to Jamila and not add to her stress when she experienced her own amygdala hijack. Third, I had to accept that *less than* 10 percent of my meaning is conveyed through the words I choose. Which meant I had to focus on the tone of my voice, which accounts for nearly 38 percent of my meaning, and my nonverbal cues, which account for nearly 55 percent of my meaning.[6] Finally, I had to be aware of when to use what Safir calls "deep listening" as opposed to "strategic listening."[7] The former is when a person speaks to be heard, to "empty their heart"; the latter is when a speaker permits us to listen and offers prompts in the form of thoughtful questions to assist them in taking steps to change some aspect of their mindset.

When Jamila felt heard and respected, I was able to build trust and goodwill with her. This allowed me to make requests of Jamila by drawing on what Safir calls the "relational capital" we had established. As I worked with Jamila, she recognized that I heard her, was not a threat, and was on her side.

Jamila had a good year in my classroom compared to years past. Her grades rose. Her confidence rose. Her negative behavior and trips to the office went extinct. She worked on several film productions in our class and became a lead editor using professional software to create several award-winning films.

In all fairness, the educational transaction that took place between us was unequal. Jamila taught me more than I gave to her. She offered grace when I struggled to listen. She provided honesty when I asked for feedback on how I was doing as a teacher. She gave me a chance to grow as a white educator even though she'd experienced so many others before me who had defined and labeled her as "challenging." What she wanted and deserved was a chance to use her mind and talents in a way that was authentic to who she was.

The final two individuals who continue to guide me on my journey are Robin DiAngelo and Dr. Ibram X. Kendi, with their books *White Fragility: Why It's So Hard for White People to Talk About Racism* and *How to Be an Antiracist*, respectively.

DiAngelo explained to me why many white folks feel uncomfortable talking about race. I was taught by my white family it wasn't a "polite" topic for mixed company, but what DiAngelo revealed was many whites avoid the subject out of fear they might look bad. DiAngelo describes how the "good-bad binary" after the civil rights movement made being a "good person" and participating in racist acts mutually exclusive because racists are widely considered "bad people."[8]

Enter the Western ideology of individualism that posits, "There are no intrinsic barriers to individual success and that failure is not a consequence of social structures but comes from individual character."[9] If I'm white and successful, it's because of the "content of my character." If Blacks as a racial group experience lower-quality employment, wealth, health, and political power, the notion of individualism frames their experience as a result of the flaws in the individuals' character and not racism or structures built to harm the racial group to which they belong. The sinister dividends of this mindset—beliefs that I am exempt from their problems and there is no need for me to change the status quo—protect white privilege and safeguard white fragility.

Kendi's words are like a Newtonian Second Law of Motion for me, an unbalanced force accelerating my thinking when he says, "There is no such thing as a not-racist idea, only racist ideas and antiracist ideas."[10]

When my students and I study science or history, discuss current events or literature, or work on civic-action projects in our community, I, as a white educator, feel enlightened and empowered by Kendi to facilitate my students' critical consumption of the information we use to inform our thinking by viewing it through the lens of anti-racism.

Race-neutrality, Kendi states, "actually feeds white nationalist victimhood by positing the notion that any policy protecting or advancing non-white Americans toward equity is 'reverse discrimination'"[11]

As an educator, I embrace National Geographic Education's mission: "We teach kids about the world and how it works, empowering them to succeed and to make it a better place."[12]

To ignore the racist or anti-racist nature of what my students study and do would perpetuate an incomplete education. It would enable yet another generation to exempt themselves and to say, "I'm not racist."

To me, that means I have an obligation to design learning experiences in which students explore and question big ideas, evaluate the veracity and bias of sources of information, critically think, and construct understandings and express them using various mediums so they can take informed actions to make the world a better place.

PERSEVERING

– Caroline Darin –

I never knew how white I really was until I became a teacher in the hood. The school I work at is in Williamsburg, Brooklyn, a neighborhood portrayed in mass media more as a white hipster utopia than the hood. The economic and cultural displacement the area has experienced has had devastating consequences for countless families. But the Brooklyn spirit persists. Take a second look, and you'll see the richness of Williamsburg's history and culture beaming through the cracks of the gentrified facade. Latinx music spills out from open windows in the summer, the scent of Fortunato Brothers' iconic Italian cookies wafts through the air, and signs in Hebrew line the bustling streets of South Williamsburg. Williamsburg teems with life.

A number of my students live in or around the school, but many come into school from other neighborhoods on the L, the train line that runs from the west side of Manhattan, through Williamsburg, Bushwick, and Brownsville, and ends in Canarsie on the east side of Brooklyn. Some used to live in Williamsburg before their families were priced out. Many live in various housing projects around Brooklyn.

My upbringing was nowhere near the hood—I grew up in an affluent family, in various suburbs across Richmond, Chicago, Los Angeles, and Boston, as well as in Southern Maine. I went to well-funded, mostly white schools and experienced immense privilege that has facilitated my journey every step of the way.

The first experience that inspired me to pursue teaching came in college. I had declared a physics major during my freshman year and though I found my classes fascinating, I struggled to connect with my classmates beyond working on problem sets together in the library. Hoping to find friends, I looked for clubs that would help me connect to my peers and find the fulfillment of community I'd been seeking. I knew some people who volunteered with an organization that brought college students to teach health classes to public school students. I applied and was accepted as a volunteer, and I began teaching sexual decision-making to fourteen- and fifteen-year-olds in Chicago public schools.

The experience was immediately jarring and humbling. Prior to my first day, I had never been the only white person in a crowded room, a fact that had never occurred to me until I entered the classroom to start my volunteer work. The realization came with a flood of questions: Will they like me? Will I embarrass myself? What will I say if they make fun of me? What if they don't like me because I'm white? What will I do if they don't listen to what I ask them to do or don't care about what I'm teaching?

All my worst fears were flooding in at once, and every single one of them has come true in my career as a teacher. And many of my fears came true that first day—but when I fumbled over modeling for students how to ask their partners to use a condom or could hear a student whispering to another one, "Why is this white lady here talking about how to have sex?" my fears weren't a deterrent but a challenge to double down on learning how to teach. Because that day I fell in love with teaching.

The joy of being a part of a young person's learning and growth is unparalleled. The awkwardness of teaching a room of students whom I had never met before about how to decide when they were ready to have sex, and fielding their inevitably surprising questions about sex, turned out to be fun. The students' curiosity about the world and their excitement, compassion, and humor were infectious. And not only that, teaching was *hard*. My privileged upbringing entailed a pretty cushy life devoid of much challenge. I always had the resources to succeed in school and live comfortably. As a teacher, for the first time in my life, I was challenged in a way I never had been before. As my fears manifested in the classroom, I had to think quickly and learn to adapt. Students made fun of me. Some were absolutely not in the mood to listen to what I had to say. Some just didn't like me. And as those challenges came up, I began to see teaching for the artful practice it was and recognized the work it would require of me. But I had fallen in love and was going to be a teacher.

After graduating college, I joined New York City Teaching Fellows (NYCTF) to become a physics teacher. I began interviewing with schools in June 2015. The assistant principal and principal from one public school, Brooklyn Preparatory High School, came to interview me during my lunch break between training sessions and classes in the cafeteria of my graduate school. I don't remember much from the interview aside from being extremely nervous, but I do remember one prompt that stood out to me: "Tell me about a time that you failed." I began sharing my prepared answer about how skilled I am at learning from my mistakes. But the principal interrupted me, saying, "That's great, but tell me about a time that you really failed and were disappointed, and there was nothing you could do about it at the moment."

After sharing a painfully honest response that felt much more raw than anything I'd ever shared in an interview, the principal looked thoughtfully at the assistant principal and back at me. He told me, "You are going to fail as a teacher. You should learn from your mistakes and work to avoid failing, but it will happen, and you need to be able to accept your failures for what they are." They called me the next day to offer me the job to teach physics and earth science, which I accepted.

Though I'd had my experiences with volunteer teaching and had taught summer school with NYCTF, I was still undeniably green in my practice as a physics teacher. I had dreams of engaging students in rigorous science debates about climate change and working with gravitational equations to map the orbits of different planets. But when I implemented the lessons I'd planned, they always fell flatter than I had imagined. While a handful of students would reliably attempt the lessons I was delivering, many others slept, texted, Snap-chatted, took selfies on their phones, talked over me, or just didn't come to my class. Many students liked me only because they saw me as more of a friend than a teacher. A small group of boys referred to me only as Taylor Swift the entire year. At twenty-three, I was so unsure of my status as a teacher, and the students' feelings toward me reflected that. This was not the case in their other classes, and I realized something was missing in mine. Though my love for science could momentarily rouse some students' interest, it was not enough to make me a good science teacher.

I remember two things my administration told me during those first few months. The first was when I was meeting with my principal about my struggles, holding back tears thinking about what a disservice I was doing to my students as such an inexperienced teacher. My principal is notorious for thoughtful pauses before he speaks—leaving the listener unsure of whether they should fill the silence. After what felt like an eternity, he started, "They are learning with you. You will grow this year and so will they. The example you set and the care you put into your work will set the tone for them."

While I still feel guilty thinking about all the ways I would have taught differently my first year had I known then what I know now, this was an important turning point in my perspective. I learned that being a good teacher means being a good student. Teaching requires adaptability and humility—you must be able to learn quickly to succeed and let go of the idea that the classroom can be controlled.

The unique combination of students and content, plus the ever changing world around the classroom, means that no classroom will ever be the same from one moment to the next. That is what makes teaching so beautiful and joyful. Teaching reflects the turbulence and growth of life itself, a fact that should be embraced rather than suppressed in favor of formulaic approaches. This reality was especially true for me, a white teacher who had vastly different experiences from my students and had much to learn about working with young people.

At that time, being the only white person in the room was still a new experience for me. Cultural differences in what seemed to be every aspect of personality arose every day between my students and me—beliefs about education, food, emotions, violence, discipline, family, and friends. Some were minor—a student asking me, "Miss, you bike to school, right? Why do white people love biking so much? And why have they started biking through my neighborhood on the weekends?" Others were more serious—a boy calling me a "pussy-ass white bitch" when I blocked the door so he couldn't go to watch the fight in the hallway. In my first year, I didn't have the language to navigate these situations as learning opportunities for myself as well as my students. But over time, as I began to see these differences not as hindrances but as opportunities for growth, connections started growing like tendrils, bridging what seemed initially to be an insurmountable gap. I recall that during my second year I was trying to convince a student to not fight another girl with whom she had been arguing for a while. Eventually, she told me, "You wouldn't get it, you're white. You're not from where I'm from." Previously, I may have shut down in the face of this comment, fearing further embarrassment or feelings of shame from what she might say next. But this time, I realized that I was missing something significant about this student when I entered the conversation, and so I responded, "Ok, you're right. Help me understand."

The other key piece of advice I was given during my first year was from my assistant principal. I had been telling her about my classroom-management practices. I am ashamed to admit they came mostly from what I was taught in NYCTF, which is largely based on a popular teacher-preparation book I'll leave unnamed. Many of the practices espoused in it centered on "controlling" students and formulaic approaches to classroom management. When I tried them, they felt unnatural to my demeanor, and my inauthenticity was off-putting to the students. When I was describing them to her, she could immediately tell I didn't have faith in the things I was saying and pointed out that I seemed woefully unsure of the techniques I was using. She told me, "I don't know you that well or what kind of teacher you are going to be. But it sounds like neither do you. You need to figure that out. Just don't pretend to be something you're not. Our kids hate that." The good news was I had honed in on the problem, but the bad news was I still didn't know what kind of teacher I was.

As I continued through my first year, I centered these pieces of advice in my practice. I persevered in my failures, trying new things in the class and building a toolbox of techniques that worked for my style. I visited and built relationships with my colleagues to see different teaching styles in action. I shed many tears in the process but kept going. And most importantly, I started focusing on building relationships with my students.

Student-centered learning is often used to refer to the teaching practice in which students actively participate in the planning and process of learning, uncovering information through inquiry. But this cannot occur if teachers don't know their students. While I had spent the first few months of my teaching worrying about making perfect worksheets and ensuring we were getting through content quickly enough, I had lost track of what I loved so much about teaching: the students. I started prioritizing my relationship with my students, inviting them to eat lunch in my room, getting to know their interests, and working to understand them more deeply. I asked questions: How do you feel about school? What is your family like? What do you and your friends like to do together? And in turn, I would share pieces of myself. I had to let go of any fear of embarrassment or how I would be perceived and instead focus on putting authentic connection at the forefront of our conversations. Of course, sometimes I did embarrass myself. I once told a student how much I love to cook, and he said, "Oh word? Bring me something you make!" The next day I brought him a small Tupperware of a vegan truffle carbonara I had made for dinner the previous night. He was deterred by the mushroom smell but took a bite anyway. He nearly threw up in the classroom trash can. Deep down, I was a little hurt. But I didn't let it show, taking it in stride and teasing him for being rude and having bad taste. Moments like this showed students that, yes, sometimes when you let your guard down and show your full self, you might get embarrassed. But it's not the end of the world if it means those who care about you see you more fully.

It was a slow recovery, but when I recentered my practice on building relationships with the students and bringing my whole self to my role as a teacher, my ability to move through other struggles began to improve as well. As I gained the students' trust, they began sharing more with me and would tell me when they liked the work or when they were struggling. As I got to know their personalities, I was better able to read the room and elicit feedback. And as I learned what was truly important to them, not just surface-level interests like music, basketball, or makeup but their families, experiences, and dreams, I saw that I could adjust my teaching to engage them on a level that was more authentic and meaningful to them. This last piece has proved to be the most difficult to master.

After learning the lessons of my first year, I came into my second year feeling confident in my progress. My school had a professional development session for teachers in which we were all encouraged to pursue our "dream projects." Mine was inspired by my earth science class, a Regents-based class that I had never taken and of which I essentially knew only the basics when I was asked to teach it in addition to physics. During my first year, I struggled to connect the content to students' lives. But after taking time to get to know my students, I had often heard them complaining about the structure of New York City—the need for places to hang out with their friends outside, the stress of the MTA, and the lack of resources invested in their neighborhoods. I saw loose connections between these concerns and the Surface Processes and Landforms Unit of the earth science curriculum. I created an urban planning project to contextualize the concepts that the Board of Regents wanted me to teach within students' lives. I collected articles and excerpts from Jane Jacobs and Robert Moses and did a case study on Black Wall Street to inspire students to envision the city of their dreams and consider how to bring that to life. It was my dream project, and after I had finalized my plans, I was so proud. But the project was a disaster. I hadn't properly supported them in reading the complex and dense texts I had assigned. One student was even furious with me for assigning Jane Jacobs because she had interpreted Jacobs's critique of the racism of project housing as a call to kick Black and Brown people out of New York. Though they were inspired by looking at Black Wall Street, they struggled to make the connections between landforms and the experience of everyday life for people living in an area.

My students had all been capable of accessing those high-level texts, given the proper preparation and support. But the concept of city planning had been completely new to them, and I had failed to properly acclimate them to the concepts and vocabulary they needed for success. This failure was a key moment in coming to a new truth in teaching: you have to meet your students where they are. In my case, I had thought incorporating their interests into my project would suffice to engage them. But I hadn't met them where they were in terms of the support they needed to be successful.

My students come into my classroom with countless different experiences. Teaching with relationships at the core of my practice helped me to build my classroom management and to open up my content and learning goals as a teacher. But it also helped me to understand *how* my students are entering the classroom. They may have been continually traumatized by a math teacher who made them feel they were incapable of ever being successful in anything remotely involving math, and now using scientific notation in physics class makes them shut down. Maybe they help their grandma with her garden in the spring and have a deep knowledge of sustainable food practices, and that has never been tapped in a science classroom. Or maybe they have only ever had painful experiences with white teachers and need time to feel comfortable in my classroom. Understanding the past experiences that have shaped my students helps me to see what they need from me as both their science teacher and an adult in their life who knows and cares about them.

Now in my seventh year, I am still far from a perfect teacher. But the lessons I learned as a new teacher have stuck with me and shaped my continual growth, and my classroom and practice are now nearly unrecognizable from what they looked like in those early years. My lessons have gotten more and more rigorous; I have a massive collection of lessons for science topics that not only engage students in high-level science but successfully prompt students to connect their learning to their own lives. My growth stemmed from each mistake and wouldn't have happened if I hadn't opened myself to the immense vulnerability of teaching. And through every moment when I am scared, angry, embarrassed, confused, or frustrated by the most arduous challenge of my life, my love for teaching propels me forward into new realms of possibility. And that's something I would never give up.

DON'T WASTE YOUR WHITE

— Corey Scholes —

The Midwest. That's where I'm from. The coast-less middle. The original land of the Kaw people. A place encompassing the complex history of Jayhawkers *and* enslavers. A place that takes "white polite" to startling levels. A place where avoiding conflict can carry more currency than telling truths. I grew up in a city with these ideals but in a household with different ones. My grandparents were immigrants, and my parents are New Yorkers. We were raised to be truth tellers (even when it's ugly) and to stay involved in our community. I was raised in a house with two loving, imperfect parents, and two siblings. We are Irish and Italian. We're loud. In my family, you must have thick skin. I'm the middle kid. The peacemaker. The bridge builder. All these pieces of my origin story shaped my future. I've dedicated my career to supporting students and educators. I have had some measurable successes and some epic failures. I have learned that you must stay in the fight and keep showing up. Make people uncomfortable if it will move the needle. Push yourself and others even when you're tired. And an important lesson I've learned in the past few years is *don't waste your white*. The notion of not "wasting" your white is based on the reality that, as a white person, you have unearned privileges based solely on the color of your skin. Use those to level the playing field for others.

I entered a Chicago classroom in the fall of 1992 as a white twenty-three-year-old who was a woefully unprepared novice. I had not spent significant time in communities of color, and I had no real relationships with anyone of color. But I'd found myself on the staff at Richard J. Daley Elementary, a K–8 school in the Back of the Yards neighborhood of Chicago. At our school, 80 percent of the staff and 100 percent of students identified as people of color—primarily Black and Latinx. Luckily for me, the veteran teachers poured love and confidence into me: Henry Martin, Vernetta White, Sandy Brown, Jacquie Jackson, and the list goes on. These amazing Black educators understood that my lack of preparation could harm kids, and they were not going to allow that to happen. While it might have been easier for them to avoid me and my naivete, they chose to use their cultural knowledge and institutional capital to engage me in hard truths that changed my practice and my life trajectory.

The most important lesson I learned from my Richard J. Daley Elementary colleagues was to *do the work*. Don't just talk, write, and think about the work, which is a passive and privileged way of existing. Do the damn work. Make things happen. Leverage everything you have to get things done. Don't complain about problems; fix them. Do for your students and community what you would do for your family and friends. When the work gets hard, keep doing it. When you fail, get back up and try again. Just don't quit. Keep pushing forward.

This is the foundation of everything I learned about becoming an effective educator. (Note: I did not learn this in either of my master's degree programs; I learned it from practitioners who were immersed in the work.) I consider these "spirit lessons," cultural artifacts imparted from my colleagues' hearts to mine. It was never my colleagues' responsibility to pour into me the way they did, but they gave me that gift and I honor that by trying to be a true accomplice in this work. My friend Sharif El-Mekki says, "Allies take up space, but accomplices take up risk." My goal became to pay forward what was gifted to me for the rest of my career, to use those lessons along with my unearned racial privileges to make education more equitable.

I was lucky to teach and learn in Chicago for a decade. After I returned home to Kansas City to teach in the public schools, administrators assigned me to work with students battling "behavior disorders" at Southeast K–8. It was there I learned many valuable lessons and was lucky enough to serve as a teacher, a vice principal, and a principal. It is a place that forever has a hold on my heart.

The biggest lessons I learned at Southeast were to advocate for others, to speak up and speak out, and to accentuate the positive of all communities. I learned these lessons from Linda Lollis.

Linda Lollis has been my biggest professional advocate and champion. She supported my growth as a classroom teacher, picked me to be her vice principal, and gave me my first job as a principal. She saw potential in me before I saw it in myself. She regularly used her power to grow mine. I was (and still am) humbled by her faith in my abilities. She is what I think of when I think of true leadership. She would breathe confidence into people and then get out of their way and watch the magic begin to glow inside them. Following Linda's lead, I have tried to cheerlead for the people I've managed. I look for the best in people and try to help them see it. I take people with me as I climb, and I try to share the lessons I learn so we can all make different mistakes instead of the same ones. Outside of the connection I have with my daughter, true connections I have with students and educators remain the greatest joy of my life, and these were modeled for me by Linda. For that, I will be eternally grateful.

Linda projected honesty. She would tell it like it is, for better or for worse. She would fight for her staff no matter the costs. When she believed the district had set unrealistic expectations, she would shield us from them and alone shoulder the blame if there were consequences.

I've tried to make what Linda did instinctually a part of my conscious leadership style. I try to lead without pretense and speak out when I perceive unfairness. I try to take the blame and share the credit. I try to use my voice, power, and position—or "my white"—to fight oppressive systems.

I put that leadership style to work at Southeast, a school with a reputation for low academic achievement and high suspension rates in a community devastated by years of racism and poverty. A local reporter once called the zip code housing our school a "murder factory." We needed to balance the narrative of this beautiful community.

We set out to do that in a variety of ways. One of the first things we did was establish a "wall of fame" inside our school to remind our students that they were part of a long line of greatness. The wall featured photos of hundreds of alumni and included their stories so students could understand their significance. The alumni ranged from current teachers to local pastors, to politicians, to world-class physicians. Each story offered a reminder of our school's legacy of excellence. Another strategy we employed involved forging deep relationships with the local news media to intentionally combat the damaging false narratives. We regularly called local TV stations and newspapers to pitch stories we thought they should share, and eventually they did. It was amazing the first time I held the *Kansas City Star* and read a front-page story about our school and community. This was the *real* story. This was who we were.

Fast forward to 2012. I have just begun working to support school systems as a director at one of the nation's largest foundations. My job allows me to work with my community to identify problems and attempt to solve them. All the lessons I learned from being in schools still matter: listen, talk to the people most impacted by problems, speak up for others, and do *real* work. I have tried to be a philanthropist that solves problems *with* communities, not *for* communities. I have tried to leverage the power of philanthropy to disrupt and change racist and inequitable systems.

In September 2016, my dear friend Winston Cox wrote a powerful article for *Education Week* entitled "Obama's Legacy for Male Principals of Color." In his article, there was a sentence I'll never forget: "No more than 2 percent of all public school teachers in the United States are Black and male."[1] Two percent?!?! I knew the percentage was low, but I didn't realize it was that low. It turns out that 71 percent of all teachers in the US are white women. That means most students receiving an education in this country get it through the lens of a white woman's perspective, her biases, and her sense of privilege. This is problematic. Winston's article also addressed how educators of color often do not stay in the profession or climb into leadership, which puts students of color at a disadvantage. There are few people at the front of the classroom who look like them and even fewer who look like them that are making building-wide and system-level decisions. When I learned this, I felt I had to do something.

I started by listening and asking educators of color what they thought. I called dozens of my educator friends and asked what they had done to attract, develop, and retain educators of color. I asked what they thought still needed to be done. I asked if they knew of people from whom I could learn. I wanted to know about any solutions.

I repeatedly was told that educators of color needed space. Space to be in community with one another. Space to have real conversations. Space to learn together. Space to experience and express joy. Space *without* white people. I understood what was meant by the word "space" but was not sure, as a white person, it was something I could create. I also wasn't sure it was something my foundation would allow. However, I've always been a big fan of asking for forgiveness rather than permission, so I proceeded.

I asked my closest friend at work, a Black woman, if we could be co-conspirators in a caper. I explained that as a white person I wasn't going to be able to attend the conference I was dreaming up and asked if she would play a lead role. It was outside her comfort zone, but she saw the vision and agreed to do it.

We convened a small group of educators of color and asked if they would serve as the steering committee, offering direction and feedback about the content and design of a conference. We asked them to help find other educators of color in the area to participate. We asked them to present and to help run the event. We organized a small but mighty group that designed it from the ground up. This structure was important. Current teachers and leaders of color needed to spearhead the effort.

With our committee in place, we looked for a name. What could we call it? We wanted the event to support and uplift educators. We wanted them to leave the event stronger and better able to do their jobs. We wanted to amplify their voices. That was it! Amplify. Let's use this platform to amplify the voices of educators of color.

We spent months debating content, keynotes, the logo, and more. We wanted *every* detail to reflect how much we appreciated the work of educators of color.

When March 3, 2017, came, we had 175 people registered! The committee wanted a social, low-key opening for the event so that people could network and get to know each other. Many attendees were of the few educators of color in the schools where they taught. The event would create opportunities for educators of color from across the city to connect.

From the moment the conference was opened, it was clear that the vision was realized. The evening went off without a hitch, and people were excited to return the next morning. After the participants left, we treated the presenters to a lovely dinner and evening of fellowship. The next morning, an amazing author, Hillary Beard, kicked things off. She tried to begin her talk but began to cry. She said she had never been in a room like this. The power of the room overwhelmed her (as it did many in attendance). Black and Brown excellence was everywhere. It was abundant, palatable, and undeniable. This was the space people had longed for.

The conference has grown over the years. Last year, one thousand people registered in ninety minutes. People crave Amplify's space and connections. It has built a reputation for being more like a family reunion than a conference. It has music, art, food, drinks, dancing, and hard-core truth-telling. The people feed the community, and the community feeds the people. Conference events include specific professional-development sessions targeting the Black and Brown educator experience, networking sessions, keynotes (Chris Emdin is the perennial favorite), and love. Lots of love. It is a space of importance that was built by an amazing group of local and national educators willing to give their time, talent, and treasure to creating a sacred space for educators of color.

Amplify was one of the first real efforts I made to "not waste my white" in philanthropy. The next big effort came when my friends, Frances Messano and

Xiomara Padamsee, funded and did the research around racism in the nonprofit sector. They unveiled what they had found in a report called *Unrealized Impact.*[2] This report was based on surveying hundreds of nonprofit organizations and getting a picture of what the sector felt like for its employees of color. I loved listening to everything they uncovered, and I wanted to do something about it. What could we do? How would we make the sector better? I could hear Mrs. Lollis in my ear.

In 2018, I had a fruitful breakfast with Xiomara and the DEI Accelerator was born. We co-created a cohort experience to challenge organizations that were impacting hundreds of thousands of students across the country to study their own data, listen to experts, and create action plans. These plans were then refined through multiple rounds of feedback from peer organizations. Finally, the participants received a years' worth of support from a coach to help implement and tweak their plan based on the specific needs of the organization. The feedback from participants was overwhelmingly positive, and the accelerator continues to support hundreds of organizations in the nonprofit sector today.[3]

The accelerator was funded, housed, and co-planned by my foundation. We sent ten grantee organizations to the accelerator to get support in becoming more equitable, but we were not going to attend as a philanthropy. I had many conversations with our senior leadership in which I pointed out that it seemed strange that we would want to hold our grantees more accountable than ourselves. With some reservations, my foundation agreed to send a team. I was excited to begin this journey. I wanted to see how we could increase our impact if we were a more purposeful, equitable foundation.

After I got the green light for us to participate, I and another white woman picked the group of people who would make up the race, equity, diversity, and inclusion team. Yes, unfortunately, you read that right. Another white woman and I picked the team. That would never happen again, but it was the reality, and it is *very* important for people to be honest about the mistakes we make in this work. When we hide the truth and only talk about the places we've succeeded, we are disingenuous to the process, and we cannot help others learn.

Our six-person team spent an entire year learning together and developing a common language and deep relationships with one another, so that we could interrogate our biases and beliefs. We started as a small, humble team and went on to lead very important work at our foundation.

A giant philanthropy has the power to influence systems of oppression. That means they can either double down and make those systems more oppressive or they can work at dismantling them and replacing them with systems that are more equitable. Thankfully, we chose the latter.

We have now been in this work for many years, and we have made many significant changes. We changed how we hire people and who we hire. This is particularly important in philanthropy because the people that work in your institution are traditionally the only people who have access to the power and privilege that come with the responsibility of disseminating hundreds of millions of dollars a year into the community. We changed how we invest and grow our assets. Our investment team paid careful attention to the racial makeup of who we invest with and made sure we were pushing for more diversity. We changed how we give grants. A small team of folks worked for years to make a more equitable grant-making process. And most importantly, for the first time in history we had a guiding principle for all of our grant-making areas: inclusive prosperity. We asked ourselves: How could our education and entrepreneurship grant making both lead to more equitable outcomes for the communities we serve? We were all rowing in the same direction for the first time.

These were giant changes that are uncommon for foundations. These changes would affect millions of people. There was a lot of pain involved in making these changes. We were always taking two steps forward and one step back, but it was worth it. If we have used the power of philanthropy to create a fairer and more just world, that's a win. To me, that is what it means to not waste my white.

PART TWO

LOCALIZED LEARNING

There are few absolute truths in teaching and learning. There are scientific and mathematical facts and dates of historical events that all teachers should know, and even dispositions, like patience and a capacity to love, that all teachers should have. However, the art of teaching and learning itself requires the teacher to be free from any conception that the way to do this work is to do things the way they have been done by and for someone else.

The magic of teaching is the recognition that you learn how to teach the people in front of you *from the people in front of you*. Their experiences, however dissimilar they are from yours, are the entry points into their soul. The only person who has the map to those entry points to their soul is that person themself.

Despite constant attempts to circumvent this truth, teaching and learning are localized activities. Ignoring this in the hopes of "scaling up" or measuring quality is responsible for many of the ills in education—standardized curriculum creates boxes that confine students and teachers, and standardized tests cement those boxes in place. When students are forced to contort themselves to fit into these mass-produced molds, they cannot and will not sit comfortably. This dis-ease becomes cause for either passive or visceral rejection of what is being forced on them.

The passive responses too often go unnoticed initially and are ultimately misunderstood. Students quietly decide that their form of protest will be to not learn any of what is being pushed upon them. This only registers on the horizon of people in positions of power when they see low test scores, which they erroneously interpret as students being incapable of learning or obstinate.

Students' more visceral rejections of standardization are sensationalized: these become the tropes dangled in front of aspiring teachers who come into urban education. Perhaps you've heard the advice, "Don't smile before Christmas," or the calls to teach students to sit up straight, listen, nod, and track the speaker—all before engaging them in any content or getting to know them. This is, of course, a negative cycle: students forced into boxes of acceptable speech, posture, and behavior, and commanded to strictly follow a curriculum that was made for another population will get angry. The "angry Black student" narrative then becomes the storyline that invites a more strict and confining curriculum and teaching style.

Each essay in this section in some way points to this reality but then offers one of the few absolute truths in this work—especially for white folks who teach in the hood: *localization opens up the doors to a living curriculum that transforms school.* Teaching locally means listening to young people and opening up the door to surrounding communities. It means leaving the physical space that is the classroom and extending the learning space to the neighborhood. It means allowing young people to use their school learning to transform their own lives and those of the people they love. Creating the space and the conditions for young people to *do* is *teaching*.

For white educators doing this work, there are some important considerations that the contributors in this section raise: How do I facilitate work in and with a community that I may not be from or not yet understand? How do I learn in ways that are not at the expense of my students or the community? When is it empowering to "let students figure it out for themselves" and when is doing so an obfuscation of responsibility?

Whoever you are, whatever position you hold, whatever forms of oppression and power you have experienced, as you read these chapters, please consider the ways these contributors have answered these questions. How have they learned from their mistakes, moved their egos to the side, interrogated who they are and what they bring to the classroom, and created the conditions for children to learn through taking meaningful action in their communities?

How can you?

FROM KIPLING TO KING

– Glenetta Blair Krause –

O n Friday, April 6, 2001, the fourteen-year-old ninth graders in my English
class were looking forward to a week-long spring break. Around Cincinnati,
front yards held every shade of green. The air wafting through our windows at
Hughes Center High School held the promise of Easter flowers. I remember we
spent that day reading "The White Man's Burden" by Rudyard Kipling. Kipling's
imperialist poem argues that white people are morally obligated to rule darker
people, or, as Kipling called them, "half devil and half child." I usually pair
the reading with a critique of the racist poem the next day—something more
uplifting. But the way the vacation fell, we wouldn't have class for another
week. So I sent my students home for a week—95 percent Black and almost
100 percent of them economically disadvantaged—with a lesson about how the
world has been racist for hundreds of years and very little hope that anything
would change.

In the early morning hours of Saturday, April 7, in Cincinnati, nineteen-
year-old Timothy Thomas was murdered by Officer Steven Roach in an alley
in Over-the-Rhine, our city's poorest neighborhood at that time. Thomas had
accumulated many nonviolent tickets and didn't pay them. These resulted in
warrants the police felt obligated to pursue. Thomas ran down an alley and
reached to pull up his baggy pants. Officer Roach thought he might be grabbing
for a gun. He shot Timothy Thomas in the chest for speed limit, parking, and
seat-belt violations.

On April 9, leaders in the Black community took their complaints to
Cincinnati City Hall and the police department, who would not reveal the
results of what they called an "ongoing investigation." This sparked four nights
of what I then called "riots." I would now call what happened something

else—rebellion, civil unrest, lament. My students spent their spring break under a city-wide curfew.

I was glued to the television as Cincinnati's local news became national news. I wanted to understand what was happening, but I was also looking for kids I knew, hoping my students weren't hurt or in trouble. I didn't go to Over-the-Rhine during those four days of unrest. I think I would have marched in a planned protest, but this didn't feel planned. It felt like a spontaneous eruption of feeling and emotion in the Black community. At least that's how it was portrayed on television. This happened before social media, before everyone had a cell phone. Most of what was happening came to me from traditional media, hours after things happened. People on the news told us to stay away, and so I did. I remember one night of our break I gathered with some coworkers for a dinner party. Our talk went late, and we realized it was past curfew. We joked that maybe we'd be arrested for breaking the law. I wasn't worried about anyone at the party but James, who was Black. I asked him to call me when he got home so I'd know he arrived safely.

When our city erupted in fire and hatred, I didn't know what to do. Everything I had originally planned for our fourth quarter seemed irrelevant. How could we go back to business as usual when our streets were still smoldering? Reading *A Midsummer Night's Dream* wasn't going to change the world. What would? There's really so little one person can do to change anything. But if everyone did what one person can do, maybe something would change. The one thing I can do is teach people.

When we got back from spring break, my lesson plan was this: listen. My ninth graders talked for at least two class periods without a particular academic objective. My objective was to make things right somehow. I knew that speaking and listening are things we needed to do in an English class, but I was assessing something more than academics. What was the state of our soul, our children, our city? I wanted to know two things: What happened? And what do you want to do about it? I had been teaching for six years, but this incident seemed more important than anything I had on my lesson plan. I remember that many of the people who marched with Dr. King were in high school at the time. This was our civil rights moment. I was confident enough in myself, in my administration. I wasn't afraid that I would be punished if I didn't "follow the curriculum." I teach English, so I teach skills, not particular content. It doesn't really matter what we read, write, or speak about. It matters that students have many opportunities to practice reading, writing, and speaking. They needed to talk. I needed to listen.

Initially, I couldn't understand what the students were saying. In my mind, I wondered why someone would run from the police. Why didn't Timothy Thomas just surrender? I guess I thought he could set up a reasonable payment plan to pay his fines. But I listened to my students, and they taught me. They told me about the harassment my honor roll students received from the police. They told me about avoiding certain neighborhoods because of racist cops. They told me about cousins, brothers, uncles, and dads who were locked away from their families for months for the same types of violations as Timothy Thomas had allegedly committed. I listened and finally started learning.

Most of them spent their spring break like I did, glued to the television. Their parents were afraid to let them out the door. One of my kids, Chadsity, said, "They burned my store down." Some ignored curfew, going out on a dare. Someone said, "My uncle got us a new refrigerator." But most wanted to talk about feelings—anger, pain, frustration, fear—and together we wondered why this kept happening again and again in our city. Between 1995 and 2001, fifteen Black men suspected of crimes were killed by Cincinnati police while in custody. During the same period—third grade to ninth grade for my students—no white suspects were killed in custody.

My students taught me about the very different experiences they had with the police. I speed constantly and occasionally get a ticket. Usually, I just receive a friendly warning. I never had to worry about how the police would treat me when they pulled me over. They called me "ma'am" and told me to be careful. Kids I knew and trusted were having very different experiences with the Cincinnati Police Department than I was. No friendly warnings. Lots of tickets. And confrontations sometimes escalated into something like what happened to Timothy Thomas.

My students told me they pay a different price for their transgressions. They were harassed by police for moving too slowly in the crosswalk, running too fast in a crowd, or just standing on the sidewalk. Some of my honor students had been handcuffed for misunderstandings. Several of my kids had been arrested at one time or another. Many of them knew someone in jail. Some of them had watched as the police dragged their fathers away. They were having a different childhood than I had. At fourteen, I wouldn't have understood why Timothy Thomas ran from the police. In fact, I still didn't. But they did. My

Appalachian family was poor and had all the societal problems that go along with that—addiction, unemployment, undereducation, debt, and depression. But I listened to my students, and I believed them. I was beginning to understand that my family's white skin protected us. In a way, our white skin was bulletproof because white kids don't get shot by police the way Black kids do.

And what do you want to do about it?

When I asked students to think of something we could do, Kamika said, "We need to write some letters." It was a perfect first step. I told the kids they should write argumentative letters to anyone they thought might have influence over the situation, advising the recipients of what they could do to help. We each wrote at least one letter, and I mailed them. We sent letters to the mayor, city council, the police chief, the president of the Fraternal Order of Police. We wrote to prosecutors and defense attorneys. We wrote to Timothy Thomas's mother, his girlfriend, his baby. We read about Black leaders in our newspaper and so we wrote to the Black United Front, the group who sued the city and police department for racially profiling our Black citizens. We wrote to the president of the Sentinels, a union of Black police officers in Cincinnati, founded in 1968 when Black officers were not allowed to advance in the ranks of the Cincinnati Police Department. We wrote to ministers. We wrote to the newspaper and to TV and radio stations. We wrote letters and poems and essays and prayers. I sent every letter, and we got a few responses back. It was the best way for my students to see the impact that their voice, their words could make. What's more, the letter assignment met every standard that I needed to cover for argumentation, and my students wrote more and better than they usually did. They were writing for more than a grade. They were writing to change the world.

Next, we connected those words and ideas with the community. I went to as many meetings and protests as I could, trying to wrap my own mind around what was happening. Sometimes I took students with me. My Unitarian Universalist church's involvement in protests connected me with many people who could tell us about how things worked, what the real story was, what was coming next, and how to combat misinformation. Our church joined with other faith communities and asked me to pull together a panel discussion. Our panel was called Young and Black in Cincinnati, and about one hundred people came to hear my students give their perspective on police brutality and growing up in Cincinnati. My students were the experts, and our community learned from them. The assignment hit all of the standards I needed for teaching a speaking unit. Shelby spoke in front of people who wanted to hear what she had to say.

She did better there than she had on any previous speech in my class because the audience was real. I gave her an A, but the real grade came from the audience, who applauded and spoke to her as an expert after the panel.

We got inspired when we read about Dr. King and the civil rights movement, so we started saving up for a trip to the National Civil Rights Museum. The ninth-grade students I taught that year were looping, meaning that I would be their teacher again for the tenth grade. So we started fundraising—we consigned our clothes, sold kitchen utensils, and worked at ball games. We held a macaroni and cheese bake-off to raise money and claim bragging rights for the best mac and cheese. I applied for grants from the Ohio Department of Education and the W. H. G. Carter Foundation at First Unitarian Church to obtain funding for kids to go on the trip.

My coworker and mentor, Diana Porter, applied for a grant to help us teach about the civil rights movement. Over the summer, teachers met with Linda Christensen of the nonprofit publisher and advocacy organization Rethinking Schools to plan units on Melba Pattillo Beals's *Warriors Don't Cry* for the following fall. With the grant funding, we were able to buy every tenth-grader their own copy of the book. Christensen and Porter put the emphasis on using memoir to help students understand the parts of history that don't always make it into the history textbooks. Christensen taught me how to help kids step into the shoes of heroes like Beals and the rest of the Little Rock Nine, the teenagers who desegregated Central High School in 1957. One technique she taught us was something she called a tea party. It's a prereading activity that has students assume the role of a character in the book. The teacher gives each kid a slip of paper that describes a particular character and their associated conflicts with minimum detail and lets those characters mingle as if they were at a party. The teacher encourages discussion between the characters, sometimes guiding them with questions. Students assume the assigned personas and find out who their characters' friends and foes are in the book. I use this technique often with my classes now. Students start to see the tensions between characters. They quickly figure out which characters are friends and which are foes. When they put themselves in the shoes of the Little Rock Nine, they quickly see how dynamics of power—money, age, politics, race—impacted history.

At the end of their tenth-grade year, our students went on a trip to Memphis, where they were able to tour the National Civil Rights Museum at the former Lorraine Motel, where Dr. King took his last breath. We went to Little Rock Central High School National Historic Site, where Melba Pattillo Beals and the rest of the Little Rock Nine went to school with National Guard protection to protect them from racists. We went to Beale Street, home of the blues. These turned out to be some of the most memorable parts of my students' high school career. Some kids were staying in a hotel for the first time. They were seeing people who looked like them revered as national heroes.

I'm still friends with many of the kids who were with me then. They're still my "kids" even though they're in their thirties and have their own kids now. I'll be teaching some of those kids soon, too, I hope. In the spring of their ninth-grade year, April 2001, we watched our city burn, and we were together again in the fall of their sophomore year on September 11, 2001, when we watched the second tower fall on the television in my classroom. Certainly living through tragedies like these bond people together. Even more so, though, I think that what truly bonds us is that we listen to each other. I love those kids and thank them all the time for making me a better teacher. A better person. They led me away from Kipling and toward King, away from fear and toward love.

INTENSIVE TENSIONS—ON THE
BLOCK AND IN THE PARK

— Jared Fox —

My co-teacher Erick Espin and I are about to begin a week-long course. Espin, who identifies as Afro-Dominican and grew up in the public housing projects a few blocks from our Washington Heights school, is viewed as an insider by our Latinx student body. To me, a white teacher, it seems that Espin is able to bond and build deep connections with our students that I cannot emulate. In truth, I'm envious. This is not to say that I have not built meaningful relationships with the students I teach but instead that, in comparison to Espin's, my connections seem more formal and transactional, whereas his seem (to me) effortless and familial. For this reason and many more (Espin is an award-winning history teacher), I'm excited to be partnered with him for the week.

Our normal schedule at school is "frozen," and instead of following our regular timetable, all students will take one class, all day, for the entire week. This change in programming, also known as "intensives," draws heavily upon the tenets of the Expeditionary Learning model our school follows. The idea is that taking only one class over the course of a week will provide students an opportunity to get outside the classroom—literally, figuratively, or both—and explore a topic in depth. This pedagogical approach also serves as a means to provide students with the opportunity to earn a credit they may need for graduation. While Espin and I (as well as the rest of our school) have debated the merits of this approach to credit accumulation and the intersectionality of academic rigor, expectations, and race, we also acknowledge the need for teaching and learning that allows for the deep exploration of a topic that may not always be possible with our regular program.

The intent of our intensive class, Restoring Highbridge, is to encourage our students to examine the history of—and participate in the ongoing rehabilitation of—the park (Highbridge) across the street from our school. In the weeks leading up to the course, Espin and I have had to find a way to mesh our respective content expertise, personal backgrounds, and educational philosophies into a cohesive and meaningful learning experience for our students. This work was not easy and was oftentimes messy. Our conversations while planning this hyperlocal course were wide-ranging and touched on education, race, income, politics, and the environment. In sum, the science-teacher-as-activist in me wanted to pursue the goal of bringing light to the environmental injustices facing our local park and the surrounding community, while Espin, ever the historian, wanted to unpack the series of past events that led to the park's decline.

In recent years, Highbridge Park's caretakers and the surrounding community have wrestled with the challenges presented by an ongoing opioid epidemic. In contrast, green spaces found in whiter and wealthier neighborhoods have been largely spared. This is not the first time that race and income have had an impact on Highbridge. Decades ago, city planners, like Robert Moses, allowed the once contiguous stretch of green along Manhattan's northeastern edge to be transected by a series of highway overpasses, favoring suburban commuters over local residents. Today, unhoused encampments have taken hold underneath the exit ramps in the now isolated pockets of the park. And thanks to the heavy traffic that cuts through the neighborhood, Washington Heights has some of the city's highest air-pollution levels.

Despite these challenges, Espin and I think that Highbridge still provides a diamond-in-the-rough teachable moment for our students. In the week ahead, we will ask them to engage in the restoration of Highbridge and envision a greener future for their neighborhood.

As our initial planning sessions leading up to the intensive week came to an end, we were feeling confident our course would attract students who were curious about how to effect change in the local community. When we received our class roster, however, we learned that most of our students did not opt in because of the course description but instead were placed with us because they needed a science credit for graduation. We entered the week unsure. This reality reminded us of past conversations on the merits of intensives and led us to wonder if the goals we had created for our course were aligned with the needs and interests of the students on our class list.

On the first day, a classroom of near-silent and tired-looking students were seated in front of us. After introductions and a quick run-through of the day, we led our students outside into the cool November air. Many students grumbled as the cold filtered through their hoodies and ripped jeans. And despite our attempts during a preclass meeting to prepare students for the upcoming outdoor learning, it's safe to say many were not enthused to be leaving the warmth of the school building.

Thankfully, Highbridge Park is only a few short steps away from our school's front door. A series of twisting trails led us to an area under a bridge littered with discarded needles, past a series of unhoused encampments, down a crumbling set of stairs, and into a field adjacent to a highway that brought us close to, but nonetheless cut off from, the Harlem River. In our planning, Espin and I intentionally chose this route so our students, many of whom had never been to this part of the park, could take in Highbridge's condition and begin to understand that despite its current state, they still had a right to access this public space.

At the end of our descent we were greeted in a grassy field by a pair of bruised pickup trucks and the local site director of the New York Restoration Project (NYRP). When I was planning the course, the director's vast understanding of Highbridge's ecology assured me he was the perfect person to help our students begin to think differently about the park. Indeed, over the past few years, NYRP had become an integral partner to the senior-level environmental science class I taught during the school year. To me, NYRP provided our students an opportunity to connect with local experts and increased the authenticity of our course. In contrast, Espin, who had yet to interact with the organization, shared that he approached our partnership with NYRP with a healthy dose of hesitancy and skepticism.

During our planning, Espin and I shared our differing perspectives on the nonprofit world. I held the position that nonprofits were inherently a part of the greater good, while Espin questioned their existence and the larger governmental, societal, and systemic shortcomings that made them necessary. From our long and nuanced discussions, I came to recognize that my initial position stemmed from me being white and not from the community in which I taught. And because of my background, I was privileged with the ability to easily overlook (and honestly not even consider) the skepticism Espin had to my proposed partnership with NYRP. Where I only saw synergistic potential,

Espin, who had lived most of his life less than a five-minute walk from NYRP's office, had never heard of their work or supposed benefit to the community. He even wondered openly if their mission to beautify green spaces would only increase the ongoing gentrification issues facing the residents of Upper Manhattan. While our initial differences in opinion could have prevented us from reaching an agreement on whether to partner with NYRP, they instead created productive tensions. These tensions not only allowed us to better understand each other as educators and people, but we hoped they also would contribute to rich discussions that would provide exceptional learning experiences for the Black and Brown students in our class.

As we listened to NYRP's director, we learned that a few decades ago, when the nonprofit's attention first turned to Highbridge, invasive plants had taken over areas of the park. Our task for the day was to assist in removing these invasive plants and, by doing so, help restore the ecosystem. We had to divide into two teams. While one team worked on trail building, the other was tasked with removing Japanese knotweed plants—an invasive species that had taken over much of the park. The trail builders were responsible for shoveling mulch into a wheelbarrow, rolling the wheelbarrow uphill, dumping the mulch on the trail, and spreading out the mulch.

While team one was building the forest trail, team two was scattered across a steep slope removing knotweed. The Japanese knotweed plant is incredibly adept at replicating itself and extremely difficult to get rid of once established. After a quick lesson on how to effectively extract knotweed's fibrous roots from the hillside, students got to work. Before long, our students had grasped the best techniques for knotweed removal and turned their task into a contest to see who could extract the longest contiguous segment of root.

As our students worked, Espin was fully immersed in working elbow-to-elbow with them. In contrast, I spent my time in a more managerial role, hopping from group to group to offer words of encouragement and to troubleshoot. Reflecting on our roles, I'm curious how this dynamic may have landed with our students. Did our differing roles as teachers that day in the park reinforce stereotypical norms of race and power, or were they glossed over as a benign occurrence? When I asked Espin for his thoughts, he suggested that I "shouldn't look for a racial element that may not have been there." And in reality, this makes sense. It was I who had the longstanding partnership with NYRP and had planned this component of the course. However, as a white educator, I nonetheless feel these reflections (and more importantly having these conversations) are necessary for true partnership with Black and Brown students and educators to occur.

After a long day in Highbridge, we met back in the classroom to debrief. As students packed their bags and shuffled out the door, we acknowledged their efforts. We reminded them that the next day would look similar, but instead of pulling invasive bushes and building trails, they would be planting trees.

Then, standing alone in our classroom, Espin and I reflected on our first day. While we unpacked the lessons we had learned from our students and began to incorporate them into the next day's plan, Espin shared that his initial skepticism about NYRP was beginning to fade. After working with the organization in the field and learning more about its mission to target underserved communities, he shared my optimism in our partnership. Looking back on this moment, it could have been easy for me to say, "Of course, Espin, you had nothing to worry about. This is a partner that I have worked with for years, and I have seen first-hand their commitment to their mission." Instead, I listened. By listening and then reflecting on this moment, I have learned that sometimes my worldview as a white person may prevent me from fully considering the thoughts, ideas, and perspectives of the Black and Brown colleagues I work alongside and the Latinx students I teach.

The next day, we succeeded at planting a number of native trees to replace the invasive plants we had removed the day before. As our course moved into its final three days, we turned our attention to beautifying the blocks adjacent to our school. On one of these days we again met NYRP's pickup trucks. This time, they were piled high with mulch outside our school's front steps. While half of our students spread wood chips around street trees, the rest went on a neighborhood walk led by community residents. While many of our students are from the community and are experts in the goings-on of the neighborhood, Espin and I thought their hearing from other adults invested in the betterment of the community would add another layer of authenticity to our course and help them meet our learning goals.

The two community members were both longtime residents from the apartments across the street from our school and were deeply invested in trying to improve the conditions of the streets around their homes. One guide, a Filipino documentary filmmaker, approached Espin and me with the vision of connecting the six schools along our street in the name of neighborhood beautification. The other guide, a Latinx parent with children in our elementary grades, was concerned about the rise in litter and drug paraphernalia to which his children were being exposed on their daily walk to our school. As our guides took our students around the neighborhood, they urged students not to accept the conditions they saw in the community. And as they shared their perspectives, many of our students disclosed that they had come to normalize the cracked concrete, the alcohol-bottle-filled tree pits, and discarded syringes on their daily commute to school. Many believed there was little they could do to effect change. However, envisioning what that change might be is exactly what our guides and our learning objectives were asking them to do. We wanted our students to consider what that change might look like. And for their final project, we asked them to share their vision with us, their classmates, and the community.

On the final day of intensives, Espin and I asked our students to take their experiences and learning from the week and create a presentation about what they would like to see added to or changed in the neighborhood. While we had initially planned on giving students the entire last day to put their presentations together, Espin came up with another idea. He shared that he thought student projects would benefit from seeing a wealthier (and whiter) part of the neighborhood. While I was hesitant to lose student work time, he maintained that getting students to see another part of the neighborhood was worth any "lost time." After going back and forth on the issue, we decided to leave it up to our students. While some opted to stay behind in the classroom with me, others joined Espin and ventured outside.

It wasn't long after Espin and his group returned to the classroom that I realized the entire class would have benefited from the walk. The students who went out shared with me and their classmates pictures of blocks with mature street trees and sidewalks adorned with neatly trimmed shrubbery. Subsequently, these images (and the lessons learned about the inequities that existed in two parts of the same neighborhood) were placed on final-project slides next to those from pictures taken closer to the school. This juxtaposition provided a powerful narrative. The students who went on the walk with Espin were able to place the photos taken earlier in the week of tree pits littered with alcohol bottles and used syringes next to those they had taken on the final day. These contrasting images told a compelling story, and as students' presentations were shared, invited guests were able to see the images as well as hear powerful remarks from students like Dayana, who told a classroom visitor, "I've lived in this neighborhood my whole life, and it is unfair that me and my family have to walk past trashed tree pits on our street that I know are not tolerated in other parts of the neighborhood." There was no doubt a fire had been sparked for the students fortunate enough to go on that day's walk.

Upon reflecting on Espin's different perspective about this final pedagogical decision, I wondered whether his firsthand experience of living in the community and sharing a background with the students provided him with insight into how to get students to grasp our big learning goals. Did I, a white teacher, who was not from the community in which I taught, have a blind spot? Why did I default to providing "work time," while Espin suggested one final excursion? Were these differences a simple matter of approach to teaching and learning or more deeply connected to our backgrounds? As someone who likes to hedge their bets, I want to say that it was likely a bit of both, but that would be a cop-out. In this instance, I must acknowledge that Espin, like our students, came to our class with an inherent understanding of the place where he was born and raised. And that I, despite my best efforts and intentions, lack the funds of knowledge gained from growing up and living in a place for one's entire life. By humbly acknowledging this, my hope is that the next time a learning opportunity like the one on the last day of intensives arises, I will be better positioned to recognize and tap into it for the betterment of the students I teach.

As final presentations and intensive week ended, Espin and I were mentally and physically exhausted but proud of the work our students had completed and what we had done together as co-teachers. All of our planning had not only provided a meaningful, hyperlocal learning opportunity for our students but also had given us a deeper collegial and personal connection. Espin shared as much when he told me that the conversations we had during our planning sessions about systemic injustices and race were topics he rarely spoke about with other white people. I was grateful that Espin felt comfortable enough to open up with me. Still, I couldn't help but feel disheartened because this meant many of the other white educators at our school were not experiencing these kinds of conversations that were making me a better colleague and teacher. Reflecting now, I realize this same scenario is likely being played out in schools across our nation. Because I know how powerful the experience I had working with Espin was and how it ultimately has made me a better teacher (and person), I, in turn, want to present a challenge to my white colleagues across the country.

I want each of you to ask yourselves, What will I as a white educator do to create spaces where my Black and Brown colleagues can show up to teach and be their full selves? If you are unsure of where to begin, I offer my experience teaching with Espin and the conversations we had openly, honestly, and often as a possible place to start. And while this suggestion of having dialogue with your colleagues may seem overly simplistic, I argue that perhaps this most humane of human interactions is exactly what we as white teachers must seek and sustain.

STUDENT LEADERSHIP

MAKING COMPLEX CHANGES
WITHOUT THE WHITE-SAVIOR COMPLEX

– Holly Spinelli –

City-As-School High School is not a traditional educational space, which helped my former colleague JP Schneider and me co-facilitate a fully student-generated, student-led, and student-centered leadership class. While sharing about this course at education conferences in New York and around the country, I have encountered educators from more traditional schools who have expressed utter disbelief that such a course could exist. I assure you the course, the administration, and the communities who supported it, as well as my co-facilitator and the students who lived the experience are all real. This course, or one like it, can manifest in school communities that trust their educators to facilitate educational experiences in which students select and lead curricular choice.

City-As-School is one of the oldest experiential-learning programs in the New York City public school system. The school's population is composed of transfer students from all five boroughs. The admissions team is deliberate, and while the process is not perfect, the goal is to create a student body that represents communities across the city, especially those that are underserved, such as immigrants, multilingual learners, members of the LGBTQIA+ community, teen parents, and BIPOC students. Once admitted, students spend time learning skills at internships across the city, and the rest of their schooling takes place in-house with educators in classrooms. An especially unique element in the City-As-School tradition is requiring students to be physically present in the building to register for their own educational experiences. They must meet each teacher and internship coordinator so they can learn more about the experiences before registering. Students select their courses and internships as well as the educators with whom they prefer to learn, a process that gives them more control over their education. An algorithm can quickly calculate a schedule to fulfill graduation requirements, but it fails to give students and educators a chance to get to know one another and to talk about preferred learning styles and content-delivery methods.

Visiting the school on a registration day might look like a strange social experiment. However, we who work there refer to the long lines of students flowing into the hallways and endless one-on-one conferencing as "controlled chaos." I dare to call it magick[1] because in the midst of a particularly busy registration period, the leadership course was (re)born.

At that time, my English classes were already full. I was diligently creating my rosters when I overheard a conversation between the school's college counselor and a Black student patiently waiting for his turn to register for a class. Their exchanges seemed lighthearted, nothing more than general chitchat, but then the conversation grew more serious. The student expressed frustration with "stop-and-frisk" tensions rising between police and Black male residents in his neighborhood. My colleague politely said, "I can see this upset you. Have you considered volunteering or talking to someone who can help make some change?" The young man smiled and said, "Miss, all due respect, but with what time? I got school and work. I wish I could, but I can't. Not unless it's a class that can get me some credit to get out of high school." I perked up and interjected, "What if it was?" The student looked stunned. My colleague turned her head and grinned. She knew my question was sincere. The student smirked and shook his head in disbelief. I asked, "What if you could take a class in which you volunteer to do things in your own neighborhood, but you earned academic credit? You'd show up? You'd take it? You'd want to do that?" The young man shrugged and said, "I guess, but do you have that?" My heart sank. "No," I murmured. He shook his head as if he understood and explained that he was almost finished with earning his credits to graduate. I thanked him for talking and went back to finalizing my rosters.

The conversation ended there, but the idea the student sparked began to crystallize. Another colleague in the office, JP, a veteran math teacher, walked over to me at the end of the day. He said, "You know, I heard your conversation. I used to teach a class called leadership, and we did pretty much what you were talking about." Despite JP's self-proclaimed "white guy from the backwoods of Maine" persona, he spent his entire career—over twenty years of teaching—in the complex system of New York City public schools and wasn't jaded. I was a young Italian American woman and had spent my life in New York City and its surrounding suburbs. I attended public schools. I grew up in a multigenerational household; my single mother and my grandparents raised my older brother and me. JP and I were different, but we were two white educators who believed students' voices belong in all school-wide decision-making. JP knew the importance of getting the adults, especially white adults, to move out of the way so kids, especially BIPOC children, could develop their own education. I shared his vision.

We immediately got to work. I grabbed a legal pad and a pen. We sat at the table in the office, and I asked JP to tell me what the leadership class was and why it disappeared. He talked about the course's student-centered philosophy and student-created projects. He spoke about the leadership class as a way to get students involved in their own neighborhoods. The course fell by the wayside with pressure from No Child Left Behind and state standards changing what constituted an "academic" experience. I knew that if we could demonstrate how the course would help students develop standards-aligned skills, we would have a solid chance to offer a course in which students would fully take the reins. We brainstormed, dreaming of what it could be. We agreed to talk to students coming in the next day for registration. We agreed that their input on the course outline mattered the most. We agreed that students, regardless of whether they chose to register for the class (if it was even approved), would be the ones to shape the course. JP and I started with the following outline:

- All projects and ideas are student generated.
- All projects and ideas have to be connected to a student's lived experience and/or desire to affect positive change in something affecting their communities and their lives.
- Students cannot select projects in which they infuse themselves, their beliefs, or their ideas into a space that isn't part of their lived experience.
- Any "outside" project requires students and educators to conduct thorough research on any organizations or leaders. Students will be required to work closely with someone with lived experience on the subject matter and allow that "expert" to lead us and guide us in the project.
- Students must create a proposal (written or verbal) and present their project ideas to one another. Proposals should address the following: the

project focus, why students chose the project, ideas for implementa-
tion, students' hopes, the project's sustainability, positive and potentially negative project impacts, possible roadblocks, and how the
project connects to students' lived experience(s).
- The work is created in small groups or with the whole class, but it is
ultimately the students' choice in determining which projects to complete or combine.
- We, the white educators in the room, must remain facilitators and
consultants only. We cannot take the lead. We support students' efforts
and help with logistics.
- It's okay if projects do not come to fruition. "Failure" for a project to
materialize does not equate to course failure.
- Reflection is an integral part of our lived experiences, and all class participants, including the educators, will reflect upon what did and didn't
work and synthesize why and how we can attempt to make the project
work with different methods.

The following day, JP and I asked students for input. Several said they liked
our ideas, but the inevitable question arose: What academic credits could they
earn? I explained specific written and oral communication standards and tied
them to the outline's requirements. JP and I spent the morning rushing between
offices, taking suggestions from students and adding their ideas to our outline.
Our excitement grew. We knew we were on the verge of something special and,
most importantly, something that authentically connected students' learning
to using their voices and skills to enact real change in their lives.

JP and I revised our proposal with the students' suggestions. We outlined
step-by-step templates to help students with research methods, planning, contact and meeting protocols, and general guidelines to facilitate community
building and open communication. We made an appointment to meet with our
principal, Antoniette Scarpinato. When we walked into her office, she looked at
the two of us and said, "What on earth did *you two* come up with?" She was half
joking but curious. JP nudged me to speak first. I explained the whole course and
how it came about, and her wry smile softened with sincerity. After presenting
our detailed outline, the course was approved with the following conditions:

1. Students must be supervised at all times, especially if we are traveling
off school grounds and/or working with the public.

2. All written communication between students and people outside of the school must be pre-approved. Verbal communication between students and people outside of the school must be supervised by a school educator or staff member.
3. Don't screw it up.

The following registration cycle, the leadership course made the list. Administration approved one section. During registration, students mostly asked about the course content. JP and I replied, "What do you want it to be?" or "What do you want to do that nobody else in your neighborhood has given you a chance to do?" Some students shrugged with uncertainty. Others lit up with excitement. A few walked away saying the class sounded like too much work. We respected all responses. Thankfully, the class was full by the end of the first registration day.

Once class began, the students, JP, and I worked on community agreements. We talked about how we wanted to communicate with each other. Students required honesty, respect, and support for each other, even when they disagreed. We talked about the kinds of responsibilities we'd have and how to hold each other accountable. *Being present* and *admitting when you need help* made the top of the list. The students agreed that a reflection after each project made sense to help us synthesize our experiences and potentially serve as a springboard for future class participants. JP and I made it clear that we were to be held equally accountable for these agreements.

When the first round of projects came about, students pitched ideas individually and then broke into small groups to talk with one another about how to make these projects happen. Not every student pitched a project. Some opted to help others with their pitches. JP and I listened and took notes. Our job was to record everything and read it back to the students at the end of each class. Afterward, the students determined the next class meeting's focus. The students took their time to weigh their options:

1. They could work in small groups to complete everyone's proposed project in the short time we had together.
2. They could select a few projects and have larger teams work on them.
3. They could rally behind one project as a class and give it our full attention.

The students discussed these options for two class sessions. Finally, they came to a consensus: they agreed to work together on one project to make it a success.

The student who pitched the idea became the project "leader." It was her job to work with her teammates to plan their project from beginning to end. The team brainstormed and often argued passionately about which ideas would work best.

That first project centered on contacting local food stores to help supplement the local food banks in Brooklyn. At the time, our nation was reeling from a recession, and food banks across the city were overwhelmed. The student who pitched the project worked in a local grocery store and was bothered by seeing groceries thrown away as they approached—but before they reached— their expiration dates. She knew students in the class had experiences using food bank services and wanted to make sure the good food reached families in need. A student in the class with food bank experience said that despite volunteers' kindness, she always wanted to shop for her own items. She had family members with health, cultural, and religious dietary restrictions, and she knew other families who used the food banks likely did too. She brought this concern to the class, and after a few disagreements, students came up with the "shopping" model: providing folks with empty bags to "shop" for their own items at the food bank.

Well before this project was complete, JP and I agreed that the students achieved success. They were collaborating. They were communicating. They were problem-solving. Students worked together to further humanize the food bank experience.

After the student who worked at a grocery store spoke to her manager, he offered to donate unexpired items. Another student from the neighborhood spoke to the person in charge at the local food bank and got them to agree to run a trial with the new model. Without hesitation, the students wrote up a proposal, made an appointment with our school administration, and got our school to host the food bank's "shopping" event on a Saturday. The event was a success. So much food was available that folks even drove in from New Jersey to pick up leftover food after someone in the neighborhood called a radio station and the DJ made an announcement about the event. A group of students was responsible for asking shoppers one anonymous "survey" question about the day's shopping experience. The attendees all said they liked having the opportunity to shop for their own items. The following week, the class celebrated their success and took time to reflect. Students agreed the project's personal connection and local focus legitimized their efforts. They agreed that they didn't need "outsiders" to come in and "solve problems" without fully consulting the community and then leaving. They took ownership of it. It was theirs.

Many projects followed in the five years JP and I co-taught the class. Two larger projects with similar successes included:

> A book-exchange program went from a small, local book exchange among Black students at their local community center to a full-fledged book-donation program that resulted in students collecting over 1,200 books— some in Swahili and French—to donate to the first public library in Rwanda.
>
> A partnership with Habitat for Humanity and local tradespeople formed to help repair affordable-housing apartments in a predominantly Black and Latino neighborhood in Brooklyn that was severely damaged after Hurricane Sandy.

The book-exchange and the Habitat for Humanity projects succeeded because the students were invested in implementing change for and with their own neighborhoods. They didn't expect their concerns in their neighborhoods to have far-reaching consequences. A few students leading the book project lived in a neighborhood with people who immigrated from or near the borderlands of Rwanda, so offering to donate books to Rwanda's first public library made sense to connect their neighbors to their homelands. Students didn't need "saving" from well-meaning white educators. These were solutions-seeking young folks who, with the right space and respect from educators, used their collective voices and talents to implement the changes they wanted to see in their communities.

When students' ideas potentially affected additional spaces in which they did not personally reside, they considered these questions:

- Which local folks and local organizations could be involved and give input?
- What goals do the local folks and organizations have for this project?
- How will this project be sustained after the initial work is complete?

These students participated in grassroots community organizing. Their work was not rooted in performative allyship or white saviorism. The students generated each project. They networked with community contacts. They worked together to achieve their goals. The students drove the curriculum. The students made the decisions. The students held each other accountable. They shared their victories and defeats. Not every project was a success. Some failed. Others did not turn out the way the students envisioned.

One project that failed to launch was a support effort for the New York City ASPCA. Students could not agree on the project's focus. Pit bulls were growing in popularity in Black and Latino neighborhoods, and the students considered helping with a pit bull education program for their neighborhoods. However, the students were indecisive and struggled to move past their differences. JP and I bickered about how much intervention we should provide. I was still new to teaching and wanted to jump in and help the students compromise. JP thought it was best to let the students identify when they wanted us to step in, not the other way around. At the time, I struggled to see his point. I thought our job was to help. JP explained that our intervention would be the two white adults taking over the project. Nearly a decade later, I see his point.

After each project, students took time to reflect together in discussion and individually in writing. They reflected on their successes, struggles, problem-solving skills, and how they could make another attempt at the project with the knowledge and experience they had as a result of their first attempt. No matter what, the students were successful because the school administration, JP, and I decentered ourselves. The students' success was a result of their teamwork, vision, personal lived experiences, and leadership.

PART THREE

LANGUAGE AND HIP-HOP

After working in elementary, middle, and high schools in urban districts for close to two decades, we have both found that—for the most marginalized young people—effective teaching is less about feeding young people academic content and more about working with them to recover what has been lost to repressive schooling experiences so that they are empowered and inspired to pursue learning. Not solving but salving. Real healing to reveal hunger for learning and growth.

Children are deeply affected by the knowledge, language, and traditions of their home communities. Each story told, each handshake given, each hip-hop lullaby heard, each kitchen calendar seen shapes the child. But then, like pieces of delicately crafted pottery, children are sent into the fire of schooling. The fire can delicately surround the clay until it firms up, or that fire can cause blemishes, burns, and breaks. Flame marks and fractures aren't necessarily bad. In the Japanese tradition of Kintsugi, cracks are painted gold and celebrated. But when the discolorations are seen as deficits and the crevices created are ignored, students suffer. No matter what is offered, if students are treated as—and therefore come to see themselves as—broken, they cannot hold what is being shared. On the other hand, if students see themselves as whole and intact, they can receive what is being poured.

Dominant forms of schooling ignore the intricacies of students, where they come from and how they were shaped. Instead they treat children like mass-produced canisters. They attempt to pour knowledge in with little regard for the receptacle. For Black and Brown students in white-culture dominant schools, what is poured in is often corrosive, which is to say it causes a chemical reaction that eats the clay from the inside out.

Hip-hop and African American Vernacular English are components of the cultural clay from which many students are shaped. When they enter schools that do not honor what they are made of, they cannot learn.

The essays in this section remind us of the value of the clay from which our children have formed. The essays illustrate the ways the earth forms to become beautiful pottery and how it can be honored and protected. When Black and Brown children are exposed to a pedagogy that is corrosive to what they are made of, each exposure burns their self-confidence, their voice, and their imagination.

Good teaching then requires (re)fortifying the ceramics. Returning students back to what they were made of. Teaching is about recovery. Before we get to content or standards, rubrics or benchmarks, our first work is to allow children to recover their language and culture, to feel the compounds and the textures they form as strong and beautiful terracotta.

Interestingly, the essays in this section are written in highly academic language, even as they advocate for the language and culture of children who have been devalued by school. Perhaps it feels necessary to lean into academic parlance in order to justify the language and culture of a population that the system has viewed as nonacademic.

Without the contributors of the following essays explicitly stating it, they have found ways to bring together the worlds they advocate for and the worlds they inhabit as white folks in academic settings. What is created in this process is a hybrid of sorts that is more nuanced than any one context would be on its own. This enmeshing of worlds can exist in gradients. Some are heavy on the academic tip. Some (through the lyrics featured) are more ratchet. Somehow, they end up moving toward what we see as ratchetdemic—equal parts ratchet and academic—while being altogether brilliant and necessary. Just like the children and the languages they vocalize and devise.

SAY IT LOUD—DECENTERING WHITENESS IN CLASSROOM DISCOURSE

– Rick Ayers –

It goes without saying, then, that language is also a political instrument, means, and proof of power. It is the most vivid and crucial key to identify: It reveals the private identity, and connects one with, or divorces one from, the larger, public, or communal identity. There have been, and are, times, and places, when to speak a certain language could be dangerous, even fatal.

—JAMES BALDWIN—"If Black English Isn't a Language, Then Tell Me, What Is?"[1]

DeAndre, a young Black man in my tenth-grade English class, is posted up in the hallway between classes, back resting against the wall, watching the flow of students and commenting on everything he sees. It's a loud public performance of greetings and call-outs, freestyling inventions, samples from tracks, improvisational jokes, and deep social critique: "Ay, Cuzzo! Why you gonna side-eye me, foolio!" . . . "Ay, teach, you lookin' fitted today!" . . . "Here come football star! I know, I know, I know . . . it's hard bein' you." . . . "Go on, little sis, you late now, you almost late anyway." The bell rings, and the hall begins to clear. DeAndre is the last one into class, slouching off his backpack and sitting near the back, silent now and withdrawn. I'm teaching English language arts—literacy, verbal expression, poetry, rhetoric, debate—all skills that DeAndre is the king of in the hallway. Yet, here he is silent. Something is wrong with this picture. I wonder how to allow him to bring his entire identity into the classroom, to leverage this performance of literacy brilliance to advance his school success. Or, better yet, to change the definition of school success to include DeAndre's powerful skills.

The struggle over language practices, and the link between language and power, burst to the surface in 1996 when the Oakland School Board declared that Ebonics, also known as Black English or African American Vernacular English (AAVE), should be recognized by teachers and honored in the classroom. This set off an explosion of pushback, with the outraged narratives filling the opinion pieces in outlets across the country, including the *New York Times*, and in letters pages in most newspapers—"Why teach ignorance. . . . School should elevate student skills . . . These teachers are lazy."

Eventually, more reflective perspectives came forward. Dr. Theresa Perry and Dr. Lisa Delpit, in articles and then a book, unpacked the deeper issues of language and power that underlie the struggle over discourse practices and exposed the coded racism in the outcries that filled the daily press.[2] I realized that I would have to teach the controversy. If my school was to be a place of culturally relevant pedagogy, or what Django Paris and H. Samy Alim call culturally sustaining pedagogy, then the raging debates about Ebonics, AAVE, and power would have to come inside the classroom.[3]

Unsure of how to take the first steps, I began a project in which my students and I would embark on an inquiry into these questions of language, discourse, and vernacular together. Being in Berkeley, a university town, we had an urban high school with BIPOC and low-income students as well as more privileged, upper-middle-class ones. My goal was to acknowledge and make a place for AAVE. I was uncertain of how I, as a white middle-class teacher raised in the world of Standard (or school) English, could advance the conversation. Indeed, to even go into this area might generate anger and distrust. Ultimately, I decided to try it out and see where we would go. I planned a unit called "Language and Power" for my tenth-grade class, which included a diverse mixture of students. We would read authors such as Lisa Delpit and Geneva Smitherman, but we would also interrogate our own discourse practices. Students would come to see that discourse was something more complex than simply "language." Discourse also involves cultural ways of knowing, communication that includes body language and inflection, and even how humor and argument are used.

As we got started, I noticed more attention from the class. This was something different than the normal march through lessons. DeAndre had seen some of the Ebonics debate on television and was incensed by it. "I'm still trying to figure out what you think about all this," he said with some skepticism after our first discussion of the issues. I left it open-ended, as I was learning at the same time. Besides doing readings, we embarked on some fieldwork. I asked students to carry a notebook out in public and to transcribe overheard conversations. This could be on the bus or the street corner or any place that worked. The pages they brought back were fascinating, containing discourse practices from all walks of life—including "valley girl" speak, youth dialect, and unhoused monologues—and we analyzed meaning and style together. Students could see that each discourse carried its own joy and creativity, its own grammar and syntax. We were exploring language and becoming metacognitive about our own practices.

I then asked students to write a short essay on their year in school so far—but to write it completely in their own home discourse, or community discourse, or friend discourse. Again, a great variety of pieces came in. As each student took the "author's chair" and read their piece, students began laughing and teasing each other. These words, these sentences, had never appeared in school work. DeAndre and his friends were laughing . . . and engaged. The joy, spontaneous metaphors, and bouncy cadence from the hallway interactions were appearing on the page.

The next step, however, was to "translate" their essays into standardized English. We discussed this discourse—how it was no better or worse at expressing ideas, that it was a signal of connection to white middle-class power, and that was the discourse often demanded in schools—and we dethroned it from a place of "correctness." Given that context, it was not so difficult for students to make this translation, to demonstrate skills at code-switching.

Too often when teachers encourage students to code switch, the process is a one-way street, another way to demand that students adopt the discourse of the white middle class. By implication, this repeats the educational myth of a cultural deficit in the Black community. But we have to remember: this dominant discourse was not created by God, and it would not always be this way.

Too many teachers are bowing down to white language practices from eighty years ago and pretending that the only way to get a job is to go along with these practices. But in the changing world of today, the new languages of academia, of journalism, and of business are in fact crumbling that edifice of the past.

Today, students can code switch in all directions. They know they have one discourse for friends, another for talking to Grandma, one for the job, and yet another for school. Ana Zentella describes middle school girls in Harlem who are adept at Spanish, Spanglish, Puerto Rican slang, Ebonics, and standardized English—and quickly code switch depending on who they are interacting with.[4]

But generally, school performance requires that students ignore, or even turn against, their own cultural and linguistic toolkit. We read a chapter of Richard

Rodriguez's autobiography in which he examines the long and lonely path to school success for him, a young child of immigrants in Los Angeles.[5] He was not a troubled or resistant student. He describes himself as the super-achiever, the "scholarship boy," the exception to his peers. And yet, he realizes many years later, each success that welcomed him into the cool rationality of school took him further from the warm and garrulous world of his parents. He ends up regretting his cruelties—correcting his parents' English, being impatient with the conversations at home. Richard Rodriguez gained a great deal by being a successful student, but he also lost something—his working-class home and family.

He says more than this, though. Rodriguez recognizes that, while he was a compliant and hard-working student, he was also a bad student. Intimidated and imitative, he failed to offer opinions of his own. He plowed through books with determination but never brought his own point of view or stance to the text. So the problem of discourse and power continued to dominate him, even as he "succeeded" and rejected his parents.

As a classroom English teacher, I recognized that young people who resisted school every day were flocking to out-of-school nonprofits that celebrated their lives and their literacies. Youth Radio, where beats and commentaries and documentaries were produced weekly, was crowded with high school kids learning the technical and narrative skills to go on the air. Youth Speaks organized spoken-word projects and slams with the slogan, "Because the next generation can speak for themselves," and was exploding throughout the country. Young people were giving their all, staying late, perfecting skills—with no promise of a grade or a college admission. What were we doing wrong in our classrooms (or, perhaps, what did we ever do right)?

Students in my Language and Power Unit had fun with their vernacular essays and then presented new versions in a pretty good version of school English. One interesting finding was that the white middle-class students would say to the class, "Well, my first version and my second version of the essay look pretty much the same." Exactly. And that was the point. They lived and thrived in the discourse that was ratified by school authorities. In other words, they were starting on third base and being told they were successful. This, then, was not just a lesson for those who are marginalized in school but a chance to explore privilege, the real core of structural racism, in school language practices.

The next project in the unit was for the students to create a slang dictionary as an exploration and study of their home discourses. Each student brought in five cards with a word on each, complete with pronunciation guide, etymology (as well as could be divined), part of speech, and sample sentence. After the words were typed up and arranged in alphabetical order, they were posted on the wall—provoking extensive debate and correction until each word was acceptable to the class. This was not a project of rejecting what has been anointed as "standard" English but rather of understanding deeply the interaction of different language practices. In addition, students were learning dictionary notation and symbols as well as productive debate skills about meaning.

Over the years as I taught this unit, the slang dictionary was updated and changed. Students participated in extended debate about meaning, implication, sourcing, and appropriateness of different terms. It was interesting to me that we were able to go deep into discussions of respect and personal rights as we encountered controversial words (like the B-word and the N-word). Of course there was slang for drugs, sometimes as a code to keep it from the snooping of adults—such as "trees" or "grapes." There were words related to robbery ("gank") and insults ("cappin") but also terms of respect and uplift ("props"). There were terms for violence ("merked") and even murder ("187"), but it's interesting to note there were many more terms for friend ("homie," "homeskillet," "cuzzo") as teens are deeply concerned about relationships and friendship. Sex was of course on their minds—sometimes in the sad impersonal way of teen sex ("hit it") and sometimes with tenderness and care ("spoonin").

Some words had their own declension, as with the superlative of "wack" being "wickety-wack." And there was joy and humor in the required sample sentences, such as the one found in this entry: "Scraper (SCRAP ur) n., An old school car, usually a Buick. Often fixed up with fancy, loud stereo systems. 'Coach Malik's baby blue scraper got slap!' [Origin, African American]." The diversity of the classroom was reflected in contributions from different cultures, such as "No mames," which was a Mexican phrase that meant "Leave me alone."

No classroom story is simply a one-dimensional report of success, and in my own efforts I committed plenty of mistakes. For instance, there was the morning class a few weeks into the language unit when Charles had just finished sharing a personal essay from the author's chair. "That was brilliant, off the heazy!" I declared with a big smile. A pained look crossed the faces of a number of students who instantly read my breach of proper diction, mixing two discourses and marking myself as trying a bit too hard. I should add that this moment, this confrontation with issues of authenticity and appropriation, had not just Black students but also many white students—who were certainly conversant in AAVE as part of their youth culture—checking my credentials.

At this point and others, I had to reflect on and check my positionality as a white middle-class male teacher in this space. It would not do to pathetically try to adopt the youth vernacular and always use it slightly incorrectly. Here in the exploration of their home and peer language practices, the students were the experts, the ones to argue over and correct the terms and usage. This gave me the chance to model being an interested outsider, the amateur willing to learn. In time, I learned that I could pepper my speech with youth slang—never in a sense of trying to pose, but rather as a curious and good-humored apprentice.

For white teachers to approach culturally relevant, culturally sustaining pedagogy, we need to learn to engage with our students' cultures as open-hearted educators, not appropriators. We need to approach our BIPOC students with humility and always as learners—positioning everyone as both learner and teacher. In other words, we can love hip-hop, we can "get" hip-hop, and we can even contribute to hip-hop, but there are so many ways to go wrong if we are trying to claim or own hip-hop. We have to learn to be respectful outsiders as well as allies, not owners or controllers or interpreters of community cultures.

My Language and Power Unit reversed power relations, first regarding classroom discussion and then ultimately in all areas because students were given the right to speak up and emerge as sources of authority and leadership in the classroom. For me, teaching this unit was the first time I broke from that nagging weight of feeling that, as a teacher, I am supposed to act as an agent of the state, expected to be the discourse police, surveilling and assessing the linguistic performance of students and often foreclosing their academic options. Schools reinforce and reproduce social hierarchies as they identify the home language practices of BIPOC students to be nonacademic.

All the students, especially BIPOC students, enjoyed and laughed throughout the unit. Instead of being a forbidding code fraught with pain and anger, language became something they owned. Students were pleased to show what they knew well—wisdom that had never previously been validated in the classroom while unleashing their curiosity about other language practices without threatening their own identity or dignity. And there is no question that after this unit students approached participation in classroom discussions, and writing, with more enthusiasm and sense of ownership. In fact, as the students learned to critique the gatekeepers of success, they were more successful in navigating them. DeAndre was able to bring his swag into the classroom and to make it a more joyful place.

The inclusion of this unit, which I continued for years, did not transform the entire school experience for students. After all, the challenges, setbacks, and the hostility of the institution to those most in need of support continued. While all children and adolescents bring important cultural resources from their home and community experiences, the cultural hierarchy reflected in schools deems the belief systems, epistemologies, learning styles, ways of making an argument, and methods of using the language of low-income and BIPOC communities as deficits. This is how the dominant group pretends to be a meritocracy, claiming that educational success rewards effort and achievement, when the knowledge examined in schools favors white middle-class practices and grades and accolades are doled out accordingly.

By disrupting the hierarchy of discourses, we are inviting everyone to the commons, to the public space of the classroom, in a more democratic way. Reflecting on all of this, it strikes me that too often white teachers think of "culturally relevant pedagogy" as simply a matter of finding a hook to interest BIPOC students, then expect that it's fine to go back to the same old white literature, history, and knowledge claims. To pursue critical humanizing education, teachers need to allow community knowledge—community genius—to take center stage in the classroom. Students need to develop all kinds of skills—but these must be skills directed toward the liberation of their communities, not simply for "access" to a retrogressive academic pathway, not to "escape" from their communities. By challenging the hegemony of white middle-class discourse, we take an important step toward making our classrooms truly inclusive and generative.

And this means that we are not just holders of wisdom and teaching strategies but that being a teacher in solidarity with our BIPOC students will change us in ways we do not even know ahead of time. If we white teachers mean to fight racism, our first responsibility is to challenge it where it originates, in the white community. If we are teaching in Black and Brown communities, we are not there to save anyone, and we are not trying to fix something wrong in our students. Our responsibility is to pursue a curriculum of questioning and to support our students in reading the word and the world in a project of humanization and empowerment.

Our students have experienced the violence of exclusion for years and have often learned survival through resistance. It is not enough to convince them to come back into the fold of hostile content and pedagogy. Immersing the class in discourse study allowed DeAndre's brilliance, which was always there, to have a place in the classroom and to thrive. White teachers who want to make a difference will need to let go of the patronizing idea that all things in our culture are the gold standard. We educators have to fight to change not only the teaching but the very linguistic markers of success, the gatekeepers that are built on standardized tests and the scholarship of dead white men. This is how we can begin to make schools places of welcome, of community empowerment, for our students.

WORKING IN THE STUDIO AND PERFECTING OUR CRAFT

— Brian Mooney —

I'm steady workin' in the stu[dio]
perfectin' my craft.

—JALEN

At 6 p.m. on a chilly evening in December, my cell phone rings, and I imme-diately recognize the number flashing on the screen. It's the security guard at the front desk of our high school calling to see if I'm still in the building. She knows I've been working in the recording studio on the third floor with several students making music. "It's time to pack it up," she says, a friendly reminder that students are not allowed in the building at this hour. When we get down to the lobby after saving our work and packing our bags, it is quiet and empty, a jarring sonic contrast to the small office space that we have converted into a recording studio on the top floor. In that room, padded with acoustic foam panels, music blared from studio monitors as students laid down multiple takes of rap vocals over instrumental beats. It's Friday evening, and we have the building to ourselves.

That recording studio became a popular space for my students and their friends. Over the course of one school year, at least ten Black and Latinx male students co-constructed and recorded music at our small public magnet high school in a large urban district in the northeastern United States. It wasn't uncommon for students to voluntarily stay late on Friday, when the building was mostly empty, to get their turn at recording original music.

This essay is an opportunity for me to engage one student, Jalen, as a case study to explore how Black male high school students use rap lyric writing to tell stories and explore emotions. It was driven by (a) my wonderings about the literacy practices of Black males who participate in and identify with hip-hop; (b) how I might work alongside them as a white collaborator through a humanizing praxis that seeks to develop the critical consciousness of both teachers and students; and (c) what it means to co-create an anti-racist hip-hop arts space through a pedagogy of radical love and care.[1]

ANTI-RACIST LANGUAGE PEDAGOGIES

Culturally sustaining pedagogy seeks to "perpetuate and foster—to sustain— linguistic, literate, and cultural pluralism as part of schooling for positive social transformation."[2] Django Alim and H. Samy Paris discuss hip-hop pedagogy as a form of culturally sustaining pedagogy but call for more critical, nuanced studies in which we engage with complexities and contradictions that are sometimes reified by youth engaged in hip-hop culture.[3] It's important for white educators to confront these contradictions alongside students.

Alim and April Baker-Bell both call for pedagogies that affirm Black language. Both scholars critique white linguistic supremacy through what Alim calls "critical hip-hop language pedagogies" and what Baker-Bell calls "anti-racist Black language pedagogy."[4] As a speaker of white mainstream English, I find it is critical for me to reflect on the ways I have internalized white linguistic supremacy, examine how it lives in me, and continuously work to dismantle those beliefs in and through my pedagogy. These theories offer us a way to see the language, literacy, and cultural practices of Black youth through a strength-based perspective while acknowledging the harmful effects of the "language ideological combat" that is being waged inside and outside of classrooms.[5]

THE HIP-HOP RECORDING STUDIO AS A SITE OF POSSIBILITY

Hip-hop is a legitimate site for labor.[6] What many educators see as "'play' is actually 'work' in the field of hip-hop."[7] Jalen's words at the beginning of this essay highlight the serious work ethic of students who recorded music in the studio. Although the studio cultivated linguistic play, experimentation, and joy, it was also a symbolic space in which the young men came to put in work.[8] Decoteau J. Irby, Emery Petchauer, and David Kirkland frame this labor through a Bordieuan theory of cultural production in which Black males have the agency to control themselves, their labor, and their products.[9] Laboring in hip-hop represents pathways to legitimate employment options and futures that often contrast with the capitalistic ways schools offer career education.

In an ethnographic study of hip-hop recording studios, Geoff Harkness described the studio as a site of hard work and emotional labor where rappers work to perfect their craft. He examined the recording studio as a "symbolic space: a 'zone' in which identity and meaning are shaped by social exchanges that occur within a culturally specific location."[10] Through interviews with professional and amateur rappers, producers, DJs, and studio owners, he documented the transformative experience that many rappers felt when stepping into the booth and the "legitimization they felt upon recording for the first time."[11]

Ian P. Levy and Edmund S. Adjapong examined the process of co-constructing hip-hop recording studios in school-counseling environments. Through an approach called hip-hop and spoken-word therapy, clinicians are provided with "a set of hip-hop–centered tools that they can use in the counseling process to support youth in exploring difficult thoughts and feelings . . . [including] lyric writing as emotive journaling."[12] The researchers highlight the recording studio as a therapeutic space of possibilities where urban youth are afforded an opportunity to share their "voice" and "message."[13] The authors' focus on how the physical design of the studio underscores the importance of creating an authentic cultural space that looks and feels like a professional studio.

Emotive journaling and lyric writing have been shown to be an effective form of counseling with male clients.[14] Research that documents the effects of emotional writing has shown favorable physical, psychological, and physiological results. Levy and Brian TaeHyuk Keum note that "At its core, great Hip-hop lyricism is emotional writing."[15] They conclude that emotional writing in the context of hip-hop may offer significant benefits for Black men to express themselves in culturally authentic ways.

CONTEXT

The story of the recording studio begins at home, where over the course of several years I acquired most of the components of a home studio, including a high-quality condenser microphone, an audio interface, studio monitors, sound isolation foam, a digital audio workstation, headphones, a mic stand, a pop filter, turntables, a mixer, and various beat-making controllers. I taught myself how to use most of the software and hardware through tutorials on YouTube, experimented with making instrumental beats in various genres, and then brought some of the equipment to my former school district, where many students of diverse backgrounds recorded music and spoken-word poetry, and learned how to DJ.

A CASE OF JALEN

During the 2018–2019 school year, I worked closely with at least ten Black and Latinx male high school students who regularly created music in the recording studio. Jalen (pseudonym) was a sixteen-year-old Black male who wrote and recorded original music in our school-based recording studio during that time. Our work together primarily happened in the recording studio during extracurricular time, mostly after school, as part of the Music Production Club.

I chose to focus exclusively on Jalen for this essay mostly because of his commitment, work ethic, and productivity, which created an abundance of material to study. He would show up early and stay late after his scheduled recording times, engage in critical listening to both his music and the work of others, and provide constructive feedback to other student rappers.

This dedication had all the hallmarks of what we label a "high-performing" student in traditional academic classes. That's why I found it so disconcerting when Jalen's sophomore English teacher—a veteran colleague—described him as "unmotivated" during a conversation we had one afternoon. I had asked this colleague how a few of the young men I worked with in the studio were performing in class. As I went down the list of names, he described nearly all of the young men, including Jalen, as lacking the very qualities that I witnessed after school in the recording studio.

Through my dialogue with this teacher, I could identify in his language the kind of deficit thinking that has historically oppressed Black males in school. This symbolic violence relegates Black male students to the margins of their educational experience while failing to recognize and build upon their many linguistic variations of brilliance. This disconnect between this teacher's perception of Jalen and my observations working with him in the studio provided a primary motivation for this essay.

I first met Jalen in the fall of his sophomore year as students were helping me construct the recording studio. He expressed his eagerness to "get in the stu" ("stu" being the abbreviation students used for "studio") and begin recording songs. Although Jalen wasn't in my English class during the day, we began to build a relationship through our work together in the studio.

I quickly found that my expertise with the technical aspects of beat-making and recording vocals in a digital audio workstation enabled Jalen and others to see me as someone with cultural capital.[16] What could amount to several hundred dollars of time in a professional recording studio was available for free to Jalen and his peers. Students who worked in the studio knew this and playfully insisted that I should charge for studio time.

Jalen knew the value of time in the studio, and he never wasted it. He came prepared with new songs every week. Sometimes he would write or finish part of a verse in the studio, but most of his writing was done beforehand. Often, he would try to rap or sing a line that wasn't quite working and then revise on the spot until it fit nicely over the beat. His process included preparation, generative writing, feedback, editing, revision, and performance—representing all of the steps in the writing process.

When Jalen's peers signed up for specific studio time but then arrived late or were unprepared, Jalen jumped in. He would seize the opportunity to record one of his new songs. He would pull out his smartphone and open the Notes application where he kept many of his lyrics. Jalen had little patience for peers who didn't take the craft as seriously as he did. For Jalen, the recording studio was where you went to put in work.

JALEN AS STORYTELLER

As a storyteller, Jalen crafted narratives that exposed many of his questions, dreams, fears, and insecurities. His command of language enabled him to construct linguistically complex and emotionally vulnerable songs. He employed rhyme, meter, rhythm, imagery, wordplay, repetition, metaphor, conflict, hyperbole, juxtaposition, mood, tone, and other literary and poetic devices to tell personal stories, explore his emotions, and make meaning of his experiences.

Jalen's lyrics can be broadly categorized into four thematic families: (a) trust, loyalty, and betrayal; (b) economic mobility; (c) hardship and struggle; and (d) hypermasculinity. The following passage, from a song Jalen titled "Anything," is a good representation of the topics that Jalen wrote about most frequently:

> To be here right now I swear it's a blessing
> Gotta make it out real fast, my momma stressin

And these streets is full of hate, gotta tote the Wesson
Your own brodies hate on you, it's depressin
I don't know who to trust, this shit ain't easy
I got big dreams to make it out, just like Houdini

The concerns that Jalen expresses include his dreams to make it out of his neighborhood, his mother's stress, the desire to protect himself, and his uncertainty about who to trust. These worries are evident in many of his songs but are often coupled with gratitude and hope, as in the first and last lines of this passage. He shows he values life, family, and friendship while at the same time expressing his uncertainty about all of the above.

The complexity in Jalen's desires shows that he values his life while at the same time promoting an action that could lead to violence or legal trouble ("tote the Wesson"). These contradictions in hip-hop, youth culture, and wider American society have the potential to create spaces in which we engage young men in dialogue about violence, emotional regulation, conflict resolution, and restorative justice. Perhaps most importantly, they provide us with opportunities to critique the structural inequities that create the conditions for violence and the need to abolish them.

Trust, Loyalty, and Betrayal

The most common themes in Jalen's lyrics include trust, loyalty, and betrayal. Jalen tells stories that reflect a worldview that he is constantly (re)constructing. He looks both inward and outward in his music while exploring relationships with himself, others, and the world around him.

Lately I can't seem to trust myself
How you gon' trust somebody else when you don't trust yourself?
Don't ever show no one you need 'em, you don't need no help
I just be stayin' on some dolo shit

These lines demonstrate a thoughtful introspection. Jalen examines the trustworthiness of his relationships and communicates a preference for independence and self-sufficiency. Grappling with the ability to trust and develop meaningful relationships, Jalen is engaged in writing as a form of emotional self-exploration.

Economic Mobility

Jalen expresses a desire to economically advance himself and his family, which he sees as connected to his career as a rapper.

I speak the truth when I be rappin, no fiction, this real
Through this rap shit won't stop grindin till I find a record deal
Gotta get momma up out these trenches
When I make it out we gon' be winnin

These lines provide insight into Jalen's determination and work ethic because he views rapping as a means to success and economic mobility. He affirms his commitment to the process and insists he won't stop working hard until he secures a record deal, which would enable him to move his mother out of the "trenches," a term he uses often to reference his neighborhood. He anticipates that when he achieves success and makes it out, the conditions for his family will improve.

Jalen looks to the past, present, and future while creating meaning through his lyrics. He sometimes looks forward to better days, but he also speaks in the past tense.

I had to make it out the hood, the fam was starving
Every two weeks we had to go to new apartments
But now my fam we is struggle free

Some of Jalen's songs, like the one here, are written as if he has already achieved stardom. This can be understood as a rhetorical strategy to transport himself into a future that has not yet come but toward which he is constantly striving—or what scholars Robin D. G. Kelley and Bettina Love have called "freedom dreaming."[17] It might also be read as a literal description of harder times that he and his family have overcome.

Hardship and Struggle

Jalen's lyrics also reflect personal and political struggles. The experiences he communicates are deeply personal, providing listeners with a window into his life in the city. At the same time, his music is highly political, describing living conditions that are byproducts of economic inequality, social injustice, and systemic racism.

Jalen is a storyteller-reporter who is documenting his own experiences, aspirations, traumas, and healing. In a song titled, "Real Ones," he raps, "see where I'm from street shit crazy / homies dyin, mommas cryin / it's daily." In these lines we see Jalen reporting on an environment where gun violence has claimed the lives of young people in the community. He acknowledges the way this affects loved ones, particularly mothers, and describes it as occurring "daily," which could mean that it's something he experiences regularly or that he sees it as a cycle that continues to repeat.

Hypermasculinity

Filmmaker Byron Hurt, in his film *Hip-Hop: Beyond Beats and Rhymes*, explores the dynamics of manhood and violence in hip-hop culture, claiming that violent masculinity is not exclusive to hip-hop but is actually stitched into the fabric of American identity. To understand the hypermasculinity in hip-hop, one must consider the history of Black men in the United States and the ways they have been physically, socially, and economically disempowered.

When analyzing Jalen's lyrics through this lens, we find a desire for power and domination manifested through (a) violent acts inflicted upon other men and (b) the sexual objectification of women. When Jalen writes about his mother, his words can be characterized by love, affection, respect, and protection. Those same qualities are present in a number of love songs that he wrote about young women in his life. The songs are intimate and emotionally vulnerable. However, there are a number of songs that sexually objectify women. Jalen uses the words "bitches" and "hoes" while describing young women as disposable.

This language reflects the way women and their bodies are commodified as sexual objects in film, music, television, and other media in a patriarchal society. It highlights the need for critical teachers, curricula, and pedagogies that provide opportunities for young men like Jalen to become more critical consumers and producers of media while examining the ways they are reinforcing dehumanizing tropes, myths, and stereotypes.

THE RECORDING STUDIO AS A MODEL FOR CLASSROOMS

Many schools lack the resources to build semiprofessional recording studios, but it is useful to discuss the recording studio as a model for what's possible in traditional classrooms. The studio in this study was co-constructed with students, highlighting the need to design classrooms and curricula in collaboration with young people. We must design literacy spaces that cultivate student voice and agency, where the environment itself encourages students to take ownership over their learning and responsibility for the physical and emotional well-being of one another. These kinds of collaborative places will resemble laboratories more than what we have traditionally understood as classrooms.

The studio classroom is collaborative by nature, and students will lead, organize, and mediate the learning that happens within it. The hip-hop recording studio values aesthetics that are conducive to creativity, collaboration, writing, and performance—such as lighting, sound, visuals, furniture, and technology. Teachers in studio classrooms should seek to create an authentic cultural environment that reflects the racial and linguistic identities of the diverse young people who learn there.

If we think about writing in terms of composition and production, we might look to the multiple literacies that are on display in the recording studio. Beat-making, recording, rapping, and using music production software require digital and media literacies that many young people have mastered outside of school. It's important to draw on the diverse literacies, languages, and ways of making meaning that students bring to the classroom.

Whiteness and Anti-Racist Black-Language Pedagogy

Jalen's words, and the space that allowed for those words to be shared, highlight the need for anti-racist classrooms and white co-conspirator teachers who will work to abolish anti-Black linguistic racism.[18] By preparing teachers of all students with anti-racist Black-language pedagogies, we can empower white literacy educators (and others) to see Black language—and the hip-hop literacies that use Black language—as an asset to be leveraged rather than a deficit to correct. Hip-hop is a cultural and linguistic identity for many Black and Latinx youth. White teachers, scholars, researchers, and teacher-educators should study and employ culturally sustaining pedagogies that recognize, cultivate, and sustain students' racial and linguistic identities.

LANGUAGE AND REFLECTION IN
WRITING CLASSROOMS

— Tessa Brown —

hris Emdin opens *For White Folks Who Teach in the Hood* in Wyoming, at the site of a teacher-education workshop he's just led. His audience is predominantly white teachers at a school where the students are predominantly Indigenous. Although he leaves confident in the teaching strategies he shared, he worries that they won't matter, since he ignored "the elephant in the room—that is, the very obvious racial and ethnic differences between the mostly white teachers and their mostly Indigenous students."[1] Driving away from the workshop, Emdin remembers the Carlisle school, an infamous boarding school in Pennsylvania that tried to assimilate kidnapped Native children into whiteness through violence. Carlisle was founded in 1879 by US General Richard Henry Pratt, who articulated his philosophy of education as "Kill the Indian, save the man."

My field of composition studies, which theorizes and teaches literacy at the college level and (like K-12 education) is dominated by white women like me, has an uneasy and evolving relationship with the colonial history of our profession. My colleague Scott R. Lyons has written that at schools like Carlisle Native students who broke the prohibition on speaking their home languages were met with physical violence.[2] By opening his book with reflections on the Carlisle school, Emdin invites white educators to be accountable to the real trauma schooling has wrought on BIPOC youth in this country. Emdin calls his teaching approach *reality pedagogy*, a teaching philosophy rooted in respect for students' realities of place and identity as grounds for co-creation of learning. In a diverse country where public school K–12 teachers are still 79 percent white and 76 percent female, Emdin's reminder of the colonial roots of American education is not as irrelevant as we might hope.[3]

Teaching writing at the college level has given me the opportunity not just to practice literacy education but to study it. In this essay, I hope to share with you some of what I've learned and tried to practice during my teaching career, particularly about language and reflection. Since my first time teaching as a graduate student, my student groups have been diverse, with kids from a range of racial, economic, and national backgrounds—some groups have been predominantly white, and others predominantly BIPOC—but all my classes have taken place at predominantly white institutions (PWIs), with a white teacher, myself, at the front of the room. My classes have something else in common—they're almost always about hip-hop, an art form and cultural movement I love deeply, as a fan and as an educator. Teaching hip-hop as a white woman has taught me some hard truths about white teachers' efforts to connect with their students and the systemic injustices that can get in the way. For me, the path forward has been a dialectic—a constant movement back and forth between understanding my students better and better understanding myself. It took a doctorate in composition and rhetoric for me to understand the depths of racist discrimination in this country, particularly how white supremacy is baked into our ideas about the inherent superiority of Standard American English (SAE). And it took a lot of reflection to understand my participation in these supremacist systems and to forgive myself for the mistakes I've made in my classrooms even as I continually work to do better.

When I taught my first hip-hop writing class, "College Writing on *The College Dropout*" (yes, it was all about Kanye West; no, I don't focus on him anymore), I was fresh out of undergrad myself. Required to teach freshman composition by the powers that be, I thought, I'll teach it about rap. I hoped I would draw students of color to my class and give them a pedagogy that was for them. I had noble intentions! I wasn't pulling students into the canon; I was reframing the canon for them. But my students were randomly assigned to my writing section, and not everyone was excited about rap, certainly not Kanye's. I had Black students from Detroit, white students from the rest of Michigan, and rich students from the East and West Coasts. It was 2009, and the economy was collapsing, but that wasn't news to Michiganders.

In my class we talked about writing, language, the Black church, gospel, sampling, redlining, racial profiling, and the students' experiences driving with the windows up or down between two parts of town. I managed to convince most of my students of hip-hop's relevance to all their lives, if not its desirability. But there was a lingering feeling, more pronounced on certain days when a white student took too long to think through their ignorance out loud, when I wondered if I was doing enough for the students of color who had to sit in that space while their white classmates learned what racism was. I didn't know key anti-racist teaching concepts yet, like the importance of decentering white students' comfort from the teacher's attention, and I wasn't yet a scholar of white women's "emotioned resistance" to critique.[4] We didn't interrogate the differences between the ways I taught my students to write and the ways the hip-hop artists we studied wrote. Language difference itself lay uninterrogated, obvious yet unnamed. In retrospect, my early classes privileged their white majorities. Hip-hop was a commodity we were dissecting, not a culture some students had grown up with and emerged from. By hyper-fixating on Black culture, I fear I silenced my Black students instead of making space for them.

After living in Michigan, I moved to upstate New York for my PhD. That's where I learned to look at writing as *situated social practice*, that is, to see reading and writing as activities we do every day in a million different ways. My doctorate program asked us to teach undergrads about their own literacies, their multilingualism, and their own writing processes and styles. My hip-hop pedagogy became infused with new possibilities: I began to see the incredible literacies of hip-hop artists themselves, young women and men whose language practices were dismissed and even criminalized even though they were the most prolific, popular poets in the world.

My students at Syracuse University were mostly suburbanites from the tristate area except for some urban students of color the admissions office had recruited from New York City and across the country. At Syracuse, the colonialism of the institution was literally built into its foundations. It was a private, majority-white school on a hill, in a region of Upstate New York with a large Native American population—I soon heard that the local lake named for them, Lake Onondaga, was the most polluted lake in the country. While the university was predominately white, Syracuse itself was a majority-Black city that had experienced white flight to suburbs whose residents then redeveloped the abandoned downtown for dinners out. In my coursework I was learning about American multilingualism and the colonial foundations of our cultural obsession with English-only reading and writing. As a hip-hop educator, I paid special attention to lessons about African American Vernacular English (AAVE), also sometimes called Black English, Black Language, Ebonics, or the language of rap. I learned about the differences between AAVE and my own variety, what's called Standard American English. I learned that SAE and AAVE were two different languages with different grammars, pronunciations, and social meanings and that there was nothing inherently less communicative about AAVE—rather, SAE's pride of place is based on the social power of SAE speakers, not inherent linguistic qualities of the language.

In my dissertation research I studied two of my own courses and two similar courses taught by a colleague, the writer Nana Adjei-Brenyah, and I realized I wasn't as radical of a teacher as I thought. For my dissertation, I took notes after my own classes, observed several of his, collected consenting students' writing and compositions, and conducted twenty exit interviews. Analyzing the students' interview transcripts, I began to understand how neoliberal ideologies of individual success had shaped their views of language and education. No matter their backgrounds, the students in my study saw their education as an investment portfolio into which they had limited resources to deposit for hopefully optimized returns, and they were skeptical consumers of nonstandard Englishes, continually reproducing the ideologies they'd internalized about the low status of Black music and Black language.

In interviews, diverse students described expecting to hate their writing class, seeing it as a distraction from the successes they'd come to college to pursue. Yet for students from disparate racial, ethnic, gender, and class backgrounds, engaging with hip-hop in class gave them an opportunity to connect with their own literacies—even as it uncovered deeply held biases toward nonstandard Englishes, biases that constrained their own range of expression. One student described how being interested in the course material led to him investing more energy in the writing process than he normally would:

> Basically if you wanna invest my time into actually doing this project, cause I'm not giving in like 2 hours after I've started writing—so it's like, this is not so bad. . . . I actually enjoy reading about the person [I'm researching], so I'm going to keep reading, keep researching, taking this information and producing something worth the professor reading basically.[5]

Another student told me the following:

> As a kid I never really liked reading. I was always, whenever they would ask me to read something in school, like, "Read this book," it was always

like I had to do it for school, I would never do it on my own. . . . But then, when we did the literacy [unit] I realized I've been reading magazines my whole life. I actually have been reading, I am reading, I just never saw it as reading because it's something I really enjoyed.[6]

Comments like these showed how students weren't taught to connect deeply to the acts of reading and writing they already did every day, how their literacy education kept their real lives at arm's length. Another student was surprised that "actually" investing in the work paid dividends beyond her grade:

Actually, I feel like if you do more research and you actually learn what you writing about your paper will actually turn out way better and you get a better grade, and it's not only benefit with your grade like its benefiting your knowledge and makes you think about certain things definitely as far as life.[7]

These students understood school as an institution that was not interested in their languages, their literacies, or their lives, and they were continually surprised by writing courses that made the effort to connect with them.

But by revealing students' anti-Black linguistic bias, even held by Black students and other students of color, the study also showed that "connecting" with students isn't enough. It wasn't enough to engage my students' attention with hip-hop; I had to make sure they understood why hip-hop language was still stigmatized, even as most of them consumed it obsessively. Early in the semester of my first class at Syracuse, my students and I had an in-class discussion about an excerpt from Jay-Z's book *Decoded* about an early night in the rapper's career. I framed the excerpt as an example of a literacy narrative in which writers describe their own writing practices and drew the class's attention to a few lines from Jay-Z's text:

I laid my little verse down, but when I went home I couldn't get [Big Daddy] Kane's freestyle out of my head. I remember one punchline in Kane's verse: *put a quarter in your ass / cuz you played yourself.* "Played yourself" wasn't even a phrase back then. He made it up right there on that tape. Impressive. I probably wrote a million rhymes that night.[8]

Attention fell to the misspelling of the word *cuz*. One student spoke up forcefully. It didn't matter how good Jay-Z found that line to be, the student said, because the misspelling would lead it to be dismissed by "the majority of people." "Who is 'the majority of people?'" I asked. He looked around at his classmates. "Just, like, most people," he said. His preoccupation with the spelling of "cuz"—delivered orally, not even written, in the story—recentered white linguistic norms and standards to suggest the text was not even worth engaging with. I reached for concepts from my own coursework, trying to explain how power functions through language, coloring our everyday assessments of writing's value. But these ideas were not in any of the course texts I had assigned. My students left the term with some revised understandings of language prestige, but they were not sophisticated. Reviewing my notes about that day, I knew my pedagogy had to change, so that students had the concepts for understanding why "cuz" was not just appropriate but, in Jay-Z's speech community and for his target audience of a rap verse, correct.

Among writing teachers, a debate rages: Should we teach our students to communicate more excellently in their home languages? Or can excellence only be achieved in the standard tongue? Hip-hop discourse shows the excellence of AAVE in every resistive couplet and internal rhyme. But for generations going back to the Carlisle school, training young people in "proper English" has been the uncontested mission of corps after corps of white women teachers. When I started my career, I did the same. Even though my students always wrote about hip-hop, in my first courses I guided them to conventional US-style papers, never problematizing the conventions of American writing styles or the "standard" dialect we espoused even as we wrote about poetics from an oppressed tongue. As a doctoral student, I learned that students have the "right to their own language," or at least that's what my professional association (Conference on College Composition and Communication) declared and ratified in 1974. But what did that right entail? Must teachers still teach their students to "code switch" into the majority variety to be taken seriously? Or do students have the right not only to use their own speech practices but also to challenge wider systems of communication and demand they be *listened to* differently as well?

April Baker-Bell discusses the limits of code-switching ideologies in her aptly titled essay "I Can Switch My Language, But I Can't Switch My Skin: What Teachers Must Understand About Linguistic Racism."[9] In the essay, the Black-language scholar and teacher-educator explains how code-switching pedagogies reinforce white supremacy by teaching students that, no matter how they speak at home or with their friends, the only way to render their intelligence intelligible in white spaces is to linguistically, which is to culturally, assimilate. Can you kill the speech and save the student? Literacy scholars today know the answer is no. As Suresh A. Canagarajah writes, "We have to teach our students strategies for rhetorical negotiation so that they can modify, resist, or reorient to the rules in a manner favorable to them."[10] For students (and teachers!) who inhabit the local linguistic majority, this also means *learning to listen differently* and becoming open and available to *negotiation* as a necessary communication skill in a globalizing and always-already hybridized world.

What H. Samy Alim has called "critical language awareness" and what others in my discipline have called pedagogies of translingualism, code-meshing, or shuttling across languages are all terms that describe teaching approaches based not just in cultural but also in linguistic realism: rejecting the lie that SAE is the only right way to speak and also the lie that speaking Standard English is the only way we can understand each other, and recognizing instead that our students speak a wide range of languages, including Englishes, and already successfully negotiate language differences every day.[11] English itself was never "a single, unchanging world language, or lingua franca, but a constellation of ever changing Englishes . . . inevitably in flux."[12] Instead of beating down our students with the "standard," we can help them become more excellently flexible across registers, thus preparing them to thrive across a wide range of future communication contexts. In my latest iteration of my hip-hop writing course, Hiphop, Orality, and Language Diversity, I began from a sociolinguistic frame that rooted hip-hop discourse in African American literacies.[13] I explicitly taught the concept that no language is more correct or expressive than any other and that standardized language practices are shaped by histories and social systems of power. By grounding my hip-hop writing courses in critical language awareness, I opened up space for my students to respectfully study the ways hip-hop discourses are appropriated, repurposed, and circulated around the globe. I also invited them to use their whole language repertoires in class, while negotiating intentionally with SAE as the lingua franca of our classroom and thus, their audience. Who they want to be, and how they want to be understood, is up to them.

Through sustained reflection, I have learned to acknowledge my own whiteness and my own SAE. I have learned not to be entitled to my students' trust but to earn it—through my course materials, which now center Black women's voices; through accessible course policies, like unlimited requested extensions;

and through my persona, as I name my own identity and language practices to make space for students to do the same. Now, on the second day of class, I ask students to share what languages they know and use. I honor the intimacy of sharing our language practices, and then I share my own story as a perpetual language learner still fluent in only one tongue, English, my grandparents' Yiddish and Russian gone with assimilation. My students' linguistic stories follow—stories of migration, family, loss, schooling, assimilation, and mastery. At Stanford, my students shared stories of how their American Englishes—SAE AAVE, and Spanglish—developed alongside dominant and discriminated-against languages from China, India, and the rest of Asia; languages from the Middle East and the African continent; and postcolonial dialects and creoles from Europe's takeover of the world. They went on to study hip-hop in almost as many tongues—languages they grew up with and languages they were studying, languages that were new to them and languages they already forgot.

Over time, I tried to build a pedagogy and a persona that were honest with my students about the contexts for their learning, inviting them to make their own decisions about what kinds of communicators they wanted to be. This is not how I first approached teaching, but this work radicalized me. I believe that if it does not radicalize you, you have not grappled with the realities of the contexts in which we teach and our students learn. The work of anti-racist teaching is personal. It is ego work—it is the work of holding on to our good intentions while confronting the realities of colonialism that have seeped into our behaviors and our tongues. It is the work of not taking history personally, while taking personally history's challenge to build something new.

ON HIP-HOP, AUTHENTICITY, AND APPRECIATION

— Ian P. Levy —

I'm scrolling through my iPhone Notes, where I've been writing rhymes sporadically for the last decade. I'm struck by a specific collection of lyrics I wrote in 2013 that read, "Hold myself in high regard, all I ever wanted was bars, hard cause it opened up the scars, charging through the darkness while the harness is on." In these lyrics I was grappling with the necessary self-work that one invites as they quest toward producing strong hip-hop lyrics ("bars"). In 2021, looking back on these lyrics is especially eye-opening because, on a personal level, I can say I am still working on embracing missteps and hard truths ("darkness") without the need to feel comfort ("a harness"). But now, I am not in the business of producing hip-hop lyrics (at least not on a full-time basis). Instead, I am working to become a better school counselor and school counselor educator. Regardless of the outcome, this process of teasing out personal vulnerabilities, biases, shame, or any other negative thought or emotion holding me back from presenting myself authentically, or holding those I am working with back from presenting themselves authentically, is something that hip-hop taught me to do. It is not something I've perfected, by any means; it's something I'm constantly pursuing.

This initial learning emerged in a college dorm room cypher, in which I fell in love with hip-hop. For those unaware, a rap cypher is a circular space where emcees take turns slinging rhymes over a beat. After sitting on the sidelines watching friends engage in a cypher, I finally decided to join and brought with me a specific set of prewritten rhymes about feelings of isolation in schools stemming from a learning disability and familial struggles. While this sounds like heavy content to suddenly introduce to a group of friends in a dorm room, it was met with an onslaught of validation and words of encouragement. As my friends praised the bars I had recited, the experience communicated to me that sharing truths I had previously kept hidden allowed me to develop stronger bonds with my peers. In that dorm room, I learned a new coping skill, a daily lifestyle mechanism to make sense of the emergence of discomfort. My prior reticence to disclose vulnerabilities was replaced by an excitement when I discovered gaps in my development because they meant that I could write a dope new song.

Hip-hop has consistently been a tool through which I've cultivated a knowledge of self, confronted deviations from my authentic self, and then worked with young people as a school counselor. For the past ten years, I have engaged deeply with the use of hip-hop lyric writing, and other multimodal hip-hop art forms, in the counseling process to support youth development. I often credit hip-hop for offering me invaluable experiential learning opportunities, each of which helped me to appreciate hip-hop culture for its complexities and to sort through stereotypical perceptions of hip-hop (i.e., that it is solely violent or misogynistic) that had been fed to me for most of my life. Hip-hop offers educators unique pathways to elicit authenticity from youth and to build the relationships we need to support their development.

HIP-HOP, SCHOOLS, AND KEEPING IT REAL

My personal experiences with hip-hop are shared by many and represent the power of hip-hop as a collectivist culture rooted in the uplifting of community in combating external and internal distress. At a cultural level, hip-hop is joyful and resilient and has been studied and integrated across education as a vehicle for accessing academic content knowledge, critiquing systems of racism and oppression, and achieving personal healing. But it took a while for me to see hip-hop as a resource, personally and in my work with youth. In fact, my upbringing taught me hip-hop was something else entirely. Through a significant amount of self-reflection though, along with direct exposure to the beauty and brilliance of hip-hop cultural practices, I learned to see hip-hop differently. For this reason, it is essential that educators have practices at their disposal to challenge biases toward hip-hop and cultivate cultural humility.

Despite being a resource for personal development, hip-hop is constantly minimized and pathologized by popular media outlets. Growing up as a white male, son of an opera singer and jazz trombonist, I was socialized to believe that hip-hop was substandard to traditional music, ways of communicating, and simply to whiteness. These ideas were pushed via statements like "Hip-hop isn't real music," "Do they have to curse in every song?" and "How can you even understand what they are saying?" We also know that mainstream hip-hop is consumed mostly by white youth, so these comments didn't stop me from listening—they were the lens through which I listened. I would silently listen to hip-hop in my headphones as a form of entertainment, hiding that I enjoyed it for fear of co-signing something taboo. Whatever interest or admiration I had at the time was upstaged by the belief that hip-hop was inappropriate. In graduate school I was exposed to writings that detailed how the demonization of hip-hop is eerily similar to the ways in which schools minimize the authentic identity expressions of Black and Brown youth and overlook what scholars like Christopher Emdin, Gholdy Muhammad, and sam seidel refer to as an innate genius.[1] Emdin's work in particular describes how the core of education is entrenched in colonialism and white supremacy, wielding assimilative praxis couched in narratives of achieving success with the intent of erasing the historical, cultural, and individual knowledge that youth and their ancestors hold.

The ways I was taught to see and appraise hip-hop as not real music, as violent, and as fun but not serious or intellectual is a reflection of the ways I was taught to see and appraise the value of Black and Brown youth. If not reconciled, white educators risk entering work with Black and Brown youth in schools believing their cultures are the antithesis of academic success and healthy identity development. This ideology then informs the use of pedagogy and ancillary schooling practices that force youth to communicate in ways that align with dominant white cultural norms perceived to be successful. I've watched many white colleagues who regularly attended local New York City hip-hop festivals write detention slips for youth who tried to start a cypher in the back of the classroom. These educators access hip-hop outside of school as entertainment but then demonize it as a way of knowing and being in their classrooms. However, notions of hip-hop as downtrodden can also impact educators who wish to use it in their classroom. Even the most well-intentioned educators and helping professionals can use hip-hop itself as a mechanism to over-portray Black and Brown youth as traumatized, broken, or in desperate need of help. Doing so risks erasing youths' internal capacities, and external community and familial networks that can be leveraged toward actualization. While Tupac wrote of the rose that grew from concrete, many educators see only concrete.[2]

SCHOOL COUNSELING

I am deeply committed to the belief that hip-hop is a vehicle through which youth can reclaim themselves. Specifically, I have worked as a professional school counselor to assist youth in using hip-hop practices to activate their authenticity and realness as necessary for living fully. It is widely evidenced that traditional approaches to counseling, much like the education system broadly, were built for and by white folks and are ill-equipped to support Black and Brown youth. With an understanding of the power of hip-hop as a healing practice and the need for hip-hop to challenge educational systems to honor youths' authenticity, I contend that community-defined hip-hop practices can inform culturally sustaining interventions. For example, a foundational belief in school counseling is that the construction of real or genuine relationships is a prerequisite for youth development. Direct participation in hip-hop spaces showed me that the hip-hop community similarly requires authentic identity presentation as a means to form connections. Scholars like Bettina Love, Adam Kruse, and Emery Petchauer have highlighted how *realness* or keeping it real is a hip-hop sensibility used by community members to maintain authenticity, access creativity, engage in social resistance, and constantly evolve.[3]

Hip-hop has taught me, and countless others who learn to earnestly interact with it, sensibilities like realness. For example, when I first began working as a school counselor, I believed that my ability to rap was the only way I was going to connect with Black and Brown youth. I used to enter a room full of new students with a beat blasting and my best sixteen bars. Sure, I got some applause, but deep down I feared that I would lose my relationships with youth if I showed them other aspects of myself that they couldn't personally relate to. I thought I needed to be "like" my students to be "liked" by my students. I have memories of students calling me corny because all I did was rap. This feedback, while hurtful in some ways, was ultimately an ask for me to show up real. Much like a cypher in which someone with a violin can pop up and add energy to the space, I needed to learn to trust in my own authenticity and in the power of hip-hop to protect authenticity. By admitting to myself that I did not know much, I could allow hip-hop to manifest authentically and invite youth to help me help them.

HIP-HOP PRACTICES FOR SCHOOL COUNSELORS AND TEACHERS

As a school counselor, I have leveraged hip-hop-based community practices to both elevate my praxis and challenge existing systemic deterrents to youth development. Hip-hop-based practices in schools aid educators in their own professional development, challenging school systems and supporting youth in reclaiming their knowledge, history, and culture. I use a hip-hop and school-counseling framework called hip-hop and spoken-word therapy, a process wherein youth write, record, and perform emotionally themed music about their lives. Salient components of this process, namely *lyric writing as emotive journaling* and *studio co-construction*, offer youth and educators valuable opportunities to challenge barriers to authentic identity presentation.

Before discussing these components, it is necessary to communicate, especially to white educators, that I do not believe actively practicing a hip-hop artistic skill (such as rapping) is a prerequisite for the use of hip-hop-based interventions in schools. What is necessary, however, is to relinquish power, listen to youth, and trust in their internal genius. There are debates within the education community and the hip-hop community (too often separately) that question who can do this work. These debates often center on tensions and questions about appropriation. This is an important consideration. What I will try to elucidate here is the need to continuously gather a deeper appreciation for the complexities of hip-hop culture, which happens by engaging with youth while questioning our own biases and judgments. For me, the best way to address questions of appropriation is by cultivating appreciation. Appropriation is the borrowing of a culture that isn't one's own and wielding it as an oppressive or assimilative practice. For example, white folks using premade hip-hop songs only for rote memorization of academic content while believing that the types of hip-hop youth engage with are unworthy of entering schools. The work of appreciation starts with understanding that youth possess what they need to develop and advocating for the use of interventions in schools, and co-creation of school spaces, that feed youths' innate ability to optimize their potential.

LYRIC WRITING AS EMOTIVE JOURNALING

Through my time working with youth, I have found one of the simplest and most effective ways of learning about who they are is by engaging with the hip-hop they digest and create. In my work, lyric writing is a narrative therapy mechanism for youth to tell their own stories and express their identities on their own terms. In so many words, *lyric writing as emotive journaling* offers youth engaging prompts to explore thoughts and feelings. Scholars like sam seidel remind us that in the design of any hip-hop curriculum, an essential hip-hop sensibility is to constantly search for ways to *flip the script*. That is, it's cool to be unique and do something no one has done before, so we must partner with youth to find creative song concepts that support emotional exploration. For example, school counselors can engage youth in writing through prompts like a time capsule song (write a verse from yourself five years from now), conflict resolution (write a verse as a letter or voicemail for someone you currently have tension with), or mirror on the wall (converse with different versions of yourself).

Lyric writing with groups of students requires initial conversations in which students and educators create a list of emotional themes they'd like to write about; collect hip-hop beats that resemble those emotional themes; and break off into pairs or small groups to co-construct songs. The iterative process of writing lyrics, sharing those lyrics with the larger group, receiving feedback that supports further exploration, and returning to writing enables youth to tap all members of the group (including the counselor) as supporters of their actualizing and healing through the presentation of complex identities and lived experiences.

There are also opportunities for bibliotherapy for those who remain on the fence about sharing. Here, educators and students listen to or read hip-hop lyrics or watch hip-hop music videos, using the artists' content as a third party through which students can begin talking through their own stories. For example, students might relate to a song by Polo G about loss, divulge a similar narrative after listening to the song, and then go find the instrumental for that beat online to lyrically explore their personal experiences with loss. Engaging in lyric writing and digesting hip-hop songs and music videos are as efficacious as counseling interventions. In fact, I have seen lyric writing lead to deep emotional self-awareness and the development of coping skills in students.

While the evocation of youth experience through a dope prompt is one essential part of the work, educators need to be able to hear and respond to the thoughts and feelings that youth communicate through hip-hop content. Therefore, I have challenged educators to develop hip-hop-based active-listening skills. This requires practice in identifying different thoughts and feelings in student lyrics, something I believe all educators can and should do in their own time. This involves listening to and discussing hip-hop songs with youth and colleagues regularly, as practice. It includes both understanding under-lying thoughts and feelings, and working to identify our own implicit biases that prevent us from unadulterated listening. For example, see the following student lyric:

> Used to power flip vernacular to make myself feel adequate/
> spectacular child raised around guns and trafficking./
> Its happening take you to that crib that pigs was passing in./
> My brothers baking work on the stove with bubbles crackling./
> Age of 6 was tackling my tactics of attacking in/
> this world made cold by every man made action./
> It would seem life would throw huge troubles like javelins,/
> and I would dodge and grab em toss that shit right back at em.

In this verse, a student is highlighting a bevy of possible emotions. In the first line the student details feelings of inadequacy and their intentional use of vocabulary to navigate those feelings. The student also describes difficult living conditions during childhood and possible traumatic experiences connected to policing and witnessing violence. However, amid the difficulties explained are also bright signs of resilience, self-efficacy, and nimbleness explained as learning to take what troubles life has thrown their way and to flip them into something greater. It is the educator's responsibility, first, to allow hip-hop to be the vehicle through which youth share narratives about their pain, joy, and resilience, and then second, to be able to see and hear complex identity expressions, ask follow-up questions to both check for and further understanding, and adequately appraise hip-hop as a way of knowing, being, and developing.

NAVIGATING APPROPRIATION

The ability of educators to hear the stories youth share in lyrics, beyond their own judgment and biases, is an essential ingredient when navigating issues of cultural appropriation. Again, I'm defining appropriation here as using a culture that is not your own in such a way that it exerts power and oppresses those to which the culture belongs. As a white male educator, I have had many moments in which a word in a student's lyric generated emotions in me that prevented me from hearing and fully appreciating their meaning and at times caused me to want to change their meaning. For a long time, I used to be against cursing in lyrics because I feared that if the administration heard a curse word on a record that I would lose my job. However, I also believe that curse words are overused when we do not have the emotional vocabulary to describe how we feel. Regardless, the sum of these judgments led to my forcing youth to utilize words that were palatable to my mostly white administration. Students hated this, with some even outwardly questioning, "Why are you trying to make us sound white?" These questions hold distinct value; youth were communicating that my judgments inhibited their authenticity. These judgments were appropriation, and comments from youth forced me and the group to reevaluate this rule. Through ongoing dialogue we collectively decided on a new rule: youth were allowed to curse if they could explain why a particular word was the best choice to describe their experience.

I recall one instance in the studio in which this rule supported a student and myself in completing an authentic record. While a student was recording a song about policing, he used a handful of curse words. As I heard them, I stopped the recording immediately and asked, "Why did you use those words?" The student responded, "Because that's how cops talk to me," and without saying more, I restarted the recording. Our ability to check our own judgments about students' words, and whether our thoughts and feelings are inhibiting students from authentically telling their stories, is essential. As educators, we want youth to develop the emotional self-awareness to use a variety of words to describe their emotional experiences. The road to appreciating students' stories requires our active self-reflection, as well as conversations with youth that help co-create norms that allow genuine emotional exploration.

STUDIOS AS BEACONS OF HOPE

When I first began working as a school counselor, I put a microphone in the corner of my office with the hopes of encouraging youth to come to my office. I imagined we would talk about thoughts and feelings, write lyrics, and eventually record songs. After a few months of referring to my office as "the studio" to students, I vividly remember a student saying, "Levy . . . this isn't a studio." Again, my individual perceptions of what youth would find engaging were not aligned with what youth actually found engaging. In fact, there was a level of phoniness students perceived because I was trying to pretend my office was something that it was not. Recognizing this, I asked students to collaborate with me on turning my office into a "real studio."

Inside of that studio was where our work happened. A dive into literature around hip-hop studios can inform the creation of school spaces that invite youth to be fully themselves. Hip-hop home studios are unique community spaces, distinct from multimillion dollar spaces with all the bells and whistles. Researchers like Geoffrey Harkness conducted interviews with hip-hop emcees and producers, who described home studios as places for identity construction, validation, and transformation.[4] If we can believe in the inherent power of studios to demand that people arrive ready to engage in the emotional labor required to create art that represents their identities, we can redefine the ways we construct school environments to foster authentic development. In reflection on studio work, I find the most honest and appropriate way for white educators to engage in hip-hop work is by pushing aside any notions that we know the right way forward and instead trusting youth as leaders and collaborators. To assess this perspective, my colleague Edmund Adjapong and I collaborated on a youth-led co-creation of a studio within a school.[5] The goal of this intervention study wasn't to engage in lyric writing; instead, it was a necessary prerequisite—the opportunity to co-design a new place within a school that invited youth to express themselves unapologetically. This process runs in direct opposition to guidance on school-counseling office design, which is basically nonexistent—but, in its rare mentions, doesn't involve youth or consider what makes a culturally sustaining environment. Our participatory action-research intervention tasked youth with researching what authentic studio spaces looked and felt like for them, leading to the clearing out of an old storage space and construction of a hip-hop recording studio. Reflections from students on this process speak volumes about its potential:

> In the studio, you could tell that there's a little piece of yourself in each sign. Like it's in a story and stuff. Like . . . I don't know. Like, you could tell the story . . . The foam and people working together and stuff, and like the wall. Painting it and just have their own creation and their own mind and nobody.

Here students describe how having autonomy in designing their own space allowed them to embed aspects of themselves into the design. These nonverbal ways of sharing stories exemplify the importance of the studio space as a physical location that invites authenticity. Further, this shows that any decision I had made independently about what would make the studio "cool" or engaging for youth would have missed out on the invaluable opportunity for the environment to be imbued with reminders of students' authentic selves. However, the creation of the studio space represented a much larger shift within the community than what it offered directly to the designers. I learned that another student indicated how the studio space could be used to support others, even after they graduated: "Even if we graduate, we could come back here and help the freshman and make them more confident to talk to the others and ask them for help." The act of co-creating a studio both enabled students to imbue aspects of themselves into the space and to consider how to leverage their environment to aid the whole school community. An essential part of this work was the belief that youth possess the knowledge and skills required to design their own spaces for healing, and that our attempts as white educators and counselors pale in comparison.

CONCLUSION

Hip-hop-based practices in schools can be integrated to engage youth in the genuine sharing of their thoughts and feelings. Theoretical and practical research affirm how essential it is that educators draw on interventions that foster youths' internal capacity to actualize. Hip-hop practices are uniquely positioned to draw out complex identity expressions. However, inviting youth to express themselves fully requires that educators are ready to respond to what they hear—which requires skills such as the ability to actively listen and actions such advocating for the changes within school buildings that youth need to actualize their full selves.

PART FOUR

DISCIPLINE/
"BEHAVIOR MANAGEMENT"

Take the word overseer, like a sample
Repeat it very quickly in a crew, for example
Overseer, overseer, overseer, overseer
Officer, officer, officer, officer
Yeah, officer from overseer

—KRS-ONE, "Sound of da Police"

Not every story has a happy ending. This section features three essays by white men who find themselves in the role of disciplinarians of Black and Brown children. All three have the critical consciousness to see how—without careful interruption—they are just perpetuating oppressive patterns of white policing of Black people. But from there, their experiences differ. One tries on a series of established teacher strategies to find the most comfortable fit. Another hands the responsibility for responding to student behavior that breaks community norms over to students by launching a student-led restorative-justice program. And the third struggles to find a path.

From stylistic to nihilistic, these contributors don't just offer a spectrum of strategies; they offer a range of outlooks on what is im/possible. What are the limitations to this whole enterprise of schooling in a racialized society?

If you are entering this section with big optimism for harmonious relationships between BIPOC students and white educators, allow yourself to see and feel the boundaries with which our contributors have collided—without jumping to solutionism about what they could have or should have done.

If you cracked open this section with skepticism about what possible paths could exist for white teachers attempting to discipline Black and Brown students, challenge yourself to slow down and truly engage with the stories and strategies being offered.

What role does discipline play in liberation?

Thus far we've offered a collective voice in opening each section of this book. The essays in this section resonated deeply with Chris, so we're offering a personal reflection from him:

FROM CHRIS

The chapters in this section bring me back to my first year of teaching. I was assigned to teach math and science in a middle school in the Bronx. On paper, I was well equipped to teach there. I was young, energetic, well credentialed, and from the same community where I was teaching. The children looked like me. We listened to the same music. They even dressed like me. In my head, I knew what they needed from me to enjoy my class. However, I also wanted to be a "good teacher." Somehow, I had been convinced that being a good teacher meant that I had to tuck away my familiarity with who they were. No one had to tell me this. It was somehow downloaded into my psyche. My commitment to this belief was reinforced when I began speaking to other teachers. They taught me that good teaching required discipline, a hyper-structured classroom, and "tough love." In the classroom, I thought that my effectiveness was based on how quiet my students were and how long I could keep them "on task" with assignments that required them to sit and work individually for as long as they could.

During that first year of teaching, I also remember being pulled over by the police for running a red light. I remember knowing I ran the light and thinking that it wasn't that bad. I would explain that the light flipped from yellow to red while I was making a turn and be apologetic. I would let the officer know I was not like the other Black men he was pulling over. I was a teacher.

After the officer walked over to my car and asked for my license and registration, I started my explanation. "I am a teacher. I am rushing home after a long day teaching. The kids were really tough today." He peered at me emotionless. No smile, no recognition of my job title. He simply and firmly said, "I have to run your license for any warrants." I nodded, and he slowly walked back to his car. After about fifteen minutes, I started to look around nervously. I looked in my rearview mirror at him and noticed he was on his phone. About forty-five minutes later, I thought about getting out of the car but realized that wasn't a good idea. About another half an hour later, he slowly walked back to my car. I had learned that this was not the time to argue for myself. I was sitting in my car livid but expressionless. He leaned into my car, took a deep whiff, then tossed my license and registration into my lap. I sat there silently as he turned around, walked back to his car, and drove away.

I had not connected this event to my first year of teaching 'til after I read the chapters in this section. The officer treated me like I treated my students. He wanted me to know that I had no power. He took power from me. He wasted my time; he provoked me to anger. I was not punished for an infraction, but punishment in the form of a ticket would have been so much more fair. In fact, I probably wasn't punished because I was a "good" offender. I didn't argue, get out of my car, or ask him what the hell he was doing. I deserved the right to argue but was robbed of it.

If a Black man with so much in common with his students replicates the oppression he experiences, becomes an enemy of children, and suppresses their right to be free and learn, white teachers without these connections who have also been fed the notion that these children are to be controlled and silenced most certainly have work to do. The essays in this section offer practical ways to engage in, stories to help us think about, and entry points into truly interrogating the concept of classroom management.

"NOT ANOTHER WHITE MAN IN CHARGE . . ."

– Adam Weinstock –

I became a teacher because I wanted all students to feel as encouraged by school as I was. I recognized racial disparities in education and sought to be an educator for liberation and social justice. Entering my student-teaching placement at twenty-two years old, I shared with my cooperating teacher my worry that I wouldn't be able to reach students who showed resistance to schooling, that having always enjoyed school and learning as a student myself would make it hard to connect with students who didn't have the same relationship with their academics. My mentor suggested that knowing what a satisfying learning experience feels like could help me foster the same for my students. That was a valuable perspective, but it didn't prepare me to navigate the dynamics of "control" in a classroom. Underlying my concern was gnawing apprehension about being responsible for managing the behavior of dozens of adolescents, mostly BIPOC students. As a white man committed to combating racism, I felt uneasy about my authority in the classroom. This insecurity contributed to early challenges for me in classrooms full of seventh graders with an instinct for pressing boundaries.

The challenges reflected themselves outwardly in class periods in which students' interest in socializing superseded attention to any learning targets I'd set for them and internally in my own corresponding angst. I tried to advance notions of a "democratic classroom." Students contributed to class constitutions. They voted on class names. I didn't overrule one seventh-grade class's vote to name itself "Looney Tunes." Subsequently, my most striking memory from that group is Shana shouting "Suck my dick!" at me when I tried to get her to stop talking at a time I expected her to be quiet. (School administrators issued Shana an in-school suspension in response to send the message that such disrespect was unacceptable.) I called class meetings to address more widespread behaviors that were detracting from my goals for the class, but these conversations did not generate the buy-in I wanted my students to have for seventh-grade humanities nor did it generate the quality of community I sought. I felt like I was battling for control of the class, but I too often found myself uncomfortable or ineffective when trying to exert control.

It was clear how resentful and defensive students could become when I grew frustrated with their behavior and instructed them to "stop talking," "go back to your seat," or any other of the countless directives I served up in response to students not meeting my expectations. As much as anyone, seventh graders do not want to be told what to do. Students who challenged me noted that I wasn't being "fair," that so-and-so and so-and-so were also talking, that they were only visiting another classmate's desk for help with their work, or that their neighbor "started it." As a white teacher wanting to advance equity at large, I was disquieted to be received by Black and Brown students as being unfair. Students perceiving me in this way also reflected an oppositional dynamic that troubled me, which was at odds with my vision of students embracing me as a facilitator of their growth and potential.

The analogy of juggling resonated with me in my first years teaching. There are so many balls to keep in the air simultaneously: paying attention to the content I'm trying to deliver, monitoring what thirty other bodies in the room are doing, managing materials, trying to respond to so many inputs at once. New to curriculum and classroom management, I lacked the automaticity with enough of the balls to keep some from dropping. As students would play off each other's off-task behaviors and amplify the distraction from what I'd planned for the class period, I struggled to wrangle the attentiveness I sought. I'm sure my frustration was evident in my eyes, voice, and posture, as my deep-seated wishes to uplift my students were confronted by what felt like their resistance to my efforts.

As I wrestled with what it meant to hold students accountable, I knew that external rewards and punishments did not match my preference for fostering intrinsic motivation; I was more aligned to restitution and what I've since heard referred to as "logical consequences." Rather than issuing "warnings" as other teachers did, I gave students "reminders," which better matched my relationship to discipline philosophy—without having a visibly different effect. Regardless of the term, three in a period added up to what the school called a classroom detention, which meant students were expected to return at the start of lunch or the end of the school day as a consequence. If the behaviors I'd classified as infractions resulted in students not completing work, detention might call for working on the incomplete assignment. And detention with me always involved having students reflect on their behavior, sometimes in writing and always in conversation.

In conversation with students, I knew that talking *at* students did not feel productive. Given we all need to process information to learn from it and to reflect on behaviors to change them, it was important to me that students articulated why they "owed" time, why I was concerned about whichever behavior led them to the conversations, what might be causing their "disruptive" actions, and what strategies we might try to support their constructive engagement in class moving forward. Each conversation felt like progress at the moment but didn't necessarily lead to different outcomes in the subsequent class periods. That said, the conversations provided a reference point for following up: "Remember what we talked about yesterday, Jon? What did we say you'd do to stay focused during reading time?" Even if Jon's focus only nominally increased on that single occasion or Noel's drumming on the desk would inevitably resume again soon, I hoped we were developing a foundation for increasing their self-awareness and self-regulation. I also believed the ongoing conversations helped us "get on the same team."

I didn't want to be in opposition to my students, but too often, I felt like I was policing their behavior. That is exactly the role I didn't want with my white-man-ness and my desire for education for liberation. So when I was able to have reflective one-on-one conversations with my students, I felt like we were working together to create a more constructive dynamic in our relationship. I was able to hear from them about their experiences in the class, what was helping or hindering their success, and how we might partner toward some common goals. Thus, fostering reflection and dialogue with students framed my response to challenges in the classroom. This reflected an effort to work *with* and not act *on* my students, which is key to overcoming the resistance of adolescents itching for autonomy.

Understanding adolescent development, tired of power struggles with twelve-year-olds, and not wanting to perpetuate oppressive dynamics as a white man in charge of BIPOC kids, I also learned to engage my students' desire for autonomy in my approaches to classroom management. "Controlled choice" became one strategy I used to reduce power struggles. My telling students to do things when they didn't want to be told what to do could be unproductive and even counterproductive if interactions spiraled into a back-and-forth duel for control. Much more constructive, I found, was providing choices for students. At its most basic, this could shift the directive, "Do your work," to a choice between doing the work now or doing it during recess, between taking responsibility in the moment for a disrespectful comment or addressing it together with their parent later. In this rudimentary form, threats were embedded in the choice, so I was advancing compliance more than engagement. In a more thoughtful iteration, I was able to provide choices grounded in the instructional purpose of a lesson. So, if the goal is for students to show their understanding of a text, they may have different options for how to do this—such as writing a conventional analytical paragraph or a letter to or from a person featured in the text, or drawing a sketch accompanied by a written explanation. Or, maybe they'd have a choice for the process—either working productively with a peer or alone—and for the place where they complete the task—at a desk or on the rug.

Controlled choices significantly reduced in-the-moment showdowns with students around whether they would follow a directive, and the strategy helped me feel more like a facilitator than an autocrat, the facilitator being a role that was more aligned to my values and vision. As a facilitator, I learned the value of responding calmly and evenly when I felt challenged by students' behavior. There were moments when I found that raising my voice strategically helped get students' attention, but this was most effective when used no more than only a handful of times in a whole year, so students were clear in those moments that I was serious about needing to honor a particular community agreement. Generally, I recognized that my remaining calm and even tempered helped me communicate respectful and respected "authority."

I've since been introduced to the adage, "Be a thermostat, not a thermometer," and this resonates with the leadership style I found most effective in the classroom. I'm not a regular coffee drinker, but on the occasional mornings I had a caffeine boost, I would greet my students enthusiastically at the classroom door, and they'd ask, "What's gotten into you today, Adam? Extra happy today?" The slight uptick in my perkiness would perk up my students too. So, in introducing curricular content, I'd want to show excitement to spark students' alertness, whereas in redirecting a behavior I'd want to exude calm to keep the temperature of an exchange low.

The thermostat analogy reminds me of mirror neurons, whereby the emotions of someone with whom we as educators are communicating turns on those same emotions in us. Being a thermostat means emitting the emotional tenor that we want students to reflect back to us. But given the way mirror neurons work, as a teacher I was susceptible to the emotional vibes my students projected my way. In a struggle for control over the direction of the classroom, I needed to show I was not losing control of my emotions when students exhibited resistance to the agenda (admittedly my agenda) at hand. I still could and wanted to name my feelings, while maintaining an equilibrium in my manner. I was modeling a controlled response, which was a more important skill to grow than any reading strategy or historical fact.

Setting the tone of how I responded to students did not mean ignoring their feelings. Finding a comfortable zone for establishing my authority meant being sure that students felt heard and that they were assured that I was invested in their well-being and success. Given the number of students in a class, I felt remiss that I was not always able to tune into their experience as much as they deserved in any given period. When something felt off to me with how a student engaged (or didn't engage) in class, I had an opportunity to check in with them after class. Even as part of a short classroom detention, I was always committed to hearing from students about their experiences. It was key for me to show understanding and to validate them as people even if I wasn't validating a particular behavior.

Of course, it was also key for me to affirm behaviors that supported our community and student learning. I learned to manage a classroom by celebrating all that students were doing to engage in their learning. Consistent with setting the desired temperature, I found much more success focusing on what students were doing "right" than what they were doing "wrong." This strategy has been named "narrating the positive" in books like *Teach Like a Champion*, but I was fortunate for teaching mentorship and an orientation to honoring kids that led me to such practices before I saw them in print.[1] Naming students and the ways they were meeting expectations for a successful class throughout a period helped affirm their efforts and served as an indirect reminder for other students of what success looked like and how they could get shout-outs too.

In my third-year teaching, my school was visited by a school climate specialist who asked me, "What if you approached your students who are off-task with the question, 'What do you need right now?'" I found this suggestion so impactful, both for illuminating the way I wanted to show up for my students— with them knowing I was really there to serve them—and in how it shifted the dynamics of interactions. For students who were simply distracted, my question "What do you need?" was often met with the response, "Nothing," followed by the students quickly shuffling their attention back to their work. Other times, students would note, "I'm confused. I don't understand what this says," or, "This book is boring." From there, I could work in alliance with them in trying to support them through whatever challenge they articulated.

When asking students what they needed didn't suit the moment, I found an axiom from the field of therapeutic crisis intervention that served my philosophy of authority: "Statements of understanding precede requests." It can be easy to feel oppositional if someone tells us to change a behavior when we're not seeking feedback. But if we feel seen and understood, we're much more likely to be amenable to coaching. I remember visiting a colleague's math class one winter, as the first snow of the season started to fall outside. Students' observations of the snow brought mild commotion, and the teacher raised her voice, "Pay attention!" Her request was ignored repeatedly. Faced with a similar situation in my classroom, I responded to the distraction by empathizing with the students' excitement for the snow: "I know how exciting it is that it's snowing . . . and I need you to bring your attention back to the lesson at hand." I have found this technique supremely helpful, both with students inside the classroom and in relationships throughout my life.

With a commitment to not perpetuate historic power dynamics through my *positional* authority, my approach to discipline relied on trying to develop *relational* authority, whereby students trusted me because they believed I had their best interests at heart, and I was dedicated to honoring their identities, interests, experiences, efforts, thoughts, and feelings. Further, I believe naming my whiteness to students and sharing my concerns about perpetuating historical dynamics of power helped my BIPOC students know that I was sensitive to using my authority responsibly, even if not always effectively.

I recall talking to my advisee, Erick, about his pattern of horsing around in the classroom, hallway, or in front of the school at dismissal, be it playful slaps at classmates or jumping on friends' backs. I shared my appreciation for the spirit and friendly intention of these behaviors, and we discussed why the behaviors may be appropriate for some settings and not others. I also noted my concern for the ways that cops might interpret some of his more rambunctious behavior on the block, based on patterns of police treatment of Black and Brown bodies, particularly young men. At the end of the conversation, I asked Erick if he was comfortable with my naming this concern connected to his race; he said he was. I'm saddened that thirteen-year-olds need to worry about being criminalized for hanging with their friends, and I wouldn't want my caution to damage Erick's or any of his peers' sense of self. Still, I believe that Erick and other students appreciated that I was "being real" with them, that I was seeing race and its corresponding injustices and thereby showing an understanding of how their experience growing up with melanin might be different than my experience growing up white.

After seven years of teaching, I took on the role of dean of students, which allowed me to focus on the intersections of school climate and adolescent development that most interested me. I remembered being a middle school student and how socially and emotionally challenging that was for me. I remember being seen and supported by my teachers and how that led to being connected to school as a community and achieving academic success. Given my commitment to trying to foster for young people the quality of school experience that I had, my work as dean allowed me to focus on school culture and practices more holistically, including advisory work and school-wide community-building events. I was also the next level up from teachers in the school's "discipline" structure. While this role did involve assigning punitive consequences (never something I felt settled in), it also allowed me to engage students in reflective conversations, facilitate countless mediations among students, foster constructive dialogue between students and teachers, and institute more restorative practices, including the pursuit of restitution as an approach to discipline that can grow students' skills and self-esteem (as well as community) rather than squash them. And I was able to apply to my work with students and teachers what I'd learned through my challenges and breakthroughs in the classroom.

My learning continued as an assistant principal and instructional coach, also in city schools with predominantly Black and Brown students. Now in the suburbs north of New York City, I continue to be invested in fostering choice, engaging student voice, and considering the dynamics of mostly white teachers in front of increasingly racially diverse classes. Since I left the classroom, my own racial literacy and understanding of equity have continued to develop; were I to teach seventh grade again, I would explore more with students the power dynamics of the classroom and school. I would explore how to collaborate to foster a greater sense of belonging and ownership for all students, with particular attention to students whose identities have been historically marginalized.

I've often been my own harshest critic, and in my initial years teaching, my shortcomings rang much louder for me than any sense of accomplishment. Immersed in the all-consuming juggling act, I lacked the perspective that years of experience can offer and hindsight might allow. In preparing to write these reflections, I was curious to learn more about how my early students remembered me as a teacher, including my relationship to "authority" and "discipline." I tagged former students on a social media post seeking their feedback. One former student with whom I felt I was always butting heads in my first full year teaching seventh grade surprised me with her positive recollections. She attributed her passion for performing Shakespeare years later to my approach to teaching poetry, which included having students read, write, and perform. Another student, who I also coached in soccer, wrote,

> As my teacher and coach you were someone I highly respected . . . you treated every one of us with respect and kindness. When I failed at soccer you were never angry, but instead you pulled me to the side and gave me nothing but encouragement. When I was under performing in school you attempted to talk to me and never washed your hands. I thank you for everything you did for me back then.

These responses suggest that my students' perspectives may also be rosier with passing years and space from any challenges we experienced in our time together. But the feedback does offer some affirmation to me, as a white man protected since birth and raised with socioeconomic security, that my growth into a relationship with authority and discipline that aligns with my vision and values enabled me to foster, at least for some Black and Brown students from "the hood," the kind of connectedness to their school experience that I cherished when I was young and that I wanted to create for them.

PEER MEDIATION

SHIFTING POWER IN SCHOOL DISCIPLINE

— Jeff Embleton —

On a Saturday morning early in October, a dozen middle school students in Brooklyn came into school, by choice, to learn with each other. The occasion was the first "train the trainer" session that eighth-grade mentors had developed and were co-leading for sixth- and seventh-grade students. The eighth-grade facilitators were already thinking about high school and wanted to pass along and teach others about peer mediation.

There were nametags and bagels outside the classroom (they'd seen enough adult "PD"), and there was light music on as the younger students who weren't really sure what to expect settled in. A couple of parents asked if we would really not be done until 3:30 p.m.—wow, on a Saturday.

The classroom was crammed with single heavy desks, perfect for rows and order.

The facilitators moved them out of the way and set up a giant circle. They weren't really sure how many students would actually show up, but there weren't many open seats by the time they turned down the music and said good morning to the room. Mind you, these weren't four regular eighth-grade facilitators. They had some superhero powers, and it was evident they had grown to understand their powers and the reach of their voice. Younger students were engaged from the moment the eighth graders opened the circle.

I was working as a dean of culture at a new school, and my role was to help build a positive school culture and also work on student discipline issues. There were a lot of ways that the school was trying to proactively build relationships with and between students and families through things like advisory groups, community meetings, and home visits. And there was still plenty of conflict.

In my first couple of years as a dean, I had received more than a thousand referrals to the office where students were sent out of class. It was my role to listen to them, help them identify and reflect on what was going on, consider the impact on the community, and make a plan if they were ready to reenter the classroom.

Almost every school has a lengthy student handbook that clearly outlines the policies and consequences for anyone who breaks the rules. We spent many hours as a staff calibrating "the rules" so that students felt a sense of fairness moving from class to class. As the frequency of students being sent out of class increases, schools often reiterate the consequences to students and families. I believe this comes from wanting to feel a semblance of control and is often justified as trying to help create a community of learning. The students who were being sent out of class (often, I would see the same student multiple times a week, sometimes multiple times a day) were *disrupting* that environment.

As a white male administrator in a space with almost all Black and Brown youth, I was acutely aware of the dynamics of my race playing out in these situations. In my role working with kids sent out of class, I was often the one who reminded them and their parents about the section of the school handbook that related to whatever rule had been broken. I was acting as a cog in a much bigger machine of the school-to-prison pipeline. I knew that this dynamic (where I was constantly reminding students and parents of rules that I was enforcing) wasn't working for the kids who were already constantly receiving the message that they didn't belong. While I valued the depth of the relationships that I was able to form with some students who were in the office almost daily, I recognized all that was being denied to them. They were missing access to knowledge, skills, and ideas that would help them become who they wanted to be, and they were being denied their right to learn.

I wasn't content to just let the discipline process be, and I wasn't okay with my part in it, so I sought alternatives. How were other schools creating welcoming and inclusive environments? What were their community norms? How did they run protocols and respond when something happened that caused harm? What was the role of the student and family in school discipline?

My colleagues and I recognized that we would have to be intentional to disrupt the power structures because they were there every day whether or not we acknowledged them. A few of us went through training with the International Institute for Restorative Practices in New York City. We read together and attended the Technical Assistance Center on Disproportionality with

Pedro Noguera and Jeff Duncan-Andrade. I can remember shifting in how I thought about school discipline policies and interpreting ed code, becoming more human centered and thinking about what my role was as a white educator to enact what Pedro Noguera called "the disciplining event":

> The disciplining event, whether it occurs in public or private, serves as one of the primary means through which school officials "send a message" to perpetrators of violence, and to the community generally, that the authority vested in them by the state is still secure. Particularly within the current political climate created by the fight against violence, the disciplining event provides an opportunity for school authorities to use those accused of committing acts of violence as an example to others.[1]

I worked with Teachers Unite around school discipline policies and learned from their documentary *Growing Fairness* and associated toolkits and training. We attended trainings with educators and students at Lyons Community School and with the director of Dream Charter High in New York City. We were learning about the contemporary and Indigenous practices of circles and restorative justice. Rather than push young people out through suspensions and expulsions, and foster schools of avoidance and compliance, we sought to build a culture that brought people in. This took more time and work, and more understanding of who students were and what was going on for them.

"Restore" implies to bring something back to a sense of wholeness. It's predicated on the idea that a whole already exists. I've both led and seen restorative practices being enacted in spaces where kids did not have relationships with one another, and therefore, the idea of sitting down and listening to how they impacted someone they didn't know didn't really matter to them. I've also had the tools of restorative justice used in settings toward a more punitive outcome.

Through all of our work, we went on a lot of school visits to see other teams in action. High school students would let us join their fairness committee meetings or take time after observing a peer mediation to debrief a move they had made as facilitators. The middle school student ambassadors really took to the process of peer mediation. That is how we ended up at school on a Saturday learning to read body language by studying silent films of world leaders and discussing how that might apply to a scenario in which two students in conflict did not want to talk.

HOW IT WORKS

Mediation is a process in which a neutral third party helps disputing parties find their own solutions to conflict. In our case with middle school students, there were two peer mediators who held the space together with two students in conflict. There was a specific way they sat so that the two students in conflict were diagonal from each other and able to see each other's eyes. Each student facilitator had their own way of opening the space to establish norms about paraphrasing, speaking with "I" statements, and not interrupting.

Peer mediation teaches students to see conflict as part of everyday life and an opportunity to grow and learn. It is a way to empower students to solve their own problems through improved communication and critical thinking. In terms of building culture, it can promote dialogue and mutual understanding of individuals and groups within a bigger community.

The eighth graders reviewed some of the key points they had learned in their own training from high school facilitators about why peer mediators were important. The written application that younger students had to complete if they wanted to be considered for a mediator role included the language:

> "Conflict is a normal part of everyday life. When it is handled in a negative way, it can have destructive results; but when it is handled in a positive way, it becomes a valuable learning experience. From middle school on, students turn to their peers when they have a problem. By using trained peer mediators, schools empower students to help themselves. When students come up with their own solution to a problem, they are happier and more inclined to live with it."

Eighth-grade students ran discussions, scenarios, and a "fishbowl" so that younger students could see a simulated mediation in real time. The sixth- and seventh-grade students were learning the fundamentals of how to have people use "I" statements, practice active listening, and work to find resolution. As an adult in the space, I had the opportunity to be led by students and shown by them what it was to be a good teacher.

WITH STUDENTS

While peer mediation may just seem like a nice thing for middle school students to do, it is much more than that. In New York City schools and elsewhere, young

BIPOC are suspended for things like "defiance" and "disruption" at a much higher rate than white students. By shifting the power away from the punitive discipline system and into the hands of students, we are creating potential for something different to happen.

I spent a lot of time learning with students outside the formal time of a school day. We came together on the weekends on multiple occasions for more workshops and tried out scenarios. And then, when these conflicts came up in real time, we had a network of student leaders who could run a mediation. As the dean, I had a whole team of students who were ready to hold a mediation in the hallway, on the yard, in the cafeteria, and even on camping trips. All this was happening in an era of "no excuses" and exclusionary disciplinary practices.

I learned that it was critical for me as a white male and as a dean to receive these students as a listener. I began to learn that I had to recognize every aspect of my identity in how I was responding. I tried to work closely with families and peers. I made hundreds of phone calls, had in-person meetings to dialogue with families, and went on home visits or met folks out in the community.

In the restorative-justice approach, we're focused on the relationship and repair for isolated incidents. As I've continued in education, I'm learning about transformative justice, which takes the work further to change the unjust conditions. It seeks to repair the larger context, and it works to uproot, dismantle, and shift the tenets upon which the system is designed.

I recently learned the meaning of the word conspire from a student. They spoke and shared the root of the word, which breaks down into the following:

CON + SPIRE
with + breathe

I ask myself regularly what it means to be not just an ally but a co-conspirator. It's the work of a lifetime.

MUCH LIKE ALL OF THE LAST

– Adam Seidel –

Land of the Free, Home of the brave? Nah
They can't let us be, we've grown from slaves
It's there if you wanna read, I mean, it's all on the page
They say it's police, I just know when it's race
And now it's thrown in our face
Maybe I'm lost signs are vital to me
Sandra Bland didn't come off as suicidal to me
Y'all play around thinking we're on safe ground
They killed Tamir Rice right and his rights, right on
      his playground.

—JOE BUDDEN, "Freedom (Freestyle)"[1]

The memory is vivid. It's a late July morning. There isn't a single cloud interrupting the crisp blue summer sky soaring above. The air is still, placid. It's quiet. For most, the day has not yet begun; the neighborhood is sleeping in after a late summer night. The sun, not yet settled high above us to bake the concrete, is peeking out over the top of the hill in Dorchester, Massachusetts, where my school sits. I'm driving, arriving early to knock out a long list of tasks to launch a new school year—preparing student and staff schedules, setting up classrooms, and doing a deep cleaning. I'm one of two school leaders in charge of a 330-student middle school. Staff return in one week for a month of professional development, and students will be here before we know it. NPR is on in the background, coming in and out as my mind races through everything I need

125

to do today. The hope of a new school year is starting to mix with anxiousness; we are in the week of summer where the idea "everything will be better next year" begins to meet the reality of what is possible. As I near the top of the hill and prepare to make the final turn before arriving, my listening settles on the newly released audio of the dashcam recording from Sandra Bland's traffic stop. I pull into the school parking lot and can't move.

My heart sinks. It's a quick clip, maybe fifteen seconds. Maybe only five. But it's unmistakable. The state trooper is me. Sandra Bland is one of my students. Sandra Bland is all of my students. My school serves 99 percent BIPOC students from inner-city Boston. I am white. In the audio, I hear how Ms. Bland's confidence and directness challenge the state trooper, and how he grasps for his lost sense of power and authority by escalating his demands and escalating his tone. In his voice, I recognize that his whole sense of self, the power and the privilege he has carried his whole life, is slipping away with each question and statement from Ms. Bland. I hear the moment when he realizes that his only way to hold onto his power is to take hers. In his initial interviews following Ms. Bland's death, he describes feeling unsafe. This was not because Ms. Bland was bigger than him, had a weapon, or even did anything wrong. But the direct confrontation of the state trooper's whiteness was too much for him to bear. He was unsafe. He found himself in a position he could not reconcile. And, as a result, she lost her life.

I can hear all of this because I've had this same interaction hundreds or thousands of times in the last few years as the leader of a high-performing charter middle school. I ask a student to comply with an expectation of the school—"Please, join the line; we are silent in the hallway"—and maybe it's ignored the first time, maybe I was unclear, or maybe it was unheard. The second time, when I step closer and lower my voice, the request is met with an audible and what feels like a purposefully loud "Huh?" that elicits snickers from the class. By the third time repeating myself, I forget our school's mantra of "purpose not power" and no longer explain the why behind my statement, saying, "In line. Silent," paired with what I may too proudly and affectionately call my well-practiced "teacher stare." Meanwhile, the blood rushes to my face. I feel frustrated, painfully aware that my authority hangs in the balance as the student decides what to do, and I'm reminded again how tenuous my power truly is and how invested I am in it. I am not going to lose it or yell, but I know that there is no way out of this situation without escalating even more—"Go to the dean's office," "I'm going to call your family," "Detention."

And while I've had some version of this interaction too many times to count, one in particular comes right back to me because it's become part of a recurring dream. It happened during my first year as a school leader, and I was leading bus dismissal early in the year. I was trying to enforce silence in the bus line, and after a few reminders and redirections, one student sucked his teeth and mumbled, "Why are you always tripping?" In that moment, my mind went blank. I couldn't access my playbook; I didn't know what to say. In the split second it took for me to utter a consequence and dismiss the line, I realized that I didn't have a real answer, and I know he knew that too. When he walked by, he looked at me with a look that said, "That's what I thought." In my nightmare, he would stare me down, and I would visibly flinch as if scared. Just like the state trooper. That didn't happen in real life, but I knew he was right. I was tripping. The whole idea of silent dismissal was tripping after a full day of silent hallways and classrooms, and yet I was clinging to it. The idea of compliance as a demonstration of values was tripping, and yet I was clinging to that too.

This is now the summer of 2015, one year after Michael Brown was killed by a police officer who was later exonerated in Ferguson, Missouri, and one year before the summer when Alton Brown was killed in Baton Rouge, Louisiana; just a week later the whole country will watch Philando Castile being murdered in front of his daughter on Facebook Live in Minneapolis, Minnesota. It's a few weeks after Ta-Nehisi Coates releases *Between the World and Me*. I'm more than ten years into a career in education, but it's my first summer as a parent. In January, my wife and I adopted our son, a dark-skinned and beautiful Black boy. And while I have always actively worked to not be a typical "white male authority figure" with my students, my journey to not just center my own experience in my interactions with students, but rather to center theirs, has just begun. Instead of just hearing the white state trooper's panic as he clung to his whiteness and privilege, or instead of hearing my own, I can start to hear and see Ms. Bland's fight to hold onto her dignity and humanity in the face of an escalating threat, in the face of whiteness. I can start to see my students, at age ten, looking to preserve some of their personhood while marching through a silent hallway to another class.

How did I land so far from my values and ideals? How had I come to see myself as a manifestation of the school-to-prison pipeline? As part of the carceral state? I always celebrated myself as someone committed to social justice. And

I worked at a school committed to the belief that education was the next civil rights movement. It was a school that I sought to work in after sitting in on an eighth-grade English language arts (ELA) lesson that compared speeches by Martin Luther King Jr. and Malcolm X and posed an essential question in a lively debate: "The ballot or the bullet?" For most of the time, I think I knew that I was not doing radical liberation work, though I don't even think I had the language for that feeling. Mostly, I held to my belief in the George Washington Carver quote that we often shared during school-wide community meetings early in the school year as we purposefully built a schema that academic achievement was self-worth: "Education is the key that unlocks the golden door of freedom." At the end of these gatherings, I would stand at the door our fifth and sixth graders exited through, smiling, nodding, giving pounds to students as they headed off to their first-period class, looking for signs that they had internalized the quote and were ready to give more of themselves to their schoolwork and to us as the adults. I believed that our school was helping a generation of young people in Boston unlock doors and access freedom that would otherwise be closed to them.

Every summer we would launch our staff professional development with a histogram that showed three data points: the college graduation rates of the lowest-income quartile, the college graduation rates of the highest-income quartile, and the college graduation rates of our school's graduates. Our students were outperforming their peers in the lowest-income quartile by more than 20 percentage points and yet their college completion rates were still below those of young people born into the highest-income quartile. We would invite observations, reflections, and commitments. Invariably, a chorus of teachers would share how proud they were to see what our students accomplished, proof that our model worked—we were proving that zip code should not determine fate. This would eventually be met with the rejoinder that the chart was both something to celebrate and a reminder that our work was still not enough. How could only four or five out of ten of our students go on to graduate from college? As soon as we got that comment and before a deeper analysis of why that might be, we would close that section with our essential rallying cry, "If we want to make sure we deliver on our promise of a college preparatory education, we are going to have to work harder to make sure our lessons are vigorously prepped and practiced, our school systems and expectations are tight, and we build a culture that celebrates academic achievement." The next three weeks of staff development were designed around those central themes and meant to build a shared passion and commitment to that vision. By design, we were working to turn passion into a pathology—one that builds on a foundational belief that "better than *is* good enough" or more specifically that "better than *is* social justice." I ultimately came to understand this pathology in the context of white supremacy. As a staff, we slid from a vision that *all students thrive with clear expectations* to asking students to perform a particular version of compliance that is rooted in white supremacy and anti-Blackness, and resulted in students internalizing that they are never enough.

Between the World and Me and Sandra Bland's death started to pierce that vision for me, as did parenting a Black boy and starting to see how the world saw him as a threat, even as a one-year-old in a sandbox at a local park. I saw it in a mom's eyes, in her clutch of her baby as mine moved closer to them. You could be Black and educated and have your dignity and life taken. My partner and I could do everything possible to nurture, love, and support our son, and none of that would protect him in the face of whiteness, white supremacy, and anti-Blackness. As Joe Budden freestyled, "Sandra Bland didn't come off as suicidal to me."[2] Sandra Bland was driving. Trayvon Martin was walking. Ahmaud Arbery was jogging. Breonna Taylor was sleeping. Tamir Rice was playing. All, along with the countless others not named, were just trying to live.

I have come to hold that good intentions are not enough. In fact, good intentions are particularly dangerous because they can obscure and shelter you from your impact. There is not a neutral path. There is only the hard work of interrogating your whiteness and anti-Blackness, actively working to dismantle it within yourself and others, and believing that we all must be liberated from the insidious and corrupting tentacles of white supremacy to truly be free. At best, we may get some kids into college, but we certainly will not get them or us free without that work.

Back to the summer of 2015. This is not a story of an immediate or radical transformation. No, this is a story about how despite my evolving transformation—the dashcam audio shook me and replayed in my head throughout the school day—I moved slowly from holding radical thoughts to taking any meaningful action.

I stayed at the school for two more years even though I couldn't unsee the impact we were having. On a micro-level, on my best days I shifted my practices, hovering above my interactions with students, listening with a closer ear to my language and how power and whiteness were held between us. But I didn't march into school that morning and revamp our summer staff professional development to hold a mirror to how our own pathology had obscured our role in propping up white supremacy and the oppression of our students. I didn't insist we scrap our student-discipline policy. I thought about it. I thought about playing the dashcam audio for everyone. I knew my colleagues needed to hear it, but I was not confident that I could create a space where staff were able to see themselves in the state trooper and use that as a reflection point. Was I calling them police? Murderers? Was I confident enough to go there? And what about my Black and Latinx colleagues? Was I ready to make a larger point about the expectations of the school and how we were *all* recreating the carceral state in our hallways? I wasn't. I wasn't confident enough to try and be wrong. The stakes feel obvious now, and I'd like to think I would do things differently if I could go back. I didn't understand it then, but whiteness and power and perfectionism were holding me back. Oppression was continuing to do its work through me—shame and fear and my need to hold onto a vision of myself as just and competent stopped me. And the momentum and immediacy of the school year propelled me—all of us really—forward, deep into another school year, much like all of the last.

PART FIVE

TEACHING TEACHERS

What they don't know won't hurt 'em.
I pledge to never be no one's burden.
Mama said never disrespect your neighbors,
'cuz next week we might have to check for favors.
That's science . . .

Keep shining.
Nobody could stop your progress,
'cuz unknown forces move some known objects.
That's magic . . .

—JAY ELECTRONICA, "Letter to Falon"[1]

We can talk all day long about what white teachers need to do, and what they can and cannot do. However, if there is no mechanism for working with them to understand the immense responsibility they carry and the power they hold to either destroy lives or build powerful new futures with young people, all these conversations lead to stagnation. That's science.

The essays in this section recognize this. They consider what teacher training and professional development should look like, offer suggestions for how to train teachers, and remind us all that there are frameworks we must utilize for teaching and training white teachers to understand their whiteness. This work cannot be haphazard and accidental. It is too important to leave to chance.

There are clear steps we must take in the never-ending journey to being our best selves for young people. This too is science.

The contributors in this section lay the steps out clearly for us. None are easy; all are necessary: study what it means to be white, learn to navigate racial stress, engage with BIPOC communities in a model of solidarity, participate in white affinity spaces grounded in accountability and action, and amid all this . . . teach.

As Lisa Graustein so eloquently writes in her essay, this work is not about being woke; it's about committing to waking up each day and doing the work to uproot the ways we have internalized white supremacy and structural racism. And then showing up and pouring love and joy and possibility into students. And being present and open to receiving it back. That's magic.

BECAUSE SCHOOL WAS BUILT FOR ME, THERE'S SO MUCH I DIDN'T KNOW

– Ali Michael –

I learned early to be afraid of "the hood." I grew up thinking the hood was the Black part of town, the scary part of town, the place I didn't belong. People I knew didn't go there, we didn't know people from there, and we told suburban legends about the dim and murky things that transpired there. Movies gave us the stereotypical visuals for these delusional stories, and rap music would make my anxious heart beat faster and harder as it evoked—unconsciously—some of my worst fears. Since my family and community didn't talk about race, these festering notions of Black places as dangerous or off-limits were never confronted.

What I love about Chris Emdin's conceptualization of the hood is that it takes this fear that so many white people have been taught to have and turns it inside out.[1] In fact, he says, we should all fear education in the hood. But not for the reasons most commonly imagined.

If you teach in the hood, you know that it's a place of light and talent, of laughter and community, of potential and power. The hood is not the one-dimensional place I imagined it to be from the distant hills of my middle-class suburb. It's not one place at all; it's many places—all complex, three-dimensional communities, places of innovation and creativity. According to Emdin, what makes the hood "the hood" is that it's a place where families send children to schools that were not designed for them.

When you're white like me and you teach in the hood, you represent and uphold a system that was not built to serve the children that you teach. That should scare all of us.

"The hood" is not a term that pertains solely to communities of Black people.[2] It includes the children of immigrants, whose parents don't have a way to communicate with the schools they attend, whose cultural and linguistic assets are undervalued or ignored. It includes Native children who attend schools that teach history in a way that actively denies their stories and values, as well as their struggles for sovereignty and survival within a system predicated on their eradication. It includes the white children of Appalachia, whose language patterns are denigrated and looked down upon. It can be located in small towns, in cities, on reservations, in the suburbs, in certain classrooms, or in one particular wing of a school.

One of the principles of anti-racist talk is that if there are broad disparities among groups, you are more likely to find solutions to those disparities if you look at the way those groups are treated disparately by systems rather than seeking deficiencies or merits in the individual members of those groups.[3] In the US, the mainstream narrative about disparities in education does the opposite: it blames individuals. The blame sounds like this: *Why is there a racialized achievement gap in schools? Well, it's because Black people don't care about education. They are more interested in sports, want to get stuff fast and easy, and are not willing to work for things.*[4] This mythology is closely aligned with stereotypes that date back to the time of enslavement: *Black people are lazy, they're more physically inclined, they are not intellectual.* This is what it looks like to blame individual members of a group for the disparities that are caused by group-level mistreatment within systems and institutions.

It is common knowledge today that race is a social construction. There is no validity to a racial hierarchy that asserts that white people are intelligent while Black people are athletic. The only difference between white people and Black people (aside from the melanin in our skin and hair) is how we have been treated by the systems that govern our lives, like the government, education, housing, healthcare, criminal justice, entertainment, law, and more. So when we blame individuals for group-level disparities, we are involved in a grave misdiagnosis of the problem. And it's racist.

When we look at our school systems, the systemic disparities in treatment of groups are profound. Again, we could do this with any "ghettoized" group, any group whose identity and concerns were not centralized as modern schooling evolved into what it is today. But if we look specifically at some of the history of Black people and schooling, we see that throughout the 1800s, before the Civil War, it was actually illegal in parts of the US for Black people to be literate; the children and grandchildren of enslaved people sought covert ways to learn, as educational historian Jarvis Givens writes in *Fugitive Pedagogy*.[5] By the time the

Emancipation Proclamation was signed in 1862, schools were beginning to be built by Black people for Black people. Throughout the 1900s, Black children were kept out of schools designed for white children. Black schools became central to Black communities, places where teachers knew families and families knew teachers, where Black excellence was expected. After *Brown v. Board of Education of Topeka*, most Black educational institutions were forced to close. Racial integration happened at the expense of Black schools. Black homecoming, Black athletic teams, Black dance clubs, and Black honors classes were disbanded.[6] A whole generation of Black educators lost their jobs. Today, schools' student bodies are largely determined by residential patterns, which means they are segregated. Most communities today are racially segregated because of policies that subsidize housing mortgages for white homebuyers while denying them to Black and Brown homebuyers. This, in addition to redlining, policing practices, housing appraisals, and overt violence, kept white and Black communities largely separate. And when we look at how schools are funded, it's by real estate taxes. Real estate, in a country where access to resources and opportunities has always been and still is deeply tied to race. We cannot look at schools in the hood and ignore the historical and systemic factors that shaped them over time.

When we break down the hood like this, it's easy to see how systemic racism shapes the schools we teach in. But when we talk about systemic racism, it starts to feel like there's nothing we can do about it. Each of us is just one person, and we don't control the system. And yet, we are always already being shaped by the system. We are each a small part of that system. And the system is also part of us. Part of creating a system that works for our students means seeing how it lives in us—and shifting our practice to make it one that is rooted in the needs, concerns, realities, assets, and contributions of our students and their communities.

When I was a new teacher, I did so much that was right. I called parents in the first month of school to introduce myself and tell them what I appreciated about their child, so that if there was a problem later in the year, we would already have a relationship. I worked hard to not let pity or the reality of what my students were up against lower my expectations of them. I tried to build relationships with all my students, especially the ones who seemed the most nonconformist, the least likely to cooperate.

But I did a lot wrong too.

I saw Black and Latinx students who I believed needed to be more like white people in order to achieve success. I believed that their leaving their communities, leaving the hood, was part of what success would look like for them. I had loads of unexamined implicit bias that shaped a too frequently patronizing and inauthentic relationship with BIPOC parents.

I remember substituting in an English class and going over the answers to a worksheet with the class. As students delivered their answers in Black vernacular, I awkwardly repeated them back to them in Standard American English (SAE), correcting them simply by stating the correct answer with no discussion of different vernaculars and no acknowledgment of the legitimacy of Black English. What was wrong here was not that I taught Black students SAE but that I did it in a passive-aggressive way without nuance or discussion, assuming that my way was right and their way was not.

When teaching middle school math, I remember my Black principal telling me I needed to be stricter. Appealing to my sense of justice, he said, "You would never let a white supremacist stand in the way of our students' learning. Remember that when you are hesitating to discipline them for standing in one another's way." He did this because I waffled on classroom management, afraid that drawing boundaries meant I would be an oppressive white person. But as a result of my fear of my own authority, no one was learning math. Resonating with the imagery he suggested, I told my Black students the next day that when they interrupt one another's learning, it was as bad as white supremacists blocking the entrance to the school building. They were—understandably—outraged.

As a teacher in my early twenties, I had traveled far from that predominantly white suburb where I grew up. I had traveled the great distance from *not knowing* what I didn't know to *knowing* what I didn't know. After four years in college studying African American literature, African history, and post-apartheid South African politics; living with a Black South African family during my study abroad; studying the civil rights movement in the South of the US with a multiracial group of students; and taking every class I could take on race or education, I went from being delightfully, naively ignorant to being both radically enraged and cautiously paranoid and tentative. I knew that what I had learned about Black people and Black communities (not to mention Native communities and Latinx communities) was wrong; it was a bias constituting dangerous weeds that needed to be pulled out by the roots. I knew much of what I had learned about myself as a white person was wrong too. But I wasn't sure what was right or how to plant new seeds. How can I be a white person who is an anti-racist educator in the hood?

In the rest of this piece, I share strategies that have supported me over the past twenty-five years to engage in ongoing anti-racist practices, to make mistakes, and to engage more in those practices. These are strategies I believe are essential for white people who teach in the hood and want to uproot habits and assumptions that live in them as a result of being a white person in a white supremacist society—a society that *was* built for them. I call this engagement a practice because it is not something that can be achieved or finished. Just like fitness, it requires an ongoing, regular commitment to training.

STRATEGIES FOR ENGAGING AN ONGOING ANTI-RACISM PRACTICE

1. Understand What It Means to Be White

Understanding one's whiteness means understanding that white people are just as much a part of the racial puzzle in the US as our BIPOC students and their families. In my own life, being white has meant seeing with a white lens, judging with a white scale, and norming behavior by contrast with white culture—all of which was largely invisible to me. When I passively yet aggressively corrected my students' Black vernacular, it was with an unconscious belief that they were the ones who needed to change in order to fit into US society, rather than that we live in a society that devalues Blackness and that the society needs to be changed. I don't mean to say here that the right answer is never to teach students SAE. Lisa Delpit suggests that absolutely we should do so in a way that is respectful of students' home languages.[7] April Baker-Bell, in contrast, suggests that Black English is denigrated in our society because Blackness is denigrated and that no amount of code-switching can erase a student's Blackness, hence rendering the teaching of SAE moot.[8] Clearly the question is complex enough to demand more complex answers than I can offer here. But racism is not a problem that belongs to the people who are victimized by it. Nor should students be made to feel inferior because they live in a society that refuses to sanction or understand their cultural and linguistic styles. As for me, it was naïve to believe that my role in those interactions was neutral as a white person. I was a part of a system that told my students the way they and their families spoke was deficient. And I possessed all of the linguistic and cultural styles that the system values because I am white and middle class.

Understanding what it means to be white means learning to see those judgments and expectations shaped by whiteness—both mine and others'. Other things I've needed to learn over time include how many of my Black colleagues have far less generational wealth than so many of my white colleagues; how many of my white colleagues have parents who live much longer than the parents of many of my Black colleagues because of the very real death gap we have in the US; and the lived experience of Black male colleagues who arrive at school thirty minutes earlier every day because they don't know, from week to week, which days they will be stopped by police on the way in. Understanding what it means to be white means realizing that the death gap, the wealth gap, the policing gap, and the achievement gap are playing out in real time in my life and in the lives of people around me all the time, every day. And it's not because white people are better, smarter, more responsible, or more health conscious. It's because of how people in our group tend to be treated—by doctors, by teachers, by police, by real estate agents, by bankers—because we are white.

I cannot know how to teach Black children without having Black colleagues, Black mentors, and relationships with Black families. But being in relationship with Black people means understanding how the system is already and always operating in my life just as it is in theirs. I cannot know how to teach Black children without examining how deeply ingrained anti-Blackness is in my own consciousness as well as our society.

2. **Engage with Communities of Color in a Model of Solidarity, Not Charity**

If I'm being honest, charity is probably the reason I started teaching in the hood to begin with. If I'm being brutally honest, charity is probably at the root of the work that I do now. I can remember watching *Dangerous Minds* with Michelle Pfeiffer and wanting—so badly—to do what she did as a white teacher to help build a school that worked for Black children. But the model portrayed in the movie gives all the credit to Pfeiffer and none to the students and their families. According to the movie, if it weren't for her, they would be wasting away, violent criminals inhabiting dangerous, common stereotypes of their various gendered and racial identities. But what I've learned since I first started teaching is that charity is an inherently inequitable model for any relationship. In a "charity" relationship, the giver has the power and the resources, and therefore the decision-making agency. They often pity and disempower the receiver. The counterpoint to charity is solidarity. In a relationship of solidarity, both parties bring, and both parties receive. The transfer of resources is based on need and is informed by both parties. It is not designed to make the giver look good or the receiver look pitiable. Engaging with students and communities in solidarity doesn't mean one has to subvert one's own knowledge and reality. But neither are one's knowledge and reality artificially elevated because of one's access to resources and power.

Developing relationships of solidarity also means recognizing that when you engage in education in the hood you are taking anti-racist action that places you in a five-hundred-year struggle that people from your school and community may have been engaged in throughout their entire lives. It means honoring the expertise that comes from life experience—particularly in regard to students' parents and family members—and working to make it count within your school community. It means honoring the assets that your students, their families, and their communities bring. It means recognizing that while you have a certain type of cultural and linguistic capital, you literally cannot do your job without people who are different from you precisely because *they do not have that same cultural and linguistic capital*. This means unlearning the myth that the way you do things (which is the way that the system has validated your entire life) is the right way or the only way.

For years I co-facilitated with an older Black male colleague who was slow and methodical in his style. In contrast to him, I tend to be fast and wordy in my style. I would get impatient with him—and he could feel it. At one point, he said this to me:

> I can't do things the way you do them. And you shouldn't want me to. If I did things the way you do them, you wouldn't need me. What's valuable about our team is our differences. You're fast; I'm slow. You're all about the books; I'm deeply intuitive. You're white; I'm Black. This is where the power of our collaboration comes in.

He was right. I couldn't do my work alone, nor could he. And if we tried to imitate one another or demanded a sameness of style, we couldn't do our work either. In order to see this, I needed to recognize how I had been taught to rank our styles and to pursue individual success. Multiracial partnerships, like the kind we need to develop to support our students and change the system, require that we value the collective and that we throw out that artificial ranking system that leads us to devalue one another's unique contributions. No amount of book smarts, higher education, or fluency with technology on my part could compare with the particular expertise of my co-facilitator.

3. **The Ability to Navigate Racial Stress Is a Matter of Competence, Not Character**

For some reason, when it comes to being a part of multiracial communities or taking anti-racist action, white people believe that we can and should be perfect. We fear making mistakes because we don't want to be hurtful, but also because we don't want to be wrong. And often we stay quiet because we don't want to speak up if we're not 100 percent sure we're right. It took me a long time to get over some of the shame I felt after I told my Black students they were, essentially, acting like white supremacists. What an ignorant thing to say to twelve-year-olds! But what we know about learning is that it's not possible without mistakes. So how do we go into classrooms where our students needed us to be racially competent yesterday and be willing to make mistakes today? How do we show up imperfectly when our students' learning is on the line?

First, let go of doing it perfectly. Consider everything you do—every action you take, every lesson you teach, to be a draft. When I write a chapter, I assume that it will go through many revisions and ultimately look completely different from when I started. But I cannot even begin to revise or get feedback on what I've written if I don't create a rough draft first. When you want to take anti-racist action, you need to begin even though it will be imperfect. When you get feedback that it's imperfect, you can take it in with the knowledge that you expected to get such feedback. The only way I can keep showing up in public as a white person trying to be anti-racist is to say to myself each morning, "I cannot be perfect. I can only be honest and authentic. And I will solicit and take in feedback that will help me get better. But the stakes are high enough that I cannot sit this out."

Second, know that your capacity to navigate racial stress will increase with practice. I used to think that I had to pretend to be competent, which meant that I would stay silent on issues of race so that no one would know I didn't know what to say. I thought that BIPOC were racially competent and that white girls like me would never be. What I have learned is that racial competence is a skills-based competency that people get better at with practice.[9] Many white people don't have practice navigating racial stress because the world doesn't place racism at our feet when we get up in the morning. For many BIPOC, racism is sitting there when they walk out the front door. They have to navigate racial stress—and make sure their friends and families know how to—in order to survive.

As a white person whose intimate relationships are mostly with white people (e.g., my partner is white, my children are white, my siblings are white, my parents are white), it is rare for me to encounter racially stressful situations that are not related to my work. This means that I am less practiced at dealing with racial stress. Not all BIPOC are good at navigating racial stress and not all white people are bad at it. But the people who are good at it are good at it because they have practiced.

Third, being racially incompetent doesn't mean you're a bad person; it means you lack skills. But—and this is a big exception—the inverse is true as well. Being a good person is not sufficient for being racially competent. And when white people are not racially competent while at the same time holding power over BIPOC (like our students), we can do real harm. Founder of Afrocentrism, Dr. Molefi Kete Asante calls this "peculiar arrogance."[10] It's when we *don't know what we don't know*, and we exercise power over others in spite of this lack of knowledge. It's the reason why knowing that we don't know—even if it makes us paranoid and tentative—is a better place to be than the delightfully naïve stage in which we don't know that we don't know.

If you count yourself in this category of people who know what they don't know, you are on the right track by reading this book. Keep up the good work. Remember that part of the system *that was not built to serve your students* is the educational certification programs that allow students to graduate without ever taking classes that deeply address racial and cultural aspects of schooling or the systemic forces that perpetuate the hood. Read books that talk specifically about the needs and concerns of groups of students that are in your classroom. Watch movies or listen to podcasts about issues that concern their communities. Listen when there are community events or meetings that can help you better understand.

Finally, solicit feedback. Ask parents what they'd like to see more of or less of. Talk to students about what works and what doesn't. Have trusted colleagues observe your teaching and give you suggestions. Feedback becomes threatening when we believe we can and should be perfect or when we want the rest of the world to think we are. When feedback merely affirms our understanding of ourselves as evolving and learning—and therefore imperfect—it becomes much more predictable and also much less scary.

4. Find a Collective to Support Your Ongoing Practice

The work that it takes to help white people, *for whom the system works*, to become teachers who can support students, *for whom the system was not built*, is transformational, long-term, and personal. For me, it was critical to have communities of practice that could help support my growth. This could include collectives of teachers who get together to discuss problems of practice or individual scenarios. It could include a white anti-racist learning space where white people who are committed to developing an anti-racist practice join together to support one another on that journey. As a beginning teacher, I had learned a lot about racism, but I still didn't quite know how to talk about it. I wasn't quite sure (as is painfully obvious from some of the examples above) how racism impacted my students or if and how I should talk about it with them. I had a small anti-racist learning group with four other white people (including my sister and my partner), and we read books about racism, watched movies, attended workshops together, and just generally practiced talking about race and developing a racial lens. We role-played scenarios, we asked stupid questions, and we created action plans that we later debriefed and revised.

The important thing is that you cultivate relationships with allies (white or otherwise) who can help support you on your own anti-racist journey. Allies can play a very particular role in your learning and growth—and they are different from friends. Allies are people who can help you develop your skills around anti-racism, who help you stay accountable to your anti-racism learning goals. My allies are also my friends, but the reverse is not true. I have friends who do not play the role of ally for me because they are not on an anti-racist path, and they are quick to let me off the hook when I am trying to hold myself accountable.

I remember taking a walk with one white friend and trying to convey my sadness and frustration when I called a Black student by another Black student's name. I recognized this as a deeply significant microaggression, even as I also realized that I needed to be able to apologize to the student and forgive myself so that I could continue to be in relationship with her rather than drown in shame (which initially seemed to be the only plausible action plan). I happened to be walking with a white friend that day, and I told her all about it. She was adamant that it was a small thing, that it didn't matter, and that I shouldn't be so hard on myself. I remember thinking, "Wow, I need to process this with an ally. This person is not getting why this matters so much." Your allies are not people who will shame you. Ideally, they will empathize, they will share a time when they made a mistake too. But they will also help you process the situation without trying to excuse you or minimize the moment.

5. Finally, Teach!

No matter how much I knew or didn't know about race, racial competency, and navigating racial stress, I also needed to learn how to teach, how to relate to middle schoolers, and how to run a classroom. As the founder and director of the Center for Black Educator Development, Sharif El-Mekki says, "The purest form of activism is teaching Black children well."[11] Learning how to teach math in a way that makes the mathematical knowledge and skill belong to students for the rest of their lives and learning how to build a school culture in which students feel safety and belonging is part of being an anti-racist teacher. This means that putting in the time to do things that may feel mundane, such as learning how to teach fractions effectively, designing equity-oriented rubrics, drawing boundaries for behavior so that everyone can learn, arranging a guest speaker from the community, or maintaining a student-of-the-week tradition, is all part of being an anti-racist educator. Building schools that are designed around the identities, needs, and concerns of the students in them is how we change the system one person, one classroom at a time.

WHITE RACIAL IDENTITY DEVELOPMENT AND RACE-BASED AFFINITY GROUPS

– Lisa Graustein –

THE TROUBLE WITH PROFESSIONAL DEVELOPMENT

As a sexuality education and humanities teacher who sat through way too many bad professional development (PD) sessions, I once wrote a blog post comparing PD to venereal disease (VD back in the day, STIs today). Both are often painful, can require awkward conversations, are shared with others, and can be a big waste of our time. PD doesn't have to be this way, especially anti-racist or diversity, equity, and inclusion (DEI) PD, but too often it is. As white staff, when we are in affinity groups, we often find our awkward, guilt-ridden silence punctuated by the sounds of animated voices and laughter from the affinity spaces of our BIPOC colleagues down the hall, intensifying our sense of inadequacy. This kind of DEI PD happens way too often and doesn't serve staff or our students.

So let's talk about what we can do instead.

RACIAL IDENTITY DEVELOPMENT THEORY

Racial identity development theory began in earnest in the 1970s, seeking to explain how BIPOC folks experience their identity and, later, with the work of Rita Hardiman and Janet Helms, how white people experience racial identity.[1] Racial identity development theory describes the cyclical stages that we move through in understanding and orienting to our own racial identity. "Cyclical" is the important word here—we cycle back, over and over again, through the different stages. We might think we are "woke" or get it, and yet a comment, uncomfortable feeling, or the witnessing of an act of racism can send us right back to an earlier stage. The usefulness of racial identity development theory comes from knowing what the stages are *so we can recognize when we are there, process our stuff, and move forward*. Let me say that again for the folks in the back: we all go through these different stages regularly, sometimes even within a given month or week. As someone who studies and teaches racial identity development theory, I still marvel each week when a thought pops in my head or a feeling swells in my chest that is coming from one of the earlier stages of identity development. It's a mistake to think we can achieve a state of being woke; it's about committing to waking up each day and doing the work to uproot the ways we have internalized white supremacy and structural racism.

WHITE RACIAL IDENTITY THEORY AND WHAT IT MEANS FOR PD

Both Hardiman's and Helms's work have a lot to offer us. Helms's model is often used in education circles. (You may have seen it in Dr. Beverly Daniel Tatum's *Why Are All the Black Kids Sitting Together in the Cafeteria?*) I'll summarize Helms's model here, but both Hardiman and Helms are worth reading.[2] Remember, this stuff is cyclical, so as you read the next few paragraphs, ask yourself, "When was I at that stage in the last week or month?" There's no shame in your answer, only learning.

Contact Stage

At this stage, we are oblivious to and lack an understanding of racism, have minimal experiences with BIPOC folks, and may profess to be color-blind. We accept most race-based stereotypes, are unaware of our internalized superiority, and see ourselves as "just people" with little to no awareness of having a racial identity.

What we need at this stage:

- Ways to help us see structural racism in bite-size parts and multiple points of engagement over time
- Modeling by other white folks of how we can expand our understanding
- Conversation and time to reflect on our own whiteness and how we learned about *our* racial identity
- Reflection on questions such as, "What were you taught about being white as a child?"
- Explicit guidance and boundaries on harmful things we are doing and saying in our work

Disintegration Stage

At this stage, we are in conflict because we are seeing or noticing something racist, and it is upsetting our worldview and *our view of ourselves*. We are starting to become conscious of our own whiteness and may experience internal conflict over white solidarity as we have experienced it. We are seeing that the system might be unfair in ways that are wrong and deeply upsetting.

What we need at this stage:

- Support from other white people in feeling our feelings and *not staying just in our feelings*
- Validation for how big and overwhelming things feel *and* concrete steps we and others can take to make change
- White people who are further along in the process to engage with us
- Questions such as, "When you saw/realized X, what did you feel?" and "How did your body respond?" that can help keep us grounded in that moment of realization and its impact on us
- Explicit guidance and boundaries on harmful things we are saying and doing in our work

Reintegration Stage

Something happens or we do some racial exploration, and what we see or feel creates enough cognitive dissonance that we back up and retrench in our white superiority. This can often look like victim-blaming BIPOC folks for racism. Much of our mainstream and right-wing media in this country supports this stage.

What we need at this stage:

- Conversation with other white people that lets us process and unpack what we are feeling
- Examination of the assumptions we are retreating into
- Well-chosen facts from people we trust that counter our retrenched narratives
- Hearing how other white people moved through this stage
- Reflective-listening questions that repeat the assumptions we are making in our statements back to us and allow us to question them
- Explicit guidance and boundaries on harmful things we are saying and doing in our work

Pseudo-Independence Stage

At this stage, we start to be curious and want to learn more about BIPOC folks and may pick up a book, talk to a coworker, or in some other way seek to engage with BIPOC folks. However, we are still really invested in feeling good about ourselves without having to do much, if any, self-examination, so we are seeking BIPOC folks who are like us, make us feel comfortable, and won't push us too hard. We want to know what *they* think or experience without having to look at how *we* are a part of creating that reality. We are keeping it intellectual and safe for ourselves.

What we need at this stage:

- Encouragement to deepen and complicate our understanding of white supremacy, structural racism, and the lived experiences of BIPOC folks
- Reminders to not expect the nearest BIPOC person to be our personal tutor
- Spaces with other white people to break down what we are learning, obtain support, and affirm our curiosity
- Continued reflection, such as through asking, "How does this resource [such as a reading/video] expand how we see structural racism functioning?" "How are my actions and choices a part of this dynamic?" and "How does this connect to our school?"
- Explicit guidance and boundaries on harmful things we are saying and doing in our work

Remember, I asked you to think about when you have been at one of these early stages in the last week or month (I can name several times when I was at one of those stages, so I'm right there with you). Being at an earlier stage might mean having thoughts like, "Why are those people doing that like that?" or "Well, if they hadn't rioted . . ." or "Oh, no, that's not what I *meant* . . ." or "I can't believe those people who stormed the Capitol." Really, take a moment and notice, feel, and breathe before continuing on with the summary.

Immersion/Emersion Stage

Now we have enough foundation to actually begin to look at our own experiences as racialized beings and the role whiteness plays in creating our shared, racist reality. We are willing to look at our own biases and privileges and are more willing and able to directly confront racism and white supremacy. We are *immersing* ourselves in identity and *emerging* in ways that allow us to begin to be real agents in the work of combating structural racism.

What we need at this stage:

- Support for our deepening work and learning *and* the invitation to seriously consider "What is *our* part in this?" with folks who can dig into that question in real and critical ways
- Invitation and skills for being in it with folks who are showing up at earlier stages
- Practice "calling in" and understanding the intra-race responsibility of that role
- Consideration of the questions "How have we internalized white supremacy culture?" and "How does it shows up in our practice and classrooms?"

Autonomy Stage

We have a fairly nuanced understanding of how white supremacy, structural racism, and white privilege operate, both outside of us and within us. We have a commitment to addressing these interlocking systems of oppression on many levels, and while we may still feel guilt, we are not stopped by guilty feelings. We are cultivating a strong, active anti-racist white identity and can show up as more effective agents for change. We can support our white siblings in addressing their and our collective, internalized white supremacy.

What we need at this stage:

- Continued opportunities to learn, reflect, and grow our practice and understanding
- Recognized responsibility to share best practices with our white colleagues
- Administrative support for serving in leadership *with* BIPOC colleagues
- Consideration of the strategies we are using to address our internalized ideas of superiority and how a particular resource [such as a reading or video] grows our ability to effectively work toward those strategies

Take a breath and a moment. What did you notice as you read this? When can you pinpoint a moment in the last week or month when you were at the contact stage or reintegration stage? What did you feel? When you felt guilt, denial, shame, embarrassment, anger (just listing *my* feelings here)—what is it you needed? How do you need other white folks to be with you in that space and at that stage?

Reflecting on our answers to these questions is the work we need to do with each other so our BIPOC colleagues don't have to do this extra emotional labor and can do their own work.

So let's talk affinity spaces and how we do this intra-racial group work.

AFFINITY SPACES: FROM COLLUSION TO ACTION AND ACCOUNTABILITY

Race-based affinity spaces—gathering people who share a racial identity in small groups—can do more harm than good if unstructured and unfacilitated. If I am in a white affinity space that is just muddling along, I am actually colluding with the aspects of racism that say we as white people can't do our own work and are not responsible for our part. If I am in a white affinity space that does nothing while the BIPOC groups dig deep and do work, I am continuing the white supremacist paradigm that BIPOC folks must educate us or that it is up to BIPOC folks to end racism. If I am in a white affinity space in which the white folks are just calling each other out and shaming each other, I am colluding in the aspects of white supremacy culture that demand perfectionism, are built on dominance, and threaten expulsion for failing to meet certain standards.[3] Nope. We are not doing this anymore.

A working knowledge of white racial-identity development combined with clear goals, facilitation, and accountability can create anti-racist, action-oriented, and successful race-based affinity groups.

Goals

"We want some affinity space" and "We'll talk about the reading in affinity groups" are *not* clear goals. Clear goals articulate the purpose with *an outcome that serves our students and families and honors our BIPOC colleagues*. For example, a clear goal is the statement: "We will use affinity space to (a) examine the ways three core aspects of white supremacy culture show up in our classrooms; (b) identify counter-moves we will replace them with; and (c) make a plan for implementing those moves with feedback." A goal like this works to change the reality for our students, honor our BIPOC colleagues' experiences, and direct us to specific steps.

Or maybe you are earlier in your collective work as a staff, in which case a goal for an affinity space might be "to process our responses to the new diversity, equity, and inclusion plan and name how we can support each other in doing the work it requires of us as white people." Doing this processing in an affinity space means we are not burdening our BIPOC colleagues with our resistance or confusion, and we are explicitly building our intragroup capacity to support each other so we are not expecting our BIPOC colleagues to do that extra emotional labor with or for us.

Both these example goals also have function and relevance for BIPOC affinity groups, though their conversations will be different. For example, as a white person, I internalize and externalize white supremacy culture as my mother tongue and as a system that keeps me comfortable and privileged. My BIPOC colleagues have internalized and externalized aspects of white supremacy culture as personal and professional *survival strategies* in a hostile dominant culture. And sometimes, the goals and structure of affinity spaces for white groups and BIPOC groups will need to be different; equity does not mean equivalence and sameness. Create your goals based on what you are truly seeking to do. Goals should accomplish the following:

- Ultimately and concretely serve your students
- Move staff along in their personal awareness *and* professional skills
- Not replicate patterns of oppression in their very structure
- Work to address concerns BIPOC students, staff, and families have raised
- Heal harm that has been done to BIPOC folks in your school

There will be white folks with no awareness, white folks who are resistant, and white folks who want to deflect their own feelings by calling out others. Create different entry points using short videos and readings ahead of time or as a self-directed "Do now." Frame them as "5K," "10K," and "Marathon" activities: "5K" being a review of key concepts, "10K" going a bit deeper, and "Marathon" for folks who are hungry to get complex and personal. We are all running, but our pace and starting points might be different.

A quick note about forming affinity groups because it's complicated. Even though I have equal parts Polish and Persian heritage, among the larger mix, my family has been white in this nation for generations; there is no complexity in my racial identity. My colleagues who are African American and second-generation

Korean American have really different experiences from each other even though they both may get named as "BIPOC"; many of my colleagues hold identities from more than one racial group. In general, I do the work ahead of time to share the goals for race-based affinity spaces and ask BIPOC folks to name groups they would like to be a part of so we can create groups that work for everyone. No one should be forced to choose only a part of themselves. In workshops I've led, this has meant everything from one single BIPOC group to multiple separate groups that define members as Black, multiracial, first generation, African and Afro-Caribbean, Latinx/Latine, and more.

Facilitation

Most white folks grow up without having many, or any, explicit conversations about what it means to be white. Many of us don't talk about our whiteness when we do talk about race. We generally don't know how to have functional, let alone anti-racist, conversations about race. We need facilitation. Facilitators hold us to functional norms, keep the conversation moving, can model vulnerability and *being with* when that vulnerability and support is absent from the group, and help us not get stuck in guilt or denial. Our BIPOC colleagues also deserve strong facilitation, supporting their growth and learning. (Pro tip: If you are an administrator, put the resources into getting skilled facilitators to help you do this work; if you are asking staff to do this facilitation, compensate them and provide them with support and training.)

Facilitators can name, model, and support call-in culture, helping people focus on the impact of their words and align their actions with their intentions. A working knowledge of racial identity development theory allows us to recognize and meet people where they are *and* help them move with us. Don't be shocked or surprised by ignorance or resistance. Ignorance is a chance to learn. Resistance is bound energy that, once released, can flow in new ways. When you hear a fellow white person expressing that they're at one of the earlier stages of their racial identity, step *in* with them. Affirm where they are and offer what you have learned that helps you move forward or hold that perspective differently. For example, use statements like "The first time I really saw how embedded racism is in my curriculum, I was totally overwhelmed. It felt too big, and I felt a lot of guilt. Focusing on one unit that I could change helped me get going. Where is a place that you can take some of what we have been talking about today and apply it? How can I help you do that?"

Accountability

While the goals for an affinity space outline the conversational and action expectations, we must also set and share clear expectations with everyone about what the share-back, confidentiality, and accountability expectations for affinity spaces are. If part of your goal is whole-group learning, then some prepared share-back from each group is appropriate. Articulating the questions that groups are expected to answer for their share-back is important and helps everyone stay focused. Whether or not there is a formal share-back, we always need to be explicit about confidentiality. There is often curiosity about what got talked about in the *other* group, particularly among us white folks. So be clear. For purposes of accountability, transparency, and creating vulnerable spaces, I generally use the following guidelines:

- Personal stories and information stay confidential to the space in which they were shared.
- The topics we discuss and our action steps can be shared and are recorded in some place publicly accessible.
- Each of us can always talk about our *own* learning and process. This looks like "I get how I am enforcing white cultural norms in my classroom that are harmful" and *not* "Wow, Chris shared this story about . . ."

For white affinity spaces, there has to be some level of public sharing. We live in a nation in which white-only meeting spaces have and continue to be harmful to BIPOC individuals and communities. When a white affinity space exists, we need to be explicit that we are meeting in this space *so that we can deepen our anti-racist understanding and practices*, part of which means some level of transparency about what we are doing; another part is an openness to aligning that work based on feedback from our BIPOC colleagues, students, and families. We should always end with time for staff to identify and plan for how they are going to *implement* the skills and content of the PD *and* make space in the coming weeks to support those steps. Support can come in the form of peer observation and feedback, dedicated time at department- and grade-level meetings, freeing up time or resources for staff to do more racial-identity work, managers actively supporting next steps, and circling back to the practices at subsequent PDs.

Finally, remember that this is not "one and done" work. We have more than five hundred years of white supremacy and lifetimes of learned behavior to uproot and change. We are not going to do that in a two-hour PD or in twenty hours of PD. We do have to commit to working on it constantly. Just like an individual's identity development is cyclical, so too is a group's learning and process. There will be steps forward as well as resistance and retrenchment. Expect it, plan for it, and keep at it.

I am writing this at the one-year anniversary of our statewide COVID-19 shut down. We know some of the many ways COVID-19 has impacted our young people and us as educators. And we will be spending the rest of our lives understanding its full impact on our education system and society. As much as many of us long for a return to "normal," that normal was never good enough, especially for our BIPOC students, families, and colleagues. We have undergone seismic shifts none of us could have imagined possible a year ago. We can bring that same creativity, tenacity, and human capacity for radical change to our work as white educators in service of anti-racist schools and schooling. We got this.

WHITENESS UPON WHITENESS

– Marguerite W. Penick and Kyle P. Steele –

INTRODUCTION

Before coming to academia, both of us taught in K–12 schools, working primarily with Black and Latinx students and in Black and Latinx communities. Since that time, we have made careers in a college of education in the Upper Midwest, where, as white folks, we prepare mostly white and mostly female teachers, the great majority of whom will end up working in schools in our region. In many ways, the demographics at play in our work are pretty typical: roughly eight out of every ten public school teachers identify as white and roughly three-fourths of teachers in higher education (professors, instructors, and lecturers) identify as white too.[1]

As a result, the stakes for Black and Latinx students in our country are remarkably high, and the dynamics of this phenomenon—white folks preparing white folks to teach—merit constant examination and scrutiny. In our current teaching on the foundations of education (we teach classes nearly every semester on multiculturalism and social justice), we draw regularly on vital lessons from our K–12 work, especially those we learned from our former students and communities. We confront the overwhelming presence of whiteness in our classrooms, at least in part, by striving to bring to life the lived realities, the love, the joy, the resilience, and the systemic inequities faced by members of our former school communities.

This chapter, as such, will flesh out the details of that work, allowing us to explain how our K–12 teaching in Black and Latinx communities is not only fundamental to the way we teach and research in higher education, but also how, in concrete ways, it permeates the content we offer to the future educators who now occupy our classrooms. While great K–12 teachers turn theories about equity into practice, this chapter uses the power of experience to enliven and bring urgency to the lessons of theory—even in college classrooms. As with our teaching, this chapter will leverage the power of vulnerability and storytelling to articulate two critical and timeless lessons we learned in the K–12 classroom years ago and now impart to our predominantly white teacher candidates. They are the means by which we offer perspective, showing the mistakes we made and the processes through which we corrected our mistakes in dialogue with our Black and Latinx students and their loved ones.

First, we learned that we needed to recognize and discard our white, middle-class, and ultimately oppressive notions of what K–12 teaching and learning should look like in favor of more inclusive alternatives. Along the same lines, we learned to truly listen to our students about what is interesting and relevant to them and then to incorporate their interests into the curriculum and in assessment. Second, we learned the power in creating deep and authentic relationships with Black and Latinx students and their caregivers, connections founded on respect and humility—often beyond the classroom. Ultimately, this chapter reveals that, although we are no longer in the K–12 classroom, our experiences working with Black and Latinx students are near the heart of what we do in higher education. We are responsible for preparing educators, and in our world predominately white educators, for a more inclusive and equitable future, and we do so—every day—with our former students in mind. It is our job to bear witness. It is our job to share the lessons our students taught us.

LESSON ONE: SUBVERT THE GRAMMAR OF SCHOOLING

If we define curriculum as the "what we teach" and pedagogy as the "how and why we teach," one thing we know is teachers tend to teach both *what* they were taught and in a manner consistent with *how* they were taught. Both things, however, are rarely synchronous with all the students in the classroom. Robin DiAngelo captures the potentially insidious effects of this phenomenon, recalling a BIPOC colleague who said, "Our students are taught by white teachers who were taught by white teachers who were taught by white teachers who were taught by white teachers using textbooks written by white people for white people."[2]

Unavoidably, every new teacher enters their classroom with an expectation of what that space should look like, sound like, and feel like. Predominantly white and middle-class schools often follow models from the past, and they tend to demand the maintenance of educational spaces where students sit quietly, raise their hands when they want to talk, and walk with complete silence down the hallways. Even white-led schools that tout their "attention to the individual," their "progressive teaching philosophies," or their "student-centeredness" still regularly fall into predictable modes when executing lessons plans: the teacher, who is most often white, is the more active authority figure—the holder of knowledge—and the student is the more passive and submissive figure—ready to receive that knowledge.

In our own K–12 teaching, we began our first years envisioning the classrooms of our white childhoods, both in arrangement and in procedure. What is more, we spent far too much energy trying to force our students to fit into the molds from which we came. We wasted far too much time trying to create spaces that rewarded and reinforced our own cultural capital at the expense of our students'. What our students showed us, however, was that nearly every facet of the classrooms from our childhood—the physical arrangement, the sound, the choreography—held *zero* intrinsic value when it came to educating them, or anyone else for that matter. For starters, what should it matter if everyone sits at their desks? Sure, some students may prefer to sit, but others may want to stand sometimes or most of the time. And while flat surfaces are usually good for handwriting (which is itself of less and less importance), some students may prefer to mix it up, spending some of the time at their desk but other parts of the day at a windowsill or at a table in the common area. With some appropriate ground rules and a respect for learning in place, who cares how the process unfolds?

Also, why should it be so quiet nearly all day long? Sure, there is a time and a place for quiet in educational settings, and we would all be well served to abide by our librarians. But other times, our students showed us, it was time for some bustling and energetic noise: for music, for open-ended dialogue, and for dispensing with the hand-raising in favor of chiming in when it felt right. They proved to us that soundlessness is not always synonymous with either peace or tranquility, as the thesaurus would have us believe. Along those lines, Kyle's fourth graders asked repeatedly, yet tactfully, if they could play music as a class during their morning journal time. After some group discussions, they settled on jazz (for its ability to dovetail with writing) and slowly began making their way through the catalog of Miles Davis, an artist who grew up less than twenty miles from their school.

Early in the "journal with jazz" experiment, Kyle looked out over his students, diligently journaling away, some swaying back and forth to "Blue in Green," and it dawned on him: he could not recall a single teacher from his K–12 days who played music inside of the school but outside of the music or band classrooms. Though he had a deep passion for music, it was his students who showed him the beauty in that simple act of schooling, an act that subverted the grammar of the institution as he knew it. And from then on, their embrace of music only grew, and they even added a permanent spot on the dry-erase board that said, "You are now listening to _____." At the urging of students once more, they added music to their daily classroom celebrations, a change that led to what was undoubtedly the most heartfelt singalong to Alicia Keys's "No One" to have ever occurred in a fourth-grade classroom.

These lessons were also applicable to the content we taught. A critical skill in teaching, we discovered, especially in the area of curriculum, is to listen. Listen with your ears, but also with your eyes, your heart, and your brain. Dr. John Igwebuike, a listening expert, says that listening is the greatest skill that is never taught.[3] Schools teach reading, writing, and speaking, but they almost never teach listening. When we are truly open to listening in a classroom, we will hear the disengagement, the lack of relevance, and, often, the single perspective being offered. We will hear that there is little attention paid to how and why the material might be important to the student's life outside the school walls.

As educators, once we learned to listen to our students and change the curriculum accordingly, we found students were more engaged. The content one chooses is critical to engaging students in learning, but even the most exciting material can become stale and boring if taught out of context. Marguerite learned this lesson teaching Shakespeare to her high school students, which was required by her district. Shakespeare, taught right, can be an amazing experience. It can also be a pretty miserable experience when read out loud, listened to, analyzed over and over, and pulled apart one iambic pentameter at a time. Be not over-tedious, the Bard warned us.

Nonetheless, by listening to her students, Marguerite found that the exploration of the essential themes of life, death, good, evil, love, hate, despair, and humor were engaging. And they could be even more engaging if, based on student feedback, she pushed her thinking about the *form* of her lessons as well as the markers of a lesson's success. What if Shakespeare was taught using call and response? Her students engaged. How about a short version, such as *Dogg's Hamlet*, which is *Hamlet* in fifteen minutes? Her students engaged even more.

How about *Midsummer's Night Dream* on rollerblades? Well, that's a little bit treacherous—but even more engaging!

LESSON TWO: RESPECT MUST BE EARNED

Working with our students confirmed for us that respect is a mutual act. Respect is not something a teacher should expect but something that must be earned. To earn our students' respect, our first hurdle was to erase all the deficit ideology, based in our whiteness, that had been poured into us in our lives before the classroom: the notion that our students were somehow "culturally deprived," the warnings about how difficult discipline—a term used explicitly in place of classroom management—was going to be, and the reminders to be prepared for a lack of engagement and expectations from our students' loved ones. Intellectually, we knew the insidiousness of deficit thinking, but confronting it regularly, as part and parcel of our practice, was an essential part of our work.

Oftentimes, we found our most meaningful chances to build relationships, based on respect and humility, took place beyond our classrooms and the school day. Marguerite, for example, served as a high school drama, debate, and forensics coach, in addition to teaching her ninth-grade English classes. Engaging in extracurricular activities comes with many added benefits for educators, namely, that it allows them to engage with their students on a personal and individual level. In those settings, Marguerite was able to work with her students on selecting debate topics that interested them, poems that reflected their feelings, and readings that spoke to their worlds. She was able to witness and assist her students' transformations on stage, where they could mesmerize their audiences and gain self-confidence. It was a process that required a special, almost spiritual, respect for students.

Further, extracurriculars gave Marguerite's students a space to introduce her to literature to bring back to her English classes, such as the speeches of Malcolm X and Ntozake Shange's *For Colored Girls Who Have Considered Suicide/ When the Rainbow Is Enuf*, both of which were well beyond the "preferred classic canon" as defined by her district requirements and white preservice program. This form of authenticity and sharing came only after spending hours and hours after school and at Saturday rehearsals engaging with her students' loved ones at performances and on the road to and from events.

Kyle similarly noticed that meaningful relationships often formed with his students outside of the classroom. Early in his first year of teaching, for example, his team teachers, both of whom were veterans, organized the "Saturday all-stars" program whereby students could earn Saturday-morning trips with their teachers to the zoo, the science center, and local museums, typically followed by a group lunch. With approval from the students' loved ones, the teachers were also able to provide transportation for the trips. While visiting local museums was fun and interesting on its own, Kyle found the in-between moments to be the most powerful: cracking jokes in the car, choosing a radio station, and discussing lunch options. While Kyle was at first prone to thinking about his job solely in terms of teaching and learning, his students, on these outings, showed him just how limited that was. Their relationship was about much more: it was about people who respected each other, people who were looking to experience joy and connect with their community, whether on a Saturday or not.

Building on this lesson from his students, Kyle looked for other ways to build mutual respect, often simply following his students' lead. Owing to the popularity of the movie *Akeelah and the Bee*, for example, his students wondered why their school failed to hold a spelling bee. So they did some research and enrolled in the Scripps National Spelling Bee program. A few months later, they held their first bee and declared their first champion. When students showed an interest in student government, they formed the school's first student council. In other cases, relationships formed in smaller, more organic ways, though they were no less profound. When a student invited him to his football game on the weekend, he went and brought his partner too. When one of his students' caregivers made time to chat—before school, on the phone, or at "Saturday all-stars" drop-off—he took this time to chat too. The relationships, he found, could not be faked. They could not be rushed. And they had to be founded on a respect that was earned.

With time, we both began to think more expansively about the bonds we were forming with our students: What if the relationships formed while coaching or setting up for the spelling bee could also become a central part of our work in the classroom? Marguerite, on this point, learned that once she decentralized her classroom, making it look more like her extracurriculars, her students became more interested, committed, and authentic in their learning. Yes, the individualization took an enormous amount of time, and the assessments were varied instead of standardized, but learning increased. When she has shared these experiences with preservice teachers, the response she's often received is "I never thought to teach that way." Or have preservice teachers not been taught to think about teaching that way?

CONCLUSION

Our Black and Latinx students taught us that, despite an unjust system, they would prove resilient—especially if we gave them encouragement, support, and love; especially if we listened to them; especially if we took the time to learn the lessons they were teaching us. We learned to create active, engaging, and relevant learning environments and lessons; build relationships both inside and outside the classroom; and never assume we had students' respect without earning it. Our students gave us countless ways to think critically and outside the box. They challenged us to be better teachers by asking questions that required answers, not circumvention.

The stories shared here, and with our preservice teachers, serve as a means of individualizing and humanizing our former students and our former school communities. They prove that listening to students may be the best pedagogical lesson one can learn. Further, we continue to honor our former students and the lessons they taught us by calling out racism, classism, sexism, homophobia, and deficit thinking in our college classrooms. And we implore our preservice teachers to do the same once they have classrooms of their own. We strive to instill in them an understanding of the deleterious effects of maintaining and perpetuating their own white privilege. We hope they, in turn, can engage in similar processes with their own students. Otherwise, the cycle of whiteness upon whiteness will continue unexamined.

PART SIX

OUT THE HOOD NOW

A RECOLLECTION FROM SAM

A few years ago, I did an escape room in New York City with my friend Marc. We had to work our way through a tight maze, finding keys to unlock doors that would take us a few steps to turn a corner and unlock another door to a long passageway, only to have to double back and find yet another door to yet another hallway. It was not until after we had finished and were sitting at a cafe that we were able to retrace our steps and draw a map of the complex labyrinth on a napkin. As we drew, we realized something that we hadn't even begun to conceptualize when we were inside the maze. Our eyes widened and we laughed (at ourselves) as we looked at the drawing on the napkin. We realized the whole complicated labyrinth was actually just a 20' x 20' square room with some walls built inside it.

There are things you can't see when you're in the middle of them that become clear with distance and intentional reflection. What can white folks (and the rest of us) who (present tense) *teach* in the hood learn from white folks who (past tense) *taught* in the hood? This section introduces five educators who each identify as white but no longer see their work as being situated in the hood. And yet, their reflections on their experiences have a tremendous amount to contribute to our conversations around race, culture, identity, the cessation of harm, and ultimately giving students in the hood opportunities to be free and learn.

The contributors in this section are able to look back at their experiences teaching in the hood through new lenses—those of a parent, an urban private school educator, a suburban educator, a researcher, and a recovering nonprofit executive. They trace some of the ways their work as urban educators informs their experiences in other roles and contexts, and in turn, how those new roles and contexts help them make sense of the experiences they had teaching in the hood.

Each of these contributors has the self-awareness to notice the insidious performative wokeness that functions as a pesticide to the organic growth processes of radical kinship and liberatory practice. They recognize and call out the uncomfortable truth that they are, in many ways, directly benefiting from the oppressions their BIPOC students experience. The question they each seem to have found their way to is: How much are we willing to give up to bang these double-edged swords of privilege and oppression into plowshares?

It doesn't have to be a zero-sum game. When we all do better, we will all live better. But doing better requires white teachers to move beyond just attempting to apply salve to their students' physical, emotional, and intellectual wounds. White teachers need to acknowledge that the privileges they are afforded are spoils of unjust pillaging and intimately related to the very injuries they are in many cases congratulated for helping their students to bandage.

You can wrap gauze around a wound, but if you keep poking at it, even through the gauze, it will not heal. In fact, it will bleed through the pretty white gauze you wrap around it and turn every pristine thing you've tried to create into a mess. Healing requires putting a stop to the violence. And in many cases, the call is coming from inside the house. In other words, the violence white teachers in the hood are working to stop is being enacted by white teachers in the hood. It's also true, though, that much of the violence that must be stopped comes from other sources outside of urban schools. This is why ending it will require white people in other contexts—such as parents, researchers, nonprofit executives, and the next generation of wealthy white people—to take thoughtful action. Getting that to happen is not simple or easy work. It is not work that will happen without material and reputational sacrifice. This is the work of the contributors of the following essays.

They challenge white teachers—and really, white people writ large—to ask how they can be in radical kinship with their students, colleagues, and communities. This is a fractal question—as soon as we lean toward it, we start to see that it is actually made up of an infinite number of more and more detailed questions: What does anti-racist work look like with white kids? What power and comfort are you willing to let go of? How can you support BIPOC students in challenging racist policies without putting them in harm's way? What daily practices are you developing to raise your self-awareness of where whiteness is showing up in your work?

FROM THE BURBS TO THE HOOD TO THE BURBS

— Tom Rademacher —

I have to start by mentioning that saying "hood" is uncomfortable for me, a super white dude whose high school had ATV and snowmobile parking. It feels like the kind of term one should use about a place only when one is from there and then only if one has never been to a Phish show on purpose. So, with all due respect to Christopher Emdin and his work, I'm going to stay away from using the word, except in titles, and even then, I will cringe a little.

Also, I should note that this chapter is no doubt influenced by the work of Barnor Hesse and his eight white identities but also honestly reflects my journey as a white dude who grew up mainly in the suburbs and ended up teaching in an urban area.

RESISTING

At my very first equity training, one month into my first year of teaching, I was *that* guy. The white guy who didn't need to be there because he knew "it all" already, and anyway not everything is about race, you know. Two months of teaching and a lifetime in an almost completely white bubble of white people, thoughts, and perspectives had taught me, surely, everything I needed to know. I "what if'd" and "what about'd" every point by the presenter and every story shared by others in the room.

How could racism be everywhere if I had never seen it and certainly never felt it? And what about Oprah? And what about Michael Jordan? And what about Jay-Z? What if I don't get a job I'm qualified for but really need? What if my dad just died, and I grew up poor enough that I know what it is to sleep with a winter coat on?

I left the training unchanged and clinging to beliefs that would enable me to perpetrate any number of micro-aggressions against my BIPOC students—assuming they needed simple assignments, trying to relate Shakespeare to Snoop Dogg to help my Black kids "get it"—because I figured that as long as I didn't say any racial slurs and otherwise taught how I had been taught, I'd be good. In my first year of teaching, it turned out, I was mostly not good.

I didn't notice until later that nearly every student I was struggling with was Black and only figured out even later that my struggle with them was mostly my fault.

Midway through that first year, things started to click. My school had, for a few years, facilitated conversations among eighth graders around race, skin color, and privilege during the spring in a combined language arts and social studies class. The Big Room, as the class was called, was a life-altering experience because as much as I could huff and puff and eye-roll at professional adult trainers, I loved these kids, even (sometimes especially) the ones who were making teaching hard. I loved them, and I listened to them, and I changed.

I heard stories about students being put in remedial-reading groups after teachers met a parent who was an immigrant. I heard stories from Black males who had never been assigned a seat next to another Black male and from students who had never had a teacher who looked like them, who was from where they were from, or who went to church where they went to church.

Slowly, painfully slowly, I was raising one of those decoder spyglasses up to my eye, starting to understand that my students had so much to teach me now that I understood how badly I needed to listen.

So, of course, I talked unceasingly about how much I was listening. Like the college kid who does a two-week summer class in Spain that becomes his whole personality for the next two years, I had experienced the very tip of an iceberg and declared myself an expert on the ocean.

I never hesitated to explain to anyone who would listen how the intersections of race, poverty, and privilege worked, and I felt not an ounce of shame (in fact, several pounds of righteousness) in calling out teachers around me, some of whom had been teaching much better and much longer than me, about all the things they obviously didn't get.

LEARNING TO SHUT UP

It took a long time to unlearn a lot of things I had been taught about what BIPOC kids, especially relatively poor and urban BIPOC kids, are capable of. I hate that that's true, that I held any of those feelings, that I expected less from many students in my room, but pretending now that my brain hadn't soaked up a whole lot of bullshit earlier in my life doesn't bring me any closer to expelling it. It took a long time and a lot of listening.

Learning to teach in the middle of our city to students who had often lived lives of deeper and more regular trauma than I could imagine meant that I first had to listen to and understand their lives; show them concern, empathy, and love with every ounce of energy I could; and then step aside and let them be fantastic. That stepping aside, that decentering of my own voice, my own plan, was the most crucial part of letting really great things happen in my room.

One student wanted her own space to work on an essay, and there was this empty room across the hall. At the end of the hour, I realized I had forgotten to check in on her at all, and when I went in to tell her the hour was over, I saw a whiteboard full of complex analysis, stuff I could never have done when I was in high school, images and themes I'd overlooked in my own reading of the text I'd assigned to the class. At the end of the day, I went and stood in front of that board for a long time, holding my rather dim expectations against the brilliance of it.

As the students got to know me and trust me enough to challenge me, they asked for a lot more than showy allyship. It took me a second to see those challenges as a sign of something good and to remember that positivity at each new challenge. Yes, we talked about performances of race as we studied *Othello*, but what was I doing about the over-suspension of Black students in my own school? What was I doing about the math teacher next to me who admitted to a class that he "didn't know how to teach Black kids"?

Make no mistake, working in urban schools is challenging for a whole host of reasons. As a white dude, though, it also meant getting a whole lot of attention and appreciation from the education community for some basic-ass stuff. You've got a Black Lives Matter sign in your classroom? Don't shrivel whenever anyone brings up race? "My god, you must be an *amazing* teacher," say the grown-ups. "I dunno, you're kind of a tool," say my students.

It was the challenges, the pushes from students, that kept me climbing the mountain. My urban students wouldn't let me pause, wouldn't let me slow down. But the adults in the city couldn't keep our school moving in that same direction, couldn't keep things stable enough to find footholds, and eventually shoved me away. I landed in the suburbs ready to work at the speed my old students demanded of me. I came at my lessons and my work with such momentum that I didn't even see the first few walls coming until I hit them.

FROM THE HOOD TO THE BURBS

On the first day of my first year teaching in a suburban school, I taught the lesson I usually did on my first day. It involves segments of identity, and I do the activity along with the students to both model it and to help introduce myself a little. When I wrote down my race on the board, explaining that students would likely want to include their own racial and cultural identities, it was like an inaudible buzz filled the room, a tension of white noise (pun mostly un-intended). In ten years of teaching, I had never felt an energy shift like that by my just bringing up the idea that we all have a racial component to our identity. It was the first of many signs that discussing race—and not just things like systemic racism, but also realities of race, different lived identities, and shared histories that impacted the literature we would read and help us understand how language operates—would be a whole lot different here.

Sprinting into Walls

I was used to students discussing the most impactful ways to address racism, for example, but I was not ready for students who were convinced that racism no longer exists. I was used to white students wrestling with the concept of white privilege. I was used to comments much like the ones I made in my first equity training as I struggled to reconcile any challenges I may have faced with a reality that very often made those challenges harder and more frequent for others. In urban schools, and in schools with a lot fewer white kids, I found those kids were a lot more willing to listen and reach for understanding from their classmates. I even got pretty good at helping coach students when they were hungry to learn.

I was not so good with larger and louder groups of white kids and families within a school community who were happy to dismiss the idea of privilege while fighting hard to protect it.

I had to do a lot of stepping back and looking at my methods, my biases, and the goals of my teaching. I had to reassess how to approach things so that even the students I fervently disagreed with had room in my classroom to learn but not to do harm to the BIPOC kids they shared space with now or in the future. I had to do that while also recognizing that I had BIPOC kids as well as groups of activism-oriented white kids, who were not just ready, but insistent that our room be a place that valued empathy, equity, and justice.

Pushing Through When Being Pulled

One of the hardest things for me about teaching in an anti-racist way in the suburban school where I now teach is that when I don't do it, my life is easier.

I have two groups of white parents who fill up my inbox whenever topics around structural or personal racism come up in class, when we read things by and about BIPOC, when we acknowledge the existence of race in the world, or when we say anything that even rhymes with the word "privilege."

There are the parents you'd kinda expect this from, parents sending PragerU videos about how white men are the most oppressed group in society and how anyone who talks about race is the real racist, who email my various bosses complaining of "reverse racism" after spending a paragraph recounting all the Black people they'd ever been friends with.

There're also the liberal social justice-y parents. I wasn't expecting the sort of constant (often nasty) feedback from them. Trying to do anti-racist work at this school has made me a point of contact for a small (and quite vocal) group of parents who seem to have lots of time to tell me how I'm doing it wrong. Fine—I'm a fan of critical partners and under no delusions that I am doing things perfectly. What's odd is that this group mostly leaves the teachers alone who are either quietly not helping or quite loudly hurting.

Whatever their aims, whatever their methods, whatever their differences, both groups serve to remind me often that the path of least resistance is to stop resisting. I could teach the same novels I read in eighth grade, teach the same grammar and writing lessons I ignored as a student, and my emails would be suddenly devoid of judgments of me as a teacher, as a parent, as a person.

Thank god for students. While most educators seem content with the status quo, I have been defined in my few years in this building by the voices of student leaders, young people who have chosen anti-racism, trans rights, and various intersectional and inspired movements to devote themselves to. It might make my interactions with colleagues easier if I just passed out "parts of a story" worksheets and had students read *Hatchet* year after year, but it would be a lot harder to look my students in the eye.

Remember the Work/Do No Harm

Like in medicine, no rule in education is more important to me as a teacher than *do no harm*. Also, I can point to every step of my career and tell stories about harm that I did because I was careless, ignorant, tired, frustrated, or just not as good at teaching as I should have been.

Most recently, in my lots-of-white-kids-but-not-all-white-kids school, I was trying to be a good little social justice teacher, and in light of the Darren Wilson trial, gave students a page of questions, a page of resources, and some time to discuss the evidence, the charges, and their own feelings about the impending verdict.

I was thinking about all the white kids who answered, "Well, kinda," when asked if they had heard anything about the trial, and about the white boy in the back of the room who got mad whenever the word "murder" was used to describe what happened to George Floyd.

I wasn't thinking about my BIPOC kids, and most especially about my Black kids, for whom the murder and the protests and the debate and the trial had been traumatizing and retraumatizing and retraumatizing, and who didn't need to read about how many minutes a knee was on a neck, didn't need to be reminded that even if the system did all it could, the world was not convinced that their lives matter.

One of my students, a Black girl in my second-period class, emailed me that night. She was careful, she was kind. She had learned how dangerous even the most "down" teachers could be when challenged. But she wanted me to know that class had been hard that day, that class had been harmful that day. These emails suck. I bet you know these emails suck. But what was true of students in my first year is still true. When students are willing to trust you enough to challenge you, you owe it to them to listen. When students are willing to risk a bad response if they ask you to do better, you owe it to them to give it your all.

WHERE THE HAND BUILDS THE MINDSET, OR REDESIGNING THE WHITE MINDSET

– David H. Clifford –

I have spent much of my career as an educator working in progressive private schools as a metal shop teacher. I am a white male teacher, and I don't teach in the hood. Early in my career, working in such a rarefied environment and coming from legacy privilege, I grappled with the assumption that in order to use my privilege and power I was supposed to teach students with marginalized identities, which, to me in the 1990s, meant poor and of color. This imperative is a common ascription often driven by the shame and guilt of us well-intended white folk.

Four years into teaching (each year, of course, exclaimed to be my last), I realized that I was teaching within a system (private schools) that has historically served students who benefited the most from white supremacy and had the least proximity to its consequences. And yet, because the particular private school I worked at strived to be "diverse," I was also teaching (and learning from) students whose families have been historically and systematically excluded from these private white spaces. It was at this moment four years into teaching that I realized I am a product of these designed white spaces, no matter how diverse they strive to be, no matter how I try to ignore my relationship to this design. I am a beneficiary of this designed exclusion. And because of this, I have a unique lens on this design's culture and construct. So I began to redirect my focus toward ways to redesign the power class's mind, my own mind—one shop class at a time.

On every back-to-school night, parents/guardians anxiously asked me, "What's the most dangerous tool in the metal shop?" Initially, I answered the lathe—a machine that moves on an axis at one thousand revolutions per minute.

It can easily remove a finger, or worse, pull you into the machine itself and never let go. As I taught more, it became clear to me that the most dangerous tool in the shop was a fearful and unconscious mind. It too can pull you into "The Machine" and never let go.

There was always the follow-up question on back-to-school nights, "How are you going to keep our kids safe?" I thought to myself, "Safe from what? The lathe? The grinder? Safe for whom? From whom? Each other? Me? You're send-ing them to a college-prep school! These are dangerous places that slowly kill all of us! (Or at least kill parts of us—our dignity, our creativity, our trust and love in ourselves and each other, our intuition, and our agency, among other parts—all in favor of the white dominant ideal of academics as supreme.)" My calming response was always the following:

> A dangerous shop is one filled with either total fear of failure or total lack of care for the consequence of one's failure, especially if it harms others. A safe shop, on the other hand, starts with a culture of joy, kindness, trust in me, trust in [the students] themselves, and trust in each other, and ultimately, each person in the shop knows that their safety, their dignity, their limbs are bound up with those of their peers. Oh, and I've been doing this for years and have never had a student injured with more than a light burn.

A somewhat natural leveling of the playing field appears in a shop class at first. Because of a fifty-year national push toward college preparation in K–12 education and the ensuing defunding—and devaluing in the mindsets of parents and educators—of shops, most students arrive with little to no building skills or experience in any kind of workshop. Depending on gender, race, neurodiversity, ability, and lived experience, so many students enter the shop with the belief that they do not belong there (that they aren't smart enough or don't have the right gender identity), and that creativity and construction don't belong on their college-bound trajectory. The students couldn't see learning beyond the oppression of academic rigor.

While they didn't quite believe shop class was a place to catalyze all that was awesome in them, I did! It was my job to wholeheartedly believe each stu-dent was capable of seeing *what was possible in them beyond the confines of white dominant culture before they've even picked up a hammer.* But my belief in them was not enough; the students had to trust that I believed in them. To do this, I had to invite, welcome, and work the fearful, unconscious minds inculcated in white dominant culture. I privileged building relationships and an equity orientation, rather than content and products.

How did this happen? Why did I choose to be an anti-racist educator in the realms of design and making? From my experience, most white men don't choose an anti-racist approach to anything. Why me? Why this white dude?

My father was a maker in his spare time, and I grew up in his shop. The shop was a place where I saw my father, a begrudging third-generation financial counselor, access his joyful self. The work he did with his hands allowed him to love himself, to skip, dance, and whistle amid seemingly impossible problems. The problems he loved to tackle most were cars. He grew up in segregated Southern California entranced by car culture; yet his car culture transcended that segregation. His car culture was tiny but mighty, built from four boys whose families came from domestics, machinists, and investment banking, whose fates were bound by a shared joy of tinkering and going fast, rather than historically designed policies of fear, redlining, and racial oppression. This bond of shared humanity wrought from greasy go-fast joy endured through the American War in Vietnam, systematic racial hatred, and school. Their bond meant that I could, as a boy, witness my father work *with* his friends toward a common purpose.

What I didn't learn was how to notice white supremacy, to name where and how it was impacting those I loved and me. The shop was a safe place to be curious. And as I grew up and noticed the antithesis of joy all around me by the hands of white supremacy in *every* school I attended or observed, I slowly grew more courageous.

Years later, my colleague Giselle Chow asked me this question after a teacher justified using the N-word while teaching *Huck Finn*: "David, what are you going to do about your people? We [people of color] can't keep carrying this work." Her sincere and brave question felt like an invitation rather than condemnation. It was an opening for me to explore my stagnant awareness of the profound inequity growing in my consciousness after learning and working for years in the privileged and politely hostile environments of private school.

When Giselle asked me what I was going to do about my people, I realized I could no longer simply sympathize, or at best empathize, with my marginalized colleagues and students who were being harmed by my people. I was no longer able to tolerate the discomfort growing in my heart *because I'd yet to do anything about it*. Giselle's question summoned my courage and sparked my realization that I *could* do something about it.

Before I could mobilize my people, I had to check myself. I am the only expert of my lived experience. I am the most proximal to my unconscious white dominant culture behaviors, yet so far from understanding them. So I started by developing a daily discipline of keeping a journal I labeled: *Racist Things I Saw/ Racist Things I Thought/and What Am I Going to Do About Them*. Holy shit! What I wrote shocked and disgusted me, not in what I saw, but what was happening in my own mind. My curiosity further led me to discover other people sharing their racial consciousness as white folks, such as Tim Wise and his book *White Like Me*. Wise's book was particularly potent in helping me to understand my whiteness and its impact. His writing was direct and not driven by shame or guilt. His book showed me a way to have some compassion for myself while continuing to mobilize and change, even when I saw my reflection in the unflattering mirror of racism. I began to see that I had some tools to grow my consciousness and extend what I was learning to my white students and colleagues.[1]

Creativity was the natural way forward in building my equity practice. Because I am a maker, I began building curricula and culture that supported more significant opportunities to invite students and colleagues into dialogue and action, particularly about whiteness. Just as I had to design shop class to be safe, relevant, and irresistible for new-to-making students, I had to design the invitation for my white students and colleagues to see building toward equity as irresistible (while maintaining an environment that was safe and nurturing for BIPOC students). I had to design for both the power-class, who saw shop as beneath them or novel, and for the few working-class students, whose families were often sending their students to this private school precisely to move away from the trades. Through multiple experiments and even more failures, I realized I was going to have to address deeply rooted and even hidden biases learned from parents, school, media, and religion. I believed that in designing curricula and culture that challenged white dominant culture, I had to design with and for both ends of the power spectrum with the belief that the students who had the most power (generally those who were white, male, and wealthy) could use their privilege and power to change (using creativity, an equity praxis with their growing ability to construct nearly anything with their hands) their own belief system and inevitably their actions as power-holding adults. The beauty of doing this in shop class was that students could literally see (and feel) their learning in their head, heart, and hands.

As teachers, whether in academics or the arts, we have the opportunity to catalyze all that is uniquely magical within each of our students. I didn't just want to teach students how to make cool-looking objects. I wanted to design an environment that built humans, humans who could see systemic oppression and its impact on others and themselves, who would seek to understand and courageously address these oppressive systems (and the objects, processes, relationships, and institutions within them), and who would maybe even solve some of the most complex problems of inequity facing their world. I wanted to design opportunities for them to *feel* the power of self-awareness, coupled with a creative mind and purposeful hands so they could imagine and enact the vastness of sheer human potential.

An excellent example of this was when a white-passing sophomore, Sarah, designed and built a chair as a way for her white peers to practice empathy and for their BIPOC peers to practice self-awareness. Her chair, along with another chair, sat atop the same platform (representing our American culture) and was separated from the other chair by a two-way mirror. One chair was extremely difficult to gain access to and was not ergonomically designed. From this chair, BIPOC students could look through the two-way mirror and see the discomfort of the white students looking at themselves in the mirror while sitting in the easily accessible and comfortable chair.

With my colleague, friend, and woodshop teacher Youssou Fall, we developed a course called Private Skill for Public Purpose. In this critical service-learning class, students utilized the skills they were learning in a private school shop to work with public schools or nonprofit organizations that worked with marginalized communities. This was a class specifically designed as a way to hold them accountable for their learning and help them do "service" that mattered beyond their college applications.

In our Private Skill for Public Purpose class, we introduced students to the history of oppression (and potential liberation) in the US education system through readings from Lisa Delpit, Paolo Freire, Horace Mann, and yes, Tim Wise, along with readings from Equity Traps and No Child Left Behind. We believed it was crucial they read these texts to check the potential for a savior mentality so common in well-intended white communities. And lastly, before we started any concrete projects or engaged with any public school (and the people within them!), the students were asked to reflect on their relationship to power, roles, and responsibilities. At one point, a white boy raised his hand amid a group of thirty-two wood-and-metal-shop students and asked, "These readings make me wonder, what if we just get rid of all private schools?" Inwardly, I had two responses. The first was "Yes, my plan is working!" My second silent response was "Yes, what if there were no longer private schools? Would this automatically rid the US of white supremacy? No. Students and their families who attend private schools still need to go to school somewhere. How do we ensure we (my white people) don't cause harm in other school settings? What harm might we continue to cause, why, and toward whom?"

A few years into Private Skills for Public Purpose, a trustee gifted one million dollars to the school. This gift would accrue interest, and that money would go toward funding this course. The goal of the course according to the trustee would be to teach students about philanthropy and encourage them to become alumni who donate to the school in the future. This was a fine intention but if unchecked could perpetuate power relationships. So, with colleagues Dr. Rebecca Hong and Dr. Anton Krukowski, we designed a curriculum called the Philanthropy Initiative: Living a Life of Consequence. This course was a cross-curricular (design/making, history, and science) class focused on developing equity-oriented humans who are critically aware of the consequences of their design decisions as a way to interrupt the cycle so often found in philanthropy: funding and the funding structure that perpetuates white dominant culture. This required, once again, to move at the rate of trust and have the students slow way down to reflect on their values and the beliefs that informed these values (family, religion, school, identity) so that they could engage authentically with schools or organizations already doing work within the realms of poverty, education, and environment. Most importantly, it was necessary for students to define their own values and beliefs, and what informed those beliefs, to use their power and privilege to challenge power, not perpetuate it through the guise of philanthropy. A decade after this philanthropy course, Saba Fazeli, the son of Iranian coffeehouse owners and an alum of this class, went on to join Beyond Meat to design, engineer, and build the machines that created this company's meat substitute made of plant protein. Beyond Meat's mission is driven by the desire to combat the effects of global warming due to meat consumption by offering a plant-based alternative.

I see my role working with white students as imperative to designing a more liberated future. Simultaneously, I am trying to redesign the white spaces of school so that the BIPOC students I have the privilege of working with feel that they have a safe haven in which to love themselves fully without question. Together, I hope all my students are rooted in their own magical lived experiences, just as my father and his friends were, nurtured in a shop filled with the magic of creativity and making.

Because of these projects and many more, over the years I've come to see schools as ecosystems that design humans. The National Equity Project starts many of its workshops with this quote: "Every system produces what it was designed to produce." So what if I co-designed a school that helps redesign young men's consciousness about their powerful place in the world? Or what if we co-designed schools with conscious and purposeful foundations that built humans with desegregated hearts and minds that can navigate complex uncertainty? What if we redesigned learning processes like design thinking or the scientific method to be more equity oriented? What if I continued to design with courage, creativity, compassion, curiosity, and a continued critical consciousness about my whiteness? And what's our responsibility knowing that "the hand is where the mind meets the world"?

I believe people can change. The beauty of making is that you can see your learning. I know from firsthand experience that mindsets, my own and my students', can change. I believe those who benefit the most from systems of oppression, white men, can change. Fred Rogers asks, "Who loved you into being?"[2] My parents loved me into being, and my friends Giselle Chow, Ilana Kaufman, Youssou Fall, Rebecca Hong, Douglas Diaz, Tarah Fleming, Van Wade, Alice Joanou, and so many others believed in me. Their belief in me loved me into being. I love my students. In many ways, my students have also loved me into being. The love of the work of equity, work that is often painful, enraging, humiliating, uncomfortable, and lonely, has also loved me into an ever-changing being.

What's going to be your invitation that calls in *your* courage?

Here are some tools I built for you to break your own status quo rules of education: www.designschoolx.org/your-tools.

I believe in you.

THE UNBEARABLE WHITENESS OF BOSTON

UNPLUGGING FROM THE
NONPROFIT INDUSTRIAL MATRIX

– Justin C. Cohen –

"The Unbearable Whiteness of Boston" has become my shorthand title for the chapter of my life when I started to reckon with my own race and privilege, but the full story begins in Camden County, New Jersey, where I grew up. The particular town, Voorhees, was named for a nineteenth-century Dutch governor, and its kindergarten was on the grounds of a one-room schoolhouse cum African Methodist Episcopal church that had once been an organizing hub for a network of Philly-based abolitionists. It was the 1980s, I was half Jewish, and I bought mixtapes by West Coast MCs at the Cherry Hill racetrack.

As a child, my connection to the city of Boston was intense but distant. My parents had met as undergrads at Boston University, where their young love was so canonically overt that a freelance photographer once spontaneously snapped a street shot of them that ended up on the front page of that year's Valentine's Day edition of the *Boston Globe*.

When that picture was printed, in 1977, my mom was at the beginning of a tumultuous, forty-year teaching career. She was posted at a middle school in Roxbury during the early, darkest years of a decade-long, violent, anti-Black uprising, triggered by court-ordered desegregation, a period that usually is euphemistically called "the busing era." Her first teaching memories are spliced with images of white families throwing rocks at her Black students.

Despite this concrete evidence that white supremacy wears a Red Sox cap just as often as a white hood, I was raised in the color-blind cocoon that coddled Caucasian kids in the 1980s. My parents moved to Jersey in the early 1980s. Compared to Boston, the South Jersey suburbs at that time contained a cocktail of extraordinary racial and ethnic diversity, along with almost no serious conversations about race. I believed that racism was, mostly, a thing of the past, even though I once watched a white gym teacher call my Black classmate "homeboy" while aggressively slamming him into the bleachers.

My intergenerational connection to public schools, coupled with my obliviousness and unexamined privilege, made me an excellent candidate for recruitment into the white-savior industrial complex. I left Jersey, went to Yale, and decided to work in education policy.

At that point, in the early 2000s, my mom had become so jaded that her only reaction to my decision was, "Seriously, what's the point?" She had arrived at that glib sincerity through honest means. Her career had dawned in desegregating Boston and hit its twilight at the inception of No Child Left Behind. Her father, a Nebraska farm boy born to Danish immigrants, had also dedicated his life to schools. He climbed the ranks of education expertise in the pre–Teach for America ways—teacher, then principal, then superintendent—and by the time he was in his sixties, Erling Clausen was elected president of the American Association of School Administrators. He cut a big figure, physically and professionally. Five decades before marketing consultants had coined the term "Common Core," Pop-Pop had written a doctoral dissertation on America's failure to embrace national standards in a globalizing world. He was the only person I knew who got Christmas cards from the White House every year, which he collected, in addition to *Playboy* magazines from the 1950s, old shot glasses, and vintage silk neckties, all of which my mom and I would load into boxes when he died in 2002.

That I followed Mom and Pop-Pop to work in public schools makes me wonder if the greatest trick white privilege plays is convincing us that we are somehow the inheritors only of our ancestors' best aspirations and not their worst delusions. As a young white recent Ivy League graduate whose only hardships in life to date were self-inflicted, I found defying Mom's wishes by taking up that career was a safe form of privileged rebellion, especially in the heady early days of what folks now call, at least cheekily, if not straight derisively, the "education reform era."

I spent the early years of my career working in schools in New York City and Washington, DC. Tolstoy said that all happy families are the same but unhappy families are unhappy for different reasons, and I found that a similar truism holds for struggling schools in historically excluded communities. I remember talking to a high school senior on the top floor of Anacostia High

School in southeast DC, with the US Capitol Building framed behind us in the school's picture window; he told me he had left his neighborhood only a handful of times. I once gave a presentation to a community meeting about a multimillion-dollar school renovation that ended with one parent asking me whether the renovation included a plan to fix the broken water fountain in the tenth-grade wing. Most days, I tried to fill the gap between reality and aspiration with charisma, but I learned that, historically, charismatic white dudes have made many more promises than they have kept.

Still, the education nonprofit sector was designed for people with my background, and by the early 2010s, I was experiencing career success. While much of my twenties had been an extension of my college experience—I acted like a child; drank too much; made suspect decisions rooted in cursorily examined privilege; and got the benefit of the doubt, consistently, because I was white and cis and male—I reached a modicum of professional achievement before age thirty. However, my maturity was accelerated by rapid career advancement and a complicated, intense, decade-long first marriage.

Before I turned thirty, I was hired to be president of a national nonprofit organization with Boston roots whose mission was to help states and districts improve schools in historically marginalized communities. This role, as an older Black mentor casually remarked, put me "in a position of more authority than any person should reasonably have so early in one's life."

His perspective ended up being prophetic.

Boston caught me by surprise. Within months of accepting the job, I realized that there were startlingly few Black people in management or executive positions in any of the education organizations in the city, not to mention the philanthropies. I had spent the first decade of my career in New York and Washington, DC, and while those places still reel from brutal segregation and institutionalized racism, there was notably more racial diversity in nonprofit leadership in those cities than in Boston.

This should not have surprised me, as whiteness in Boston is more refined than it is anywhere else in the United States. One clue is that the city is the cultural center of a place that calls itself, unironically, New England. From the seventeenth century on, the primary tradition that Boston has etched upon the world's ethnographic landscape is that of the WASP. Being a white Catholic is considered somewhat outside the cultural norm in Boston. Boston is so white. . . .

Okay. You get it.

That Boston is unbelievably white and unusually racist is the sort of casual observation that everyone agrees with, except, of course, white people who live in Boston. White people who live in Boston, the vast majority of whom self-identify as the liberal's liberal, have sworn a blood oath to make excuses for, ignore, obfuscate, minimize, or take oneself out of this reality. White liberals in greater Boston will buy a house in a town that is 97 percent white, on purpose, and then put a Black Lives Matter sign on the lawn. An older white colleague in Boston once told me, "Boston isn't racist, it's tribal," and then several months later used the N-word in front of a young woman of color, ostensibly to describe what someone else had said, even though uttering the slur appeared to give him pleasure.

This less-than-covert sort of racism is enabled, in large part, by other white men like me. Passive acquiescence is the fuel that feeds white supremacy in the nonprofit industrial complex, which is mostly white led, white financed, and white governed. Meanwhile, the white folks in this professionalized savior sector, myself included, conduct extraordinary mental gymnastics to convince ourselves that this series of arrangements does not imply "white serving." That racism of all varieties—interpersonal, institutional, systemic—goes unexamined in these spaces is the worst kept secret in America.

My first reaction to Boston's monochromatic nonprofit sector was to try and "fix it," which is how privileged white men are trained to respond to challenges of any size. I unironically called people I knew from New York and Washington, DC, and asked them to move . . . to Boston. One former colleague laughed at me over the phone, saying, "I am an unmarried Black woman in her forties. On what planet do you think me moving to Boston is a good idea?"

Valid point.

Despite this being an uphill effort, within three years the organization I worked for moved from a staff that was almost 100 percent white to one in which white folks were in the minority. This fleeting moment, during which I got to be part of a truly diverse team that sometimes played a role in hastening extraordinary improvements in schools that had been written off, was one of the most joyous experiences of my life.

Once some modicum of diversity was achieved, though, bigger, more complicated dimensions of institutional racism started to reveal themselves. Creating an inclusive environment at work meant making space for the awful experiences encountered by educators and children at the hands of not just the nonprofit industrial complex and school systems but also the various other institutions that intersect to oppress historically marginalized people. I started speaking about this in more public ways, not because I was an expert, but because as a white nonprofit leader, I constantly found myself in rooms of all white people where nobody else ever mentioned the topic of race.

This reputation—of being the relatively young white guy who would talk about race all the time—did not make me popular with the old guard of corporate philanthropy and institutional grant making in Boston.

Eventually, my stridency caught up with me. It's hard to pinpoint the exact moment everything collapsed, but several scenes replay in my head year after year.

Scene 1, spring 2012. It's just a few weeks after Trayvon Martin is murdered, and I'm sitting in my office, across the table from a colleague, Anthony, who is Black and in his twenties. My mood is sad and detached, his direct and visceral. He says, "It could have been me, in a hoodie, on the streets of Boston." I look at him, and after thirty years of thinking that somehow, some way, things have gotten better in this country, I realize that he is right, and that I am delusional if I disagree.

Scene 2, spring 2014. We have started an organization-wide book club, and we are discussing Tony Lukas's *Common Ground* at a large boardroom table. The book chronicles the anti-Black, white supremacist uprising that people in Boston still quaintly call "the busing fiasco," and it happens to be the fortieth anniversary of the events in the book. The story follows three people, one of whom is an upper-middle-class white Ivy League–educated technocrat who oversees busing from his privileged perch in the mayor's office. I try to describe to the rest of the book club the feeling of repeating this person's mistakes against the backdrop of my own family's intergenerational participation in a wretched system, and I start sobbing at the table.[1]

Scene 3, summer 2014. Our organization's founder and board chair, an older white man who is my boss, decides to hold a "lunch and learn" session about the history of redlining and segregation in Boston. During that session, a young Black woman employee asserts that many of the problems that we've discussed still exist today and are perpetuated by white folks in the city hoarding privilege. The founder tells her she is wrong. I speak up to agree with her, and he berates both of us in a way that is both unnecessarily cruel and insulting. Later that week, I am moderating a panel about community organizing while he sits in the audience; he stands up, uninvited, in the middle of the discussion, and lectures the whole room about his disagreement with one of the panelists, an older Black man. As the moderator, I ask him to sit down, and after he does, I say to the audience, "In these discussions, racism and privilege are always lurking as subtext, but we should probably acknowledge that, just now, it came to the surface." I watch him seethe from his seat in the audience while a few audience members audibly agree with my sentiment.

(There's a simpler version of that last scene wherein my simmering anger and shame leads to a Hollywood moment in which I confront racism in my own organization, causing me to lose my job in a chaotic, public way, but reality is far more complicated than the harsh blowback from faux-heroics.)

In hindsight, I remember that moment in the summer of 2014 as the beginning of the end, not just of my relationship with that particular boss but of my career as a nonprofit leader. At that point, I was a young executive, juggling ever expanding professional responsibilities within an organization that had recently lost many of its senior leaders due to a combination of philanthropic chicanery and internal strife. The decision to confront my own boss about his perpetuation of white supremacy culture in front of an audience of several hundred people that included state and district chiefs who had hired my organization was self-destructive, yes, but it was not an off-the-cuff, *Jerry Maguire* moment. It was the consequence of years of anger, rage, and self-hatred growing inside of me. He was the target of my anger, but I was no less complicit in the system. I was in over my head, wrestling with my own whiteness, surviving the final throes of a collapsing marriage, and isolated from my friends and family in a city that reminded me every single damned day of the intergenerational trauma that whiteness and white supremacy exact on all of us.

In short, when I decided to publicly shame the man who signed my checks, I was done, not just with him, but with the version of myself I had been.

Our tension came to a coda the Friday before Thanksgiving later that year, when the old man and I had a final face-to-face confrontation that went . . . poorly. I left the office that day knowing that I would never go back. My soon-to-be ex-wife was so frustrated with the situation that she asked me to leave the house. I slept in the guest bedroom that night, with a bottle of whiskey and a pack of Camel cigarettes. I had no job, my marriage was obviously over, and I had no idea what I was going to do, having burned a whole variety of bridges. At some point in the middle of that night I drunkenly stumbled into our backyard and screamed at the sky to give me a sign about what I ought to do next.

While there was no immediate answer to my heavenly inquiry, the universe started sending unsubtle hints. As I sat up alone that night, I watched the uprising in Ferguson flare up after prosecutors declined to prosecute Darren Wilson for murdering Mike Brown. I drove to New York the next day in a mint-green Fiat with a twenty-pound turkey in the trunk. In November of 2014, New York City was still reeling from the police killing Eric Garner, and during my best friend's birthday celebration at a Thai place on Seventh Avenue in Manhattan, an enormous Black Lives Matter march materialized outside of the restaurant. I apologized to the group, left my bags with them, and joined the protest. I circled back later, for the after-party, at a fusion wing joint called Seoul Chicken, owned by our high school friend.

After Thanksgiving, I returned to Boston and started writing about my personal reckoning with race. I started a blog in which my writing was sincere, sloppy, scattered, and riddled with the sort of holy-shit revelations about racism that caused one friend, a Black woman, to remark that I was "processing the world like a Black adolescent who sees slights around every corner." I still do not think this was a compliment.

I wrote personal narratives about my upbringing, interviewed Black and Brown leaders in public education, and tried to shock white folks into doing the kind of work that I had only been able to learn through painful personal experience.

Several months after I started blogging, childhood friends on Facebook noticed what I was doing. CB, whose wing joint had been the site of the Black Lives Matter march/birthday-dinner after-party, called me to talk. "How are you gonna write a whole blog about race and not ever talk to me about that thing that happened in high school?" he asked.

I panicked and flashed back to gym class in the 1990s. There I saw CB, pressed up against the bleachers by our gym teacher, the older white man spitting in his face, calling him "homeboy" over and over again. It had been awful, and I wasn't the one being assaulted.

"How have we never talked about it?" I repeated back to him, knowing that this one particular incident, with its racism so overt, had been the single biggest source of cognitive dissonance about race inside my young white skull. The adults had told us, in the 1980s, that racism was over, and yet I had seen white supremacy, wearing a cheap track suit, beating and berating my Black classmate.

So CB and I finally talked about it. A lot. And it brought us closer. CB had almost been expelled for the incident, which I didn't know. The gym teacher had lied about what happened, and when the principal asked me to corroborate the teacher's version of the story, I refused. The whole situation could have been a learning experience for me and other white kids at the school, but the principal, a white woman, asked me to "keep this whole situation to yourself."

"Wouldn't it have been great," I asked him, twenty years later, "if we had been able to learn from that moment?"

"Justin," he said, "my trauma can be a lot of things, but translating it into a learning experience for my white peers was not a priority as a fourteen-year-old."

He was, of course, correct.

I have come to believe that this disconnect is the great paradox of racial equity for those of us raised in the era of color blindness: through cosmetic integration, we encountered more opportunities than any generation before us in achieving justice, but because our understanding of each other was so shallow, it was more convenient to maintain lukewarm proximity than to create true kinship.

My approach to school reform up to that point, not to mention public policy in general, had been rooted in a combination of intellectual stimulation about technocratic complexity, coupled with an unabashed curiosity about humanity. It was not, however, rooted in the sort of radical kinship and love that is necessary to transform our culture into something untethered from racial caste.

Just a few days after CB called, I found out that the white Boston city official whose work on busing and desegregation was captured in *Common Ground* had moved back to Boston after many years of heading up a liberal arts college. I made contact with him through a mutual friend, and he agreed to talk to me. I left out the fact that his decades-old story had triggered my personal meltdown, because that might have been, you know, creepy and weird.

When we got on the phone, the man assumed I wanted to talk about education policy, which he wasn't eager to discuss. He hadn't thought much about K–12 education for years, but I didn't care about all that. I wanted to know how he felt, forty years after his work described in the book, looking back on his role as a privileged white man trying to remedy the inexorable problem of racism in America, which was well beyond the boundaries of any sort of technocracy that he or I was prepared to wield.

"You want to talk about that?" he asked. "Why now, and why me? I left that behind years ago, and I left it a mess."

"Yes," I said, "but there aren't many white men who have even tried hard enough to fail, and I was hoping to talk to one who has."

He paused for a while, and when he spoke, his tone was different, more secure. "You have to see the whole complexity of the system to really do anything," he began. He continued:

> If you push it in one place, it moves in another. That's what people get wrong about systemic change, and why I caution most people against trying it; it's not for everyone. But everyone can—actually must—go talk to ten people in their own community and change how relationships work.
>
> If we all did that, that would be the truly radical thing.

WHITE BOY/DISRUPTING WHITENESS

– Eli Tucker-Raymond –

L et me be up-front: I am no longer a K–12 teacher. I am an education researcher and a sometime university teacher for people in the education and
learning sciences fields. I have taught preservice and in-service teachers, and I
have taught graduate school. When I did teach in K–12, it was for five years as
a mostly middle school teacher in Chicago and in San Pedro Sula, Honduras.

I grew up in Cambridge, Massachusetts. Cambridge is an ethnically and
economically diverse city and was probably more so when I was a child. People
from Cambridge like to boast about how many tens, or hundreds, of languages are
spoken at the public high school. White, mostly middle-class parents advocate
for equality for everyone until it comes time for the resources to apply to their
child, or not. Middle-class and well-off white parents take up preschool spots
meant for working families. They make sure Advanced Placement classes remain
at the high school their children attend even though very few Black and Brown
children are recommended for them. These white parents are often the type to
send their kid to public elementary school because the classrooms are diverse,
so as to expose their child to different cultures, and then to turn around and
remove their children for middle school because some of the middle schools,
in characterizations based in racism, are not seen as academically rigorous.

I started kindergarten in 1978, just a couple of years after court-ordered
school integration and racist resistance in Boston, just across the Charles River
from Cambridge. The school I went to was, in part, created to address Cambridge's own integration needs. It was an alternative public magnet school created to attract white students to a building that served a neighborhood student
population that was about 70 to 80 percent Black. Our alternative school, placed
alongside the existing school, was meant to represent the city as a whole, and

the children who attended were from an ethnically and economically diverse pool of families. That meant that although there was one building, there were two different schools, each with their own student populations. I stayed in that magnet school from kindergarten through eighth grade. While we learned about the civil rights movement, the curriculum was more about togetherness and similarity than difference.

From sixth grade on, about when I became intentional about representing my identity, my class had a core group of Black boys that outnumbered the white boys. I was a young person becoming aware of my gender identity, what it meant to be a boy. I wanted to be seen as a boy, as a b-boy no less (a break dancer), so those were the classmates I bonded with. We hung out. We joined the same soccer team, close to the school. Eventually, I came to learn that many of their families were part of a group of Black families that had known each other for some time and were educators and activists. Through elementary and high school, my critical awareness of racial issues would grow through my authentic relationships with people, an expanding, multicultural group of friends—not relationships that were formed on the basis of learning from one another or some ulterior purpose or that served me and not others but real relationships based on shared interests, values, and worldviews. Through those relationships, I learned. Yes, those were childhood friendships, and they are hard to replicate as adults. We are still friends, which is even harder to replicate. Some of my friends work in education-related fields. Some work for the same school district where we went as children. Not everyone still has a core group of friends from elementary or high school, but everyone can form authentic relationships. These relationships mean putting ourselves in positions to be invited to spaces where we are learning but where we also have something to offer. Friendships, good ones, are mutual. Be a resource, recognize your limitations and others' strengths, and celebrate them all.

Probably around seventh or eighth grade was when I began acknowledging or more deeply understanding racism as a structural issue. Facing History and Ourselves, which focused on the Holocaust and the power of ideology and group think, was our year-long curriculum for seventh grade. And in eighth grade, *Eyes on the Prize*, a multipart documentary about the Black civil rights movement, came out, and we watched it in class. It so happened that one of our classroom parents, Bob Moses, was a civil rights leader and appeared in the film. He was also our math teacher, as we were in the beginning stages of piloting the Algebra Project. At that time, the goal of the Algebra Project was to provide high-quality mathematics learning for every single child. We all learned algebra in seventh and eighth grade. There was no other expectation. I bring up these two experiences because they were when I began to understand the difference between racism (structural), prejudice (personal), and discrimination (one of the effects of either). They are also when my school and my teacher explicitly engaged us in those discussions. I began to see the intersections between politics, freedom struggles, and education. Discussions of racial politics and inequities are necessary for everyone, not just for white kids. That thought might not be popular in some places. Many school districts want to curtail or deny "politics" in teaching. Paolo Freire wrote that teaching itself is a political act.[1] And not teaching about racism, about civil rights, or about a plurality of identities is also a political act. It simply reinforces the status quo—the structure of white supremacy culture.

Don't get me wrong, I know difference based on skin color is a fallacy. In many ways there is no such thing as being white. But socially, growing up white meant benefitting from a system of whiteness. Whiteness is a structuring function of institutions in the United States, baked right into the US Constitution. Legal scholar Cheryl Harris argues that whiteness is property.[2] That is, the Constitution afforded white people the right to hold property and determined Black people as part of that property. While white people could own land, Indigenous folks had no rights to that land and were forcibly removed. Some of my ancestors were initially "granted" land by the English Crown in 1634 for settling in what is now Massachusetts. They didn't buy their first land. They were given it. I own land. I didn't buy it. I was given it. In one of my family's genealogies, my own English ancestors, in 1643, "purchased" some eighty square miles of land in Massachusetts from the Indigenous people living there, Nashaways, under the condition that they "not molest the Indians in their hunting, fishing, or planting place." In 1675, King Philp's War began, removing the Europeans from that place for a time. Don't worry, my family found other land to grab.

So, that was a long time ago, right? But I benefit from that legacy. It is my job as an educator, as a white person, to lay that bare and to work with others to undo it. The idea of whiteness as property is about actual property. Taxes on property values fund schools. Schools in higher-value districts have more access to resources. Racial-discrimination tactics, such as redlining (creating boundaries where Black people can live) and predatory lending, contribute to differences in who can own homes and where. That is a legacy of whiteness as property. It also includes anything of value. Since the founding of the

Constitution, which associated whiteness with property, what counts as property has become more abstract, including the benefits of education.[3] Whiteness as property continues to legitimate white power, to legitimate white domination over institutions like schools and over disciplines like science and mathematics, and to legitimate the exclusion of others.[4] Ideas of a white racial identity and its misalignment with the right to property and ownership continues to create inequitable learning conditions disproportionately harming young BIPOC in schools. Domains like science and mathematics are aligned with the idea that they are fields of white racial identity; they belong to white people.

Personally, this has meant that I have dedicated my research life to undoing whiteness as property in education. In one project, I worked with a seventh-grade teacher, Maria Rosario, in Chicago's historically Puerto Rican Humboldt Park neighborhood to help Black and Latinx (many of whom also identified as Black) students explore relationships between gentrification in their neighborhood, globalization and colonialism in Puerto Rico, and racial and ethnic identities.[5] Students, in their terms, took up what it meant to be Black, Puerto Rican, and white. Through Socratic seminars in which they debated topics and built meanings together, interviews they conducted with neighborhood residents, and arts-based projects, they placed themselves within the struggle for the right to be in place and to be educated the way they chose. They created their own counternarratives about who they were and the place where they lived. As their home lives permeated school, they found power in their histories and themselves.

This project began in 2009, right after Barack Obama had been elected president. Students wrote a column to the school newsletter about their experiences and warned the community that racism was still rampant, even though there was a Black president. They were told by the principal to redact the portion on racism because it might offend some staff. I would receive the same warning in 2018 when my then boss asked me to remove a line from a publication in which I pointed out that Black students were being blamed for their underrepresentation in STEM just as they were blamed for being shot by police. In my case, I was able to refuse, but the students were not. Silencing those perspectives maintains whiteness as property and any benefits from schooling and STEM as belonging to whiteness. Structures are powerful. Sometimes we have to work outside them.

In work both inside and outside of schools, my colleagues and I have pushed to center positive racialized identities in science class and at the same time disrupt what it means to do science or engineering or mathematics in the first place. I have continued to work with the Young People's Project (YPP), an out-of-school-time organization affiliated with the Algebra Project.[6] At YPP, the young people, including high schoolers and college students, are the teachers. They are centered as knowers and doers, as leaders and organizers. Young BIPOC people teaching other young BIPOC people at YPP disrupts whiteness as property in several ways. It positions mathematics learning as a continuation of the Black Freedom Struggle, as a fight for civil rights. Young BIPOC, not institutions structured in whiteness, design and implement the lessons; they take ownership over what is to be learned and how, and they create the space for teaching, learning, and sharing. The near–peer mentoring structure also creates a family atmosphere. The youth call each other "uncle," "aunt," "sister," or "son." That configuration disrupts the straight handing down of property as well as the idea of who gets to know and of the fallacy of individual achievement. It makes achievement a collective and loving effort, like being part of a family. Additionally, instead of starting from a point of negation, of what Black and Brown and Asian and Indigenous people are not, or a focus on the obstacles people face (although not ignoring them), it starts from a place of affirmation. It recognizes people's tremendous capacities and pushes them to push themselves. As a white person, my role is to provide assistance when I am asked. I know how to write grants, so I write grants to bring in money when I can. I know how to explain to other people the impact of the program on learning and identity, so I do that. I have slowly learned to walk beside young people. In doing so, I learn to help others make their own space for leadership.

It took me a while to learn this perspective. I didn't start teaching from a place of affirmation. While I was teaching, and even while conducting my first research project with teachers, I wanted to explore injustice, right the wrongs, upend discriminatory practices, and disrupt dominant ideologies that supported inequality. I saw myself as a partner in the struggle, but I had my own agenda. Sometimes, this put my students in harm's way.

I taught English language arts and social studies to multiethnic classrooms of seventh and eighth graders in Chicago public schools. All eighth graders had to pass a test on the US Constitution. We studied the constitutional amendments by relating them to contemporary issues. At the time, Chicago had an anti-gang law that forbade youth from congregating on the street and subjected them to regular stop-and-searches. We studied the Fourth Amendment, which is the right not to be searched without probable cause. One year, just as we were studying the amendments, the city experienced an uptick in gun violence, particularly gun violence after school, near or on school grounds. Many schools were installing metal detectors, and my principal had decided to search all of the seventh and eighth graders' backpacks before they entered the classroom. The students and I talked about how this decision was similar to the stop-and-search practices used by police on the street, which some of them had also been subject to. Some of the students must have talked with the principal because he came up to me one day while I was on recess duty, extended his hand to shake mine, squeezed my hand hard, and told me in so many words not to mess with his authority. I tried to explain the Supreme Court case we were studying, and he let me know, with an increased squeeze, that it didn't apply to his school. I knew I was doing the right thing because what the principal was doing was upholding the status quo, the power struc-ture based in whiteness, based in white people's perceived authority to police Black and Brown people.

What I may have inadvertently done was put my students in the way of more harm as they resisted his racist policies and faced disciplinary action. I did not expect them to go to the principal. Nor did we talk about or practice how they might approach their displeasure with the policy. And so, even in that work we think is righteous, we need to consider who it impacts and in what ways. We need to act both with care and responsibility. We need to critique systemic barriers, and we also need to support students on pathways to hope and trans-formation. We need to support their brilliance and their beauty. So what does it mean as a white person to support Black and Brown power? To support Asian or Indigenous power? To support other people in ways that decenter ourselves as white people and deconstruct whiteness as property? It means taking risks, dwelling in uncertainty and contradiction, and trusting in the power of people.

Below, I have included some snippets of actions I try to take as a white educator and scholar working with BIPOC communities and questions I ask myself about how to take that action. They are related to the previous parts of this essay. They include:

1. Be in Community

Be in deep authentic relationships. I have tried to engage with the community where I am working, with people who do not look like me. That said, I do not get a pass because of proximity. I need to acknowledge my positionality, to be ready and humble enough to be called in and called out when I mess up. I ask myself: Since "community" can mean so many things, what does it mean to me, and what are my communities? Why am I doing work with BIPOC communities? What are the relationships I have in the communities in which I am working?[7] Do I only have a relationship with one person in a community where I am working? Multiple people? Multiple people of all ages? How are those relationships powered?

2. Be a Resource

BIPOC communities are rich in resources.[8] Still, I recognize my responsibility to be a resource where I can and not simply an agent of extraction. How do communities in which I am working want me to reciprocate? Money? Material resources? Labor? Political advocacy?[9] Who am I bringing with me? This work is not about my personal gain or my advancement. Am I working with newer Black, Latinx, and Indigenous educators and scholars in a professional development capacity? How am I uplifting the work of Black, Latinx, and Indigenous scholars? In my arguments, have I cited the work of Black, Latinx, and Indigenous scholars?

3. Be Political

As a designer of learning environments, I ask what in the environments that my colleagues and I design is assimilative and what is transformative? By assimilative, I mean the ways we ask learners to change themselves to fit in or to learn canonical (and disciplinary) ways of being that have historically limited who can bring their whole, true selves into learning spaces. By transformative, I mean the ways we change the conditions of learning. The purpose of learning becomes the learners' purpose through reflecting, responding to, and building on their whole, true selves and at the same time working to dismantle inequitable structuring of participation.

4. Be Humble, but Don't Neglect What You Know

As a white person, I know that I am not able to fully appreciate the activities and meaning making in which people engage.[10] Am I collaborating with BIPOC scholars and educators to help create more robust learning environments? Are there things others know that I do not? Where are the places I can contribute?

5. Be a Learner

Learning about other people's histories and perspectives is a lifelong process. It is not something that starts and ends with a book group. At the same time, to learn means to change. What am I willing to change? What can I change about my views? My attachment to power? My material life?

There is not a right time to ask these questions. They are not always explicit. Some questions are broader and more long-term (What communities am I a part of?) and some are more site specific (How am I acting as a resource?). The answers change. Asking them is a daily commitment that I try to make part of my work. At my best, I help educators and young people create opportunities for themselves and others by recognizing and affirming their strengths. However, I can also cause harm through my assumptions or by not thinking through consequences for others who do not share my identity as a privileged white male. The more humble I can make myself, the more I learn and the more I have to offer. It is my short-term and long-term goal to disrupt the caste system through which people benefit or are oppressed through whiteness.

THE MISPLACED OUTRAGE OF WOKE WHITE PARENTS

— Jonathan Osler —

I was angry, though not surprised, when the crude signs began popping up around our Oakland neighborhood. "Urgent" the signs read, threatening us that our school might be merged with a "challenged" school in the neighborhood. No information accompanied the sign to identify its author; there was only a call to voice concerns at an upcoming community meeting. Over the next year, this hostile message, dripping in coded, racist language, was repeated in emails, at community meetings, and finally in public by white parents from our school. Each parent expressed the same thing: outrage.

I too have felt outrage before. I had felt some version of outrage as a teenager when I noted how my progressive public school in Cambridge, Massachusetts, tracked classes, segregating students along racial lines and transforming my privilege into tangible opportunities while hindering my BIPOC peers from achieving their true academic potential.

In the early 2000s, as a new math teacher at a public high school in Williamsburg, Brooklyn, I felt outraged as I saw white people flood into the neighborhood, driving rent sky-high for the Black and Brown families whose children attended our school. Years later, as a math coach at a high school in South Central Los Angeles, I was outraged watching first-year educators struggle to teach classes of more than forty students, many of whom sat on the floor. And as a high school principal in the Bay Area, I felt outrage upon learning that BIPOC students were prevented from taking Advanced Placement classes by guidance counselors who didn't believe in their potential and cranky teachers who balked at enrolling them.

Experiencing outrage at these inequitable conditions, while continuing to learn about racism and white supremacy, helped shape the type of educator I strived to become. I had a novice understanding of how, even unintentionally, I was complicit in the systems that contributed to these inequities for my students. As I worked through my white guilt and developed clearer ideas about how to be a white anti-racist educator, I still was not done raging.

In my first year working at a public high school in Oakland, three of my students were murdered, multiple students were incarcerated, and dozens of others stopped showing up at school. I raged at the conditions that made these realities possible: underprepared and mostly white teachers like myself from outside the community, budget cuts to schools already grossly underfunded, lax gun laws that led to a flood of weapons into our city, and pervasive economic divestment that impacted many of the families in the community.

I felt outrage the day I showed up to school and found the body of a murdered man had been dumped in front of the building. I felt outrage when a young Black man was shot and killed by our school police officer outside of a nearby high school dance. Through my own anger, I recognized the trauma that many of my students, for whom these conditions were almost normalized, were experiencing. For these young people, rage seemed to simmer just below the surface much of the time.

These experiences informed my limited understanding of what young people from low-income BIPOC communities from across the country faced as part of their educational journey. So it was against this backdrop that I felt shock when my wife and I sent our own daughter off to kindergarten in the same Oakland district to a school that seemed almost untouched by any of these challenges.

In 2019, the school we sent our daughter to, Peralta, was the most requested elementary school in the Oakland Unified School District.[1] Most homes surrounding the school had a value well over one million dollars.[2] Not coincidentally, the percentage of white students, like our daughter, at the school had nearly tripled in just over a decade.[3]

Among other things, my daughter's school benefitted from an active parent group that annually raised over $300,000, roughly $1,000 per student.[4] These extra funds paid for field trips, classroom aides, grants for teachers, and additional staff to provide music, sports, and arts. Large numbers of parents volunteered at the school each week helping in classrooms, writing grants, planning the annual auction, and tending to the garden. I often wondered whether these folks knew how good our kids had it there and whether they cared about the kids in our community who didn't have all our kids had.

Actually, I think many of them had a sense of how good we had it. Only four blocks away sat a very different school that many Peralta parents were uncomfortably aware of, as if a giant mirror were projecting our privilege back at us, warts and all. Sankofa Elementary School, designed on Afrocentric principles, served more than 90 percent BIPOC kids and children from low-income families. Despite strong parent opposition, the school district had closed Sankofa's middle school in 2017, and rumors swirled that district staff continued to steer prospective families toward other schools.[5] While Peralta faced two applicants for every one slot, enrollment at Sankofa had dropped 64 percent, from over 362 students in 2015 to 132 students just four years later.[6]

Peralta families knew about the disparities between the schools. Roughly 20 percent of the Peralta families actually lived in Sankofa's enrollment zone.[7] Our local radio station ran a program called "Two Moms Choose Between Separate and Unequal Schools in Oakland" that stated, in blunt terms, "When you concentrate poverty and wealth . . . it creates separate and unequal schools, like Sankofa and Peralta."[8]

The radio program created a great deal of discussion and presumably discomfort among many in the Peralta community—especially among us white people who considered ourselves progressive.

"What can we do to help?" Peralta parents wondered. One suggested volunteering at Sankofa as reading tutors. Another suggested raising money; a handful of families chipped in one year but only came up with $2,000. Well-intentioned as they were, these were all quick-fix, Band-Aid solutions, rather than actions that would actually address the deeper structural issues at play. And along the way, many of my fellow white parents conveniently fell into a state that stalls so much meaningful action: confusion. A Peralta parent wrote on a local listserv, "We were invited to a working group of families/parents that care about diversity and don't exactly. know. what. to. do."

Ernest Owens, a Black journalist writing for *Philadelphia* magazine, offered us a clear suggestion: "Apologizing isn't enough. Giving money isn't enough. Saying Black Lives Matter isn't enough. Relinquishing power and reducing the space you take up in society as white people is good."[9] I wondered if we would actually be willing to relinquish some of our power if given the chance. As it turned out, a clear opportunity to do just that soon presented itself. But would we seize the moment or fight to maintain the status quo?

In October 2017, our local school board representative circulated a memo that mentioned the possibility of Peralta and Sankofa merging as part of a city-wide effort to improve educational outcomes for students while also reducing costs in the face of pending budget cuts. Rather than viewing this rumored merger as an opportunity to create more equitable access to high-quality schools throughout our community, many Peralta parents reacted with rage.

A Peralta parent wrote in an email to our local board member, "Because of [Peralta's] small size there is a wonderful intimacy that creates an environment free of bullying behaviors, where every child is seen and known. I would surely leave [the district], if this merger takes place." Our school newsletter, trying to forestall the palpable growing white fear, attempted to reassure the parent community that any potential merger was a long way from becoming a reality by using the headline "It's Not Freakout Time" (insinuating that "freaking out" would be appropriate if and when the proposal gained more traction). And signs, like the one I saw, popped up around the neighborhood with a dire warning: "Urgent: Peralta may be merged with Sankofa, a challenged nearby school. If you seek to keep Peralta independent, now's the time to make your voice known." Outrage was beginning to simmer at the idea of desegregating our neighborhood schools.[10]

For some context, most parents at Peralta would likely consider themselves to be progressive and maybe even "woke." Many white families—mine included—were attracted to Oakland because of its diversity, lefty politicians, and long history of activism (the Black Panthers were founded not far from our school). My fellow parents took pride in the school's arts-infused curriculum; attended an annual diversity dinner; championed the use of restorative justice and socioemotional programming; volunteered in the cafeteria, encouraging kids to eat from the salad bar; and supported teachers who used anti-racist, project-based curricula.

Despite our collective "wokeness" and plethora of cool Oaklandish hoodies, the backlash to the proposed merger with Sankofa grew louder. At a parent meeting, an angry white father shouted at district representatives that it was impossible to work toward the three goals of "social justice, high-quality schools, and financial savings. You have to choose!" he yelled, "It isn't Peralta's job to save Sankofa." Another community member, an older white woman, yelled,

> I've had my son and grandchildren at Peralta. There are generations of parents who have put sweat into this campus. This campus and facility

are a very attractive school, so to just pass it off after parents have worked so hard . . . it's astounding and shocking and disrespectful to generations of people.[11]

The dots were laid out for us and should have been easy to connect: concentrating advantages in one school was harming another. But instead of connecting them, many in the community pointed their fingers at convenient targets everywhere but inward. While these angry Peralta parents would have been delighted to see conditions improve at Sankofa, they could not accept that our school was part of the problem—and could even be part of a solution. Parents were adamantly unwilling to support systemic reforms that might have improved educational outcomes across our neighborhood if it meant changing anything about our own school. It seemed we were just fine continuing to hoard opportunities for our own kids and were angered by the suggestion that we should be sharing our power and access.

And it all seemed pretty outrageous to me.

A year before whispers of a merger began swirling, I had helped start a racial justice group at Peralta. We'd coordinated implicit-bias-awareness training for parents, advocated against budget cuts at low-income schools in the district, and facilitated teach-ins about the history of school segregation in Oakland. Some of us had also forged relationships with staff and families at Sankofa. When the merger conversations began, our group members spoke regularly with Sankofa parents about the outcomes they wanted in order to ensure that our advocacy would be aligned with their goals. It was clear: the families at Sankofa were afraid that their school—depleted of resources and facing a shrinking student body—would be closed entirely unless they merged with another school. And so we began advocating for the merger.

We were aware of how our pro-merger stance might be construed as thinly veiled white saviorism. Some might criticize us for acting as if we (mostly white people) were going to gallantly try to "save" a mostly Black school community. Saviorism is a very real and dangerous pitfall of trying to do anti-racism work as a white person. We tried to combat it by forging trusting, albeit precarious, relationships with the Sankofa community, and we were intentional about listening deeply and getting our advocacy strategy vetted by Sankofa before taking action.

Eventually, we began advocating to our school board and our superintendent, explaining why we believed a merger was the best course of action for our school communities. Our letter, which was ultimately signed by forty-eight Peralta parents, made clear our support for the merger and encouraged the school district to do the following:

> Do what will be best for Sankofa's current students and families, based on their input and guidance. If you make decisions based on what other families want, you will likely let those already in positions of privilege and power continue to shape the system to benefit their (and our) children at the expense of Sankofa students.[12]

Our letter had an impact. Within days we learned that the school board was seriously considering the merger. But our cautious optimism didn't last long.

Up until this point, Peralta's white-led parent-teacher association had played the aspirationally neutral role of convening community members to meet with district officials, learn about the proposal, and give feedback. However, due to the PTA's hierarchical structure, among other factors, this powerful body skewed heavily toward a mostly white group of "insiders" with a stake in preserving the school they'd invested so much time and money into already. The night before the school board was to meet and vote on the merger, the co-chairs of our PTA decided to end their "neutrality" and used their bully pulpit in the form of an email sent to the full school community:

> We have written to all the board members to let them know that we think it would be unfair and unwise to include Peralta in any vote tomorrow. The District told our school community repeatedly that we were no longer being considered for a merger. To vote now on any scenario involving Peralta without giving us the consideration of proper public notice would be outrageous.

Their email was followed the next morning by a similarly damning message from our principal, who informed the community that she'd also written to the school board and superintendent asking them not to merge the schools:

> This last minute effort to force an outcome that is clearly based more on an agenda than it is on any real understanding of how learning communities

actually work is both disgraceful and unfortunate. I am saddened by the attempts of members of our own school community to usurp the process in order to see their personal vision realized potentially at the expense of the community at large.

Between the angry-parent emails that were sent off to school board members at the encouragement of our PTA and our principal's public stance against the merger, the message that Peralta should be considered "untouchable" was confirmed. The merger was voted down.

What transpired in the following months was both sad and predictable. The school board selected a different school to be merged with Sankofa, and the response from many of their parents was outrage. White parents spoke passionately at school board meetings about how sending their kids to the merged school would be "traumatic." Parents claimed, in racially coded language, that the merged school would be "unsafe." Many threatened to pull their kids out of the district. Several filed a lawsuit trying to stop the merger and launched a petition to recall our local school board representative. In the end, only 51 out of the 265 students from the school the board had selected enrolled in the merged school.[13]

James Harris, a Black school board member at the time, reflected recently on the outrage displayed by these parents:

In Oakland, a lot of the time we say we want equity or we say we want what's best for all children, but do we really mean we want what's best for our children as long as we are not personally inconvenienced?

What I noticed in my time on the school board is that when people with time, access, and privilege are worked up about an issue, disruption happens, and it usually leads to change. So I am by no means against peaceful protest, but I do want to know who is going to protest for the children no one seems to speak for—those who haven't missed out for a year, but those who have been missed and overlooked for decades?

On average, about 3 out of 10 Black children in district-run and charter schools in Oakland read on grade level. Is that not worthy of protest, right now?[14]

I wondered if many of the parents from Peralta and the other school that was selected to merge with Sankofa could find the time and energy to fight against the proposed mergers, why had they not used this time and energy to protest the systemic mistreatment of Black students in the months and years prior? Where had they been when Sankofa was losing students, teachers, and funding? Maybe if more of them—and more of us—had used our power to help the Sankofa community get the support it deserved earlier, the district wouldn't have had to talk about shutting schools to stay afloat. But unfortunately, this problem we had all been living with became a real concern only when it reached the steps of our schools, and by then it was too late to solve it.

There are thousands of white families like mine in Oakland who have used our privilege to get our kids into the best-resourced and highest-performing schools in the district (even if by no other means than renting and buying some of the most expensive homes in the city). I speak as an insider when I say that most of us consider ourselves to be proud proponents of social justice. We have Black Lives Matter signs in our windows. We attend protests decrying police killings of Black people, read Robin DiAngelo's *White Fragility* in our book clubs, and lament the growing lack of diversity in our schools. We gobbled up the podcast "Nice White Parents." We have advanced degrees in performative wokeness. And when given an opportunity to really act as if Black lives mattered by parting with some of our advantages, by divesting some of our own power and resources, we found and channeled our outrage—just at all the wrong things.

An ugly truth that most of us with privilege don't want to acknowledge is that the *disadvantages* faced by some people in our community are directly related to the *advantages* held by a small portion of the rest of us. When it comes to our children's educational opportunities, these advantages are highly concentrated within a small number of school communities like mine, built up and normalized over generations. Yes, the fact that many Black and Brown kids in Oakland have had abysmal educational experiences can be blamed on the institutionalized racism that has been pervasive here for decades. And individual white and privileged families are certainly not at fault for all of this mess. But we must have an honest conversation with ourselves and each other about the roles we play in maintaining inequitable systems that simultaneously help our children while harming others.

Kelsey Smoot, a Black doctoral student, asked a provocative question in *The Guardian*: "If the white people in my life could hit a button and instantly remove the privileges afforded to them along racial lines, would they hit that button?"[15] Smoot's question gets at the heart of the white outrage displayed here in Oakland and in countless other communities. Although many of us want to be seen as allies to the Black community, not only are we unwilling to push this button; we actively resist when someone else tries to. Smoot sees right through this hypocrisy:

> The truth is, genuine allyship is not kindness, it is not a charitable act, nor is it even a personal commitment to hold anti-racist ideals—it is a fall from grace. Real allyship enacted by white Americans, with a clear objective to make *equitable* the lived experiences of individuals across racial lines, means a willingness to *lose things*.[16]

If we—liberal and woke white people—truly care about the outrageous educational mistreatment of BIPOC communities, then we must act accordingly. But we cannot tinker toward utopia. There is an important and necessary role for us to play in using our access, resources, and power to advocate for structural changes in school funding, local enrollment policies, and other institutionalized practices that maintain inequality. But just as critical, if not more so, is our responsibility to help end the concentration of advantages that we are currently benefiting from.

When opportunities arise (or when we help create them) for structural change that could help schools other than the ones where our children attend, even if on their face they could chip away at our kids' advantages, we should not cry, "Outrage!" These are the moments for us to demonstrate to our children, our fellow parents, and our communities that we will act in the best interest of the collective. Because, if we allow ourselves to believe in the myth that things will get better for others while we maintain the advantages for our own families, the inequities we profess to care so much about will persist.

So you can keep your Black Lives Matter sign in your windows, curate a racially diverse bookshelf, and take other symbolic actions that lead to marginal and short-lived benefits for others. But good deeds will not end systemic oppression. What we're truly being called to do as white people is to take bold action that will ultimately lead to the desegregation of opportunities in our schools.

Anything less would truly be outrageous.

FAREWELL

We are living in an unparalleled moment. It has presented a confluence of once-in-a-lifetime events, each of which alone should cause the world to take pause. Together they created what just days earlier would have seemed impossible interruptions to life as we knew it. A global health crisis and racial reckoning brought much of the world to a halt and screamed for us to reflect on the value of life and the purpose of our work. For those who teach, though, we were not afforded the luxury of stopping, and many of us could not carve out the time to reflect. Instead, we found ourselves in nearly impossible situations, fighting against threats to our students' safety and personhood. But, caught in our defensive postures, too often we were not quite sure what exactly we were fighting *for*. Extending online instruction or getting back to being in person? Using our limited time with students for catching up on missed academic content or social-emotional connection? Meanwhile, the chokehold white supremacy has on schools and schooling went—and still goes—largely ignored. So, if you haven't already, it's time to answer the following: *What exactly do you stand for?*

Are you anti-racist? Or are you pro-freedom? Of course this is not a binary choice. We cannot ignore the systemic, interpersonal, and internal violence that is inflicted on Black and Brown people. And we also have to be careful how much of our identities we orient around what we are not and what we do not wish for the world.

White supremacy is like devil's ivy. It grows in the shadows. White educators have the responsibility to shine light on how whiteness shapes their understanding of themselves, their students, and the world. This takes vigilance and vigor.

White educators should hold themselves to the highest standards when it comes to interrupting racism. (Is any particle of oppression acceptable?) At the same time, we must acknowledge that perfectionism and urgency as well as the belief that there is only one right way to do things (and "I am the only one who can do them") are all tenets of white supremacy culture.

The beautiful challenge is to not let a reaction to racism become white teachers' full definition of themselves, their only way of viewing their students, or the only frame through which they peer at the world. When white teachers get so hyped about acknowledging racism that they force it into every crevice of their existence (and every conversation with BIPOC students, colleagues, and passersby), they deny the fullness, soul, and humanity of their BIPOC students and colleagues—and of themselves.

We both know from personal experience that a look in the mirror as an educator is a powerful thing. If we look at students' behaviors in any classroom, we can see reflections of their teacher's pedagogy. Youth from the hood hold plane mirrors up to teachers all the time—offering us direct reflections of what we project. There can be a glassy smoothness to what they give, which might be summed up by the simple statement, "I will match your energy." They give us both the beauty and the ugliness that we project. If you refuse to glance in that mirror, you will be left with delusions of what you actually look like as a teacher. White saviorism in urban schools is simply an attachment to a vision of your likeness that is not reflected in reality.

White teachers often hold carnival mirrors up to students. The reflections are distortions of the real students. The students show you who you are, and you show them misrepresentations of themselves. In so many ways students tell us: "When you highlight my brokenness and tell stories of all you are doing to save me from myself, you are not looking at an accurate reflection of me or yourself. You are only seeing and showing a distortion of me that comes from your carnival mirror."

Distorting mirrors have the uncanny ability to manipulate our appearances in appealing ways. The right mirror can make you look slimmer. The right lighting attached to it may make your complexion seem smoother. Over the last several years, we have seen many white educators enter the field seeing their role as—to put it slightly more crassly than they might—fixing broken children and communities. They arrive armed with a carnival mirror that no matter what they do shows them as "fixer," even as students hold up more accurate reflections.

We have also seen (and been a part of) many of those white educators who initially see themselves as fixers discovering the layers of racism all around them. They shift from wanting to fix the broken kids to wanting to fix the broken system. This is a much healthier orientation but still obfuscates the fact that the work can begin only when they see and fix themselves.

Repair is certainly necessary, *but why are white educators so fixated on fixing everything?*

We want to challenge white educators—all educators really—to define themselves not in relation to anyone's or anything's brokenness. When we let ourselves dream most wildly about what our students deserve and look at ourselves most clearly, what are we inspired to do?

It has become popular for white folks to call themselves "co-conspirators" and "accomplices" to express their desired alliance with BIPOC to interrupt dominant racist paradigms. Does creating a liberatory experience for Black and Brown children require *conspiracy*? Why do we voluntarily choose language commonly ascribed to "plotting to do something harmful" to describe our role in work that can and should be generative and affirming? This is a particularly odd word choice for white educators trying to express an alliance with populations of people who are already unjustly criminalized.[1] This is avoiding the plane mirrors held in front of us by students while aiming carnival mirrors at them.

So much talk about mirrors. Our wish is for this book to function as a different type of glass: a clear pane—a window that allows you to see the experiences of our contributors. We hope that by reading their stories you are provoked to think about where you have come from, where you are now, where you are headed, and what it is you stand for.

Some people are born to fight. We've never been ones to back down easy. But we also don't want the essence of our existence to be about fighting a thing someone else built to divide and dominate us. If there is anything to fight, let's make it our false visions of ourselves and others. If there is anything to shatter, let it be the distorting mirrors we hold up for our students.

Let's look directly at the plane mirrors young people are holding up and at the young people holding them. Then let's build with them. Let's cook with them. Let's spit hot fire with them. Let's celebrate with them. Why define ourselves by our nightmares when we could define ourselves by what we dream?

CONTRIBUTORS

MAYA PARK taught seventh-grade history and coached teachers for six years in Brooklyn, New York, where she grew up and still lives in beloved community. Currently, she is a teacher-educator through Harvard's Teaching and Teacher Leadership Program and a PhD student at the CUNY Graduate Center's Urban Education program, exploring the intersection of teacher-mentorship and abolitionist freedom dreaming.

JAMIE WILBER has been teaching in New York City public high schools since 2009. Jamie is best known for teaching classes about horror movies.

JIM BENTLEY is an educator, a National Geographic Explorer and Education Fellow, a member of the PBLWorks national faculty, and a KQED Media Literacy Innovator and PBS Digital Innovator All-Star who empowers students to understand the world and how it works so they can make it a better place.

CAROLINE DARIN is in her eighth year teaching physics and AP environmental science at Brooklyn Preparatory High School and is a PhD candidate studying gender and science education at Teacher's College, Columbia University.

COREY SCHOLES is a lifelong educator and proud mom.

GLENETTA BLAIR KRAUSE helps students and teachers in Cincinnati find their voice.

JARED FOX, PhD, taught for seventeen years in New York City public schools and is the founder of the recently launched Fox EduConsulting.

HOLLY SPINELLI is an advocate for inclusive, culturally responsive educational practices, and she strives to co-create community-inspired work as a public high school English teacher and as an executive board member of the New York State English Council.

RICK AYERS is a former high school teacher at Berkeley High School and is a professor emeritus of education at the University of San Francisco.

DR. BRIAN MOONEY is a teacher-educator, a poet, a scholar, and an author from New Jersey who is currently an assistant professor of literacy education at Fairleigh Dickinson University.

TESSA BROWN, PhD, is the CEO and cofounder of Germ Network, a start-up fostering healthy digital communication.

DR. IAN P. LEVY is an associate professor in school counseling as well as the chairperson of the Department of Counseling and Therapy at Manhattan College, and he is an emcee.

ADAM WEINSTOCK is a lifelong educator committed to the unrealized potential of public education and is passionate about helping teachers be as impactful as possible. Raised in Cambridge, Massachusetts, he has taught, coached teachers, and helped lead schools in New York City, and he now continues the pursuit of his calling from just north of NYC.

JEFF EMBLETON is executive director of Forest & Tree (www.forestandtree. org), an organization in Oakland, California, working to support equitable opportunities for young people to have transformative outdoor experiences.

ADAM SEIDEL is a third-generation educator, a parent (of two humans and many plants), and a partner who lives with his family in his childhood home and roots for the Celtics.

ALI MICHAEL, PhD, uses her life, parenting, and research to engage the inquiry "What can white people do about racism?" She is the co-director of the Race Institute for K-12 Educators and the author of multiple books, including *Our Problem, Our Path: Collective Antiracism for White People* (2022).

LISA GRAUSTEIN (she/her) is a queer mother, artist, former middle and high school teacher, Quaker minister, and DEI facilitator of European and Persian heritage living on Neponset Band of the Massachusett land.

MARGUERITE W. PENICK, PhD, is a professor of educational leadership and policy at the University of Wisconsin–Oshkosh and a co-editor of several books, including *The Guide for White Women Who Teach Black Boys* and *Teaching Beautiful Brilliant Black Girls*.

KYLE P. STEELE is an assistant professor in the Department of Leadership, Literacy, and Social Foundations at the University of Wisconsin–Oshkosh.

TOM RADEMACHER is the 2014 Minnesota Teacher of the Year, a middle school teacher of sixteen years, and an author of two books on teaching (with jokes and swear words).

DAVID H. CLIFFORD takes on whatever form is needed to challenge white dominant culture in schools: designer of tools to break status quo rule, shop teacher, leadership coach, sparkly ray of sunshine, edu-agitator, or a mere catalyst for people's equity-centered creative courage.

JUSTIN C. COHEN is a Brooklyn-based dad, author, and activist.

ELI TUCKER-RAYMOND is research associate professor at Boston University's Wheelock College of Education and Human Development.

JONATHAN OSLER spent twenty years as a public school teacher and principal in Brooklyn and the Bay Area, and cofounded two parent groups in Oakland, California, that organize for educational equity. His essays on education, whiteness, and parenting can be found at www.jonathanosler.com.

NOTES

CAN WE WATER OUR STUDENTS AND OURSELVES AT THE SAME TIME?

1. In creating pseudonyms, I adopted the approach Savannah Shange outlines in *Progressive Dystopia: Abolition, Antiblackness, and Schooling in San Francisco* (Duke University Press, 2019): "Within Black naming traditions, the genres stay the same: Arabic-derived names are replaced with the same, while Black vernacular names are like-wise remixed with the assistance of the most common Black names on the census registry. . . . Place-names (Kinshasa, Savannah, Asia) are relocated, while biblical names stay somewhere in the Good Book. Across the board, I tried to alter the number of syllables in a name such that John might become Elijah and Chauniqua might end up as LeNae."

THE PATH TO FORMING MY IDENTITY

1. "Our District," Elk Grove Unified School District, https://www.egusd.net/District/About-EGUSD/Our-District/index.html, retrieved February 28, 2023.
2. E3: Education, Excellence & Equity, https://e3educate.org, September 21, 2023.
3. Shane Safir, *The Listening Leader: Creating the Conditions for Equitable School Transformation* (New York: John Wiley & Sons, 2017), 38.
4. Safir, *The Listening Leader*.
5. Safir, *The Listening Leader*.
6. Safir, *The Listening Leader*, 112.
7. Safir, *The Listening Leader*, 109.
8. Robin DiAngelo, *White Fragility: Why It's So Hard for White People to Talk About Racism* (Boston: Beacon Press, 2020), 71–73.
9. DiAngelo, *White Fragility*, 10.
10. Ibram X. Kendi, *How to Be an Antiracist* (New York: Penguin Random House, 2020), 20.
11. Kendi, *How to Be an Antiracist*.
12. "Bring National Geographic Resources into Your Classroom," National Geographic, n.d., retrieved from https://www.nationalgeographic.org/education/?utm_source=kids.nationalgeographic.com&utm_medium=referral&utm_campaign=ngp-ongoing&utm_content=ngp-page-footers, accessed September 21, 2023.

DON'T WASTE YOUR WHITE

1. Winston C. Cox, "Obama's Legacy for Male Principals of Color," opinion, *Education Week*, September 20, 2016, https://www.edweek.org/leadership/opinion -obamas-legacy-for-male-principals-of-color/2016/09.
2. Xiomara Padamsee and Becky Crowe with Lyle Hurst, Erin Trent Johnson, Leslye Louie, Frances Messano, and Tanya Paperny, *Unrealized Impact: The Case for Diversity, Equity, and Inclusion*, Promise 54, July 2017, https://www.promise54.org /wp-content/uploads/2020/09/Unrealized_Impact-Final-072017.pdf.
3. "DEI Accelerator: Using Data to Drive DEI and Racial Justice Priorities," infographic, Promise 54, 2021, https://www.promise54.org/wp-content/uploads/2021 /05/Learn-More-Promise54-DEI-Accelerator.pdf.

STUDENT LEADERSHIP: MAKING COMPLEX CHANGES WITHOUT THE WHITE-SAVIOR COMPLEX

1. Magick is defined as an intentional action and practice to move toward an intended outcome and is differentiated from the term "magic" that is associated with performance or entertainment. See Aleister Crowley, "A Lecture on the Philosophy of Magick," in *The Revival of Magick*, ed. Hymenaeus Beta, Richard Kaczynski, and S. A. Jacobs (Tempe, AZ: New Falcon Publications, 1998), 207.

SAY IT LOUD—DECENTERING WHITENESS IN CLASSROOM DISCOURSE

1. James Baldwin, "If Black English Isn't a Language, Then Tell Me What Is?" July 29, 1979, *The New York Times on the Web*, www.nytimes.com/books/98/03/29 /specials/baldwin-english.html, accessed September 21, 2023.
2. Theresa Perry and Lisa Delpit, *The Real Ebonics Debate: Power, Language, and the Education of African-American Children* (Boston: Beacon Press, 1998).
3. Django Paris and H. Samy Alim, "What Are We Seeking to Sustain Through Culturally Sustaining Pedagogy? A Loving Critique Forward," *Harvard Educational Review* 84, no. 1 (2014): 85–100.
4. Ana Celia Zentella, *Growing Up Bilingual: Puerto Rican Children in New York* (Malden, MA: Wiley Blackwell, 1996).
5. Richard Rodriguez, *Hunger of Memory: The Education of Richard Rodriguez* (New York: Bantam, 1983).

WORKING IN THE STUDIO AND PERFECTING OUR CRAFT

1. Paulo Freire, *Pedagogy of the Oppressed* (New York: Continuum, 1970).
2. H. Samy Alim, "Critical Hip-Hop Language Pedagogies: Combat, Consciousness, and the Cultural Politics of Communication," *Journal of Language, Identity & Education* 6, no. 2 (2007): 161–76, doi.org/10.1080/15348450701341378.

3. Django Paris and H. Samy Alim, *Culturally Sustaining Pedagogies: Teaching and Learning for Justice in a Changing World* (New York: Teachers College Press, 2017).

4. Alim, "Critical Hip-Hop Language Pedagogies," 161; April Baker-Bell, *Linguistic Justice: Black Language, Literacy, Identity, and Pedagogy* (New York: Routledge, 2020), 8.

5. Alim, "Critical Hip-Hop Language Pedagogies," 164.

6. Geoff Harkness, "Get on the Mic: Recording Studios as Symbolic Spaces in Rap Music," *Journal of Popular Music Studies* 26, no. 1 (2014): 82–100, doi. org/10.1111/jpms.12061; Decoteau J. Irby, Emery Petchauer, and David Kirkland, "Engaging Black Males on Their Own Terms: What Schools Can Learn from Black Males Who Produce Hip-Hop," *Multicultural Learning and Teaching* 8, no. 2 (2013): 15–36, doi.org/10.1515/mlt-2013–0009.

7. Irby, Petchauer, and Kirkland, "Engaging Black Males on Their Own Terms," 19.

8. Harkness, "Get on the Mic."

9. Irby, Petchauer, and Kirkland, "Engaging Black Males on Their Own Terms."

10. Harkness, "Get on the Mic," 85.

11. Harkness, "Get on the Mic," 90.

12. Ian. P. Levy and Edmund S. Adjapong, "Toward Culturally Competent School Counseling Environments: Hip-Hop Studio Construction," *Professional Counselor* 10, no. 2 (2020): 266–84, doi:10.15241/ipl.10.2.266.

13. Levy and Adjapong, "Toward Culturally Competent School Counseling Environments," 273.

14. Ian Levy and Brian TaeHyuk Keum, "Hip-Hop Emotional Exploration in Men," *Journal of Poetry Therapy* 27, no. 4 (2014): 217–23, doi.org/10.1080/08893675 .2014.949528.

15. Levy and Keum, "Hip-Hop Emotional Exploration in Men," 4.

16. Pierre Bourdieu and Jean-Claude Passeron, *Reproduction in Education, Society and Culture*, trans. Richard Nice (London: Sage, 1977).

17. Robin D. G. Kelley, *Freedom Dreams: The Black Radical Imagination* (Boston: Beacon Press, 2002); Bettina Love, *We Want to Do More Than Survive: Abolitionist Teaching and the Pursuit of Educational Freedom* (Boston: Beacon Press, 2019).

18. Baker-Bell, *Linguistic Justice*.

LANGUAGE AND REFLECTION IN WRITING CLASSROOMS

1. Christopher Emdin, *For White Folks Who Teach in the Hood . . . and the Rest of Y'all Too: Reality Pedagogy and Urban Education* (Boston: Beacon Press, 2017), 2.

2. Scott R. Lyons, "There's No Translation for It: The Rhetorical Sovereignty of Indigenous Languages," in *Cross-Language Relations in Composition*, ed. Bruce Horner, Min-Zhan Lu, and Paul Kei Matsuda (Carbondale: Southern Illinois University Press, 2010), 127–41.

3. "Characteristics of Public School Teachers," National Center for Education Statistics, 2020, last updated May 2023, https://nces.ed.gov/programs/coe/indicator/clr/public-school-teachers.

4. Cheryl E. Matias, *Feeling White: Whiteness, Emotionality, and Education* (Leiden: Brill/Sense, 2016); Tessa Brown, "Constellating White Women's Cultural Rhetorics: The Association of Southern Women for the Prevention of Lynching and Its Contemporary Scholars," *Peitho: Journal of the Coalition of Feminist Scholars in the History of Rhetoric & Composition* 20, no. 2 (2018): 233–60.

5. Tessa Rose Brown, "Schooled: Hiphop Composition at the Predominantly White University," PhD diss., Syracuse University, 2017, https://surface.syr.edu/etd/764.

6. Brown, "Schooled."

7. Brown, "Schooled."

8. Jay-Z, *Decoded* (New York: Spiegel & Grau, 2010), 16.

9. April Baker-Bell, "I Can Switch My Language, but I Can't Switch My Skin: What Teachers Must Understand About Linguistic Racism," in *The Guide for White Women Who Teach Black Boys*, ed. Marguerite W. Penick-Parks et al. (Thousand Oaks, CA: Corwin, 2017), 97–107.

10. S. A. Canagarajah, "A Rhetoric of Shuttling Between Languages," *Cross-Language Relations in Composition*, ed. Bruce Horner, Min-Zhan Lu, and Paul Kei Matsuda (Carbondale: Southern Illinois University Press, 2010),158–79.

11. H. Samy Alim, "Critical Language Awareness in the United States: Revisiting Issues and Revising Pedagogies in a Resegregated Society," *Educational Researcher* 34, no. 7 (2005): 24–31.

12. Bruce Horner, "Introduction: From 'English Only' to Cross-Language Relations in Composition," in Horner, Lu, and Matsuda, *Cross-Language Relations in Composition*, 1–17.

13. Elaine B. Richardson, *Hiphop Literacies* (London: Routledge, 2016).

ON HIP-HOP, AUTHENTICITY, AND APPRECIATION

1. Christopher Emdin, *For White Folks Who Teach in the Hood . . . and the Rest of Y'all Too: Reality Pedagogy and Urban Education* (Boston: Beacon Press, 2016); Gholdy Muhammad, *Cultivating Genius: An Equity Framework for Culturally and Historically Responsive Literacy* (London: Scholastic, 2020); Sam Seidel, *Hip Hop Genius: Remixing High School Education* (Lanham, MD: Rowman & Littlefield Education, 2011).

2. Tupac Shakur, *The Rose That Grew from Concrete* (New York: Simon and Schuster, 1999).

3. Bettina L. Love, "Complex Personhood of Hip Hop & the Sensibilities of the Culture That Fosters Knowledge of Self & Self-Determination," *Equity & Excellence in Education* 49, no. 4 (2016): 414–27; Adam J. Kruse, "Being Hip-Hop: Beyond Skills and Songs," *General Music Today* 30, no. 1 (2016): 53–58; Emery

Petchauer, "Sampling Memories: Using Hip-Hop Aesthetics to Learn from Urban Schooling Experiences," *Educational Studies* 48, no. 2 (2012): 137–55.

4. Geoff Harkness, "Get on the Mic: Recording Studios as Symbolic Spaces in Rap Music," *Journal of Popular Music Studies* 26, no. 1 (2014): 82–100, doi.org/10.1111/jpms.12061.

5. Edmund Adjapong and I collaborated on a youth-led co-creation of a studio within a school (2020).

"NOT ANOTHER WHITE MAN IN CHARGE . . ."

1. Doug Lemov, *Teach Like a Champion: 49 Techniques That Put Students on the Path to College (K-12)* (Indianapolis: John Wiley & Sons, 2010), 203.

PEER MEDIATION: SHIFTING POWER IN SCHOOL DISCIPLINE

1. Pedro A. Noguera, *The Trouble with Black Boys . . . and Other Reflections on Race, Equity, and the Future of Public Education* (San Francisco: John Wiley & Sons, 2009), 97.

MUCH LIKE ALL OF THE LAST

1. Joe Budden, "Freedom (Freestyle)," Genius, July 12, 2016, https://genius.com/Joe-budden-freedom-lyrics, retrieved February 28, 2023.

2. Budden, "Freedom."

PART FIVE: TEACHING TEACHERS

1. Jay Electronica, "Letter to Falon," from *Act II: Patents of Nobility (The Turn)*, released 2020, Genius, https://genius.com/Jay-electronica-letter-to-falon-lyrics, accessed September 22, 2023.

BECAUSE SCHOOL WAS BUILT FOR ME, THERE'S SO MUCH I DIDN'T KNOW

1. Christopher Emdin, *For White Folks Who Teach in the Hood . . . and the Rest of Y'all Too: Reality Pedagogy and Urban Education* (Boston: Beacon Press, 2016).

2. Emdin, *For White Folks Who Teach in the Hood.*

3. Ibram X. Kendi, *How to Be an Antiracist* (New York: Penguin Random House, 2020).

4. In recent years, I've had the opportunity to co-edit both *The Guide for White Women Who Teach Black Boys* and *Teaching Brilliant Beautiful Black Girls.* This means that many of my ready examples are about white/Black relationships. For the sake of specificity, I use those relationships in this piece, but a discussion about education in "the hood" could be about white teachers and Latinx students, Native students, immigrant students, economically impoverished students, or many other groups.

5. Jarvis R. Givens, *Fugitive Pedagogy: Carter G. Woodson and the Art of Black Teaching* (Cambridge, MA: Harvard University Press, 2021).
6. Vanessa Siddle Walker, *Their Highest Potential: An African American School Community in the Segregated South* (Chapel Hill: University of North Carolina Press, 1996).
7. Lisa Delpit, *Other People's Children: Cultural Conflict in the Classroom*, 2nd ed. (New York: The New Press, 2006).
8. April Baker-Bell, "I Can Switch My Language, but I Can't Switch My Skin: What Teachers Must Understand About Linguistic Racism," in *The Guide for White Women Who Teach Black Boys*, ed. Marguerite W. Penick-Parks et al. (Thousand Oaks, CA: Corwin, 2017), 97–107.
9. Howard C. Stevenson, *Promoting Racial Literacy in Schools: Differences That Make a Difference* (New York: Teachers College Press, 2014).
10. Molefi Kete Asante, *The Afrocentric Idea* (Philadelphia: Temple University Press, 1987), 4.
11. Roxanne Patel Shepelavy, "Teaching Black Teachers," *Philadelphia Citizen*, March 28, 2022, https://thephiladelphiacitizen.org/teaching-black-teachers.

WHITE RACIAL IDENTITY DEVELOPMENT AND RACE-BASED AFFINITY GROUPS

1. W. E. Cross, "The Negro-to-Black Conversation Experience," *Black World* 20, no. 9 (1973): 13–27; Rita Hardiman, "White Identity Development: A Process Oriented Model for Describing the Racial Consciousness of White Americans," PhD diss., University of Massachusetts–Amherst, 1982, publication no. AAI8210330, ScholarWork@UMass Amherst; Janet E. Helms, "An Update of Helm's White and People of Color Racial Identity Models," in *Handbook of Multicultural Counseling*, ed. J. G. Ponterotto, J. M. Casas, L. A. Suzuki, and C. M. Alexander (Thousand Oaks, CA: Sage Publications, 1995), 181–98.
2. Beverly Daniel Tatum, *Why Are All the Black Kids Sitting Together in the Cafeteria? And Other Conversations About Race* (London: Hachette UK, 2017).
3. Tema Okun, "White Supremacy Culture," dRworks, n.d., https://www.dismantlingracism.org/uploads/4/3/5/7/43579015/okun_-_white_sup_culture.pdf, accessed September 22, 2023.

WHITENESS UPON WHITENESS

1. "Characteristics of Public School Teachers," National Center for Education Statistics, last updated May 2023, https://nces.ed.gov/programs/coe/indicator/clr/public-school-teachers; "Race/Ethnicity of College Faculty," National Center for Education Statistics, 2020, https://nces.ed.gov/fastfacts/display.asp?id=61.

2. Eddie Moore Jr., Ali Michael, and Marguerite W. Penick-Parks, eds., *The Guide for White Women Who Teach Black Boys* (Thousand Oaks, CA: Corwin, 2017).
3. John Igwebuike, "Effective Listening: The Secret Sauce of Diversity Consultants," in *The Diversity Consultant Cookbook: Preparing for the Challenge*, ed. Eddie Moore Jr., Art Munin, and Marguerite W. Penick-Parks (New York: Stylus Publishing, 2019), 47–49.

WHERE THE HAND BUILDS THE MINDSET, OR REDESIGNING THE WHITE MINDSET

1. Tim J. Wise, *White Like Me: Reflections on Race from a Privileged Son* (Berkeley, CA: Soft Skull Press, 2011).
2. "Fred Rogers Acceptance Speech—1997, The Emmy Awards," YouTube, posted March 26, 2008, https://www.youtube.com/watch?v=Upm9LnuCBUM&feature=youtu.be.

THE UNBEARABLE WHITENESS OF BOSTON: UNPLUGGING FROM THE NONPROFIT INDUSTRIAL MATRIX

1. J. Anthony Lukas, *Common Ground: A Turbulent Decade in the Lives of Three American Families* (New York: Alfred A. Knopf, 1985).

WHITE BOY/DISRUPTING WHITENESS

1. Paulo Freire, *Education for Critical Consciousness* (New York: Seabury Press, 1973).
2. Cheryl I. Harris, "Whiteness as Property," *Harvard Law Review* 106, no. 8 (1993): 1707–91, doi:10.2307/1341787.
3. Subini Ancy Annamma, "Whiteness as Property: Innocence and Ability in Teacher Education," *Urban Review* 47, no. 2 (2015): 293–316, doi:10.1007/s11256-014-0293-6.
4. Felicia Moore Mensah and Iesha Jackson, "Whiteness as Property in Science Teacher Education," *Teachers College Record* 120, no. 1 (2018): 1–38.
5. Eli Tucker-Raymond and Maria L. Rosario, "Imagining Identities: Young People Constructing Discourses of Race, Ethnicity, and Community in a Contentious Context of Rapid Urban Development," *Urban Education* 52 (2017): 32–60, https://doi.org/10.1177/0042085914550412.
6. Young People's Project (YPP), https://www.typp.org, accessed September 22, 2023.
7. Robert P. Moses and Charles E. Cobb Jr., *Radical Equations: Civil Rights from Mississippi to the Algebra Project* (Boston: Beacon Press, 2002).
8. Tara J. Yosso, "Whose Culture Has Capital? A Critical Race Theory Discussion of Community Cultural Wealth," *Race Ethnicity and Education* 8, no. 1 (2005): 69–91.

9. Ariana Mangual Figueroa, "La carta de la responsibilidad: The Problem of Depar-ture," in *Humanizing Research: Decolonizing Qualitative Inquiry with Youth and Com-munities*, ed. Django Paris and Maisha T. Winn (Los Angeles: Sage, 2014), 129–46.

10. H. Richard Milner IV, "Race, Culture, and Researcher Positionality: Working Through Dangers Seen, Unseen, and Unforeseen," *Educational Researcher* 36, no. 7 (2007): 388–400.

THE MISPLACED OUTRAGE OF WOKE WHITE PARENTS

1. "Demand Rates: 1st Choice On-time Applications for Entry Grades TK, K, 6, 9," Oakland Unified School District, n.d., https://dashboards.ousd.org/views/Demand Dashboard/DemandDashboard?%3AshowAppBanner=false&%3Adisplay_count =n&%3AshowVizHome=n&%3Aorigin=viz_share_link&%3AisGuestRedirect FromVizportal=y&%3Aembed=y, retrieved February 27, 2023.

2. "94609 Home Values," Zillow, n.d., https://www.zillow.com/home-values/97811 /oakland-ca-94609, retrieved February 27, 2023.

3. "Official Enrollment Over Time," Oakland Unified School District, n.d., https:// dashboards.ousd.org/views/Enrollment/Historic?%3Aembed=y&%3AshowApp Banner=false&%3Adisplay_count=n&%3AshowVizHome=n&%3Aorigin=viz _share_link, retrieved February 28, 2023.

4. "Peralta Parent Teacher Group Budget: Where the Money Will Go," infographic, Squarespace, 2018, https://static1.squarespace.com/static/521d4503e4b06c 0489929bb2/t/5b62550d562fa72518558203/1533170957900/PPTGExpenses 1819.pdf.

5. "Washington Elementary School," LocalWiki, n.d., https://localwiki.org/oakland /Washington_Elementary_School, retrieved February 27, 2023.

6. "OUSD School-Based Strategic Regional Analysis: 2017–18," Oakland Unified School District, n.d., https://dashboards.ousd.org/views/SRA1718_SchoolBased /Choice?iframeSizedToWindow=true&%3Aembed=y&%3AshowAppBanner =false&%3Adisplay_count=no&%3AshowVizHome=no, retrieved February 27, 2023; "Official Enrollment Snapshot," Oakland Unified School District, n.d., https://dashboards.ousd.org/views/Enrollment/Snapshot?:embed=y&:showApp Banner=false&:display_count=n&:showVizHome=n&:origin=viz_share_link, retrieved February 27, 2023.

7. "Live/Go: LIVE," Oakland Unified School District, n.d., https://dashboards.ousd. org/views/LiveGo2015–16ForwardPUBLIC/LGMAP1/rattana.yeang@OUSD .ORG/1d4a3b23–1528–4521-a93d-95dab5b2f54c?%3Aembed=y, retrieved February 27, 2023.

8. Zaidee Stavely, "Two Moms Choose Between Separate and Unequal Schools in Oakland," KQED, August 30, 2016, https://www.kqed.org/news/11059974/two -moms-choose-between-separate-and-unequal-schools-in-oakland, retrieved February 27, 2023.

9. Ernest Owens, "White People, I Still Don't Believe You," *Philadelphia* magazine, June 8, 2020, https://www.phillymag.com/news/2020/06/08/white-people-anti -racism, retrieved February 27, 2023.

10. "Letter from Peralta Parents in Support of Potential Sankofa/Peralta Merger, Aug 2019," letter to OUSD school board and superintendent, Google Docs, 2019, https://docs.google.com/document/d/1EDYw9DJ8ff0fF0NojT8PsayEM2KGDfZD 5hqBWPUSiFU/edit, retrieved February 28, 2023.

11. "PPTG and Leadership Committee Meeting Minutes, Peralta Elementary," Peralta Elementary School, n.d., https://www.peraltaschool.org/pptg-meeting -minutes, retrieved 2022.

12. "Letter from Peralta Parents."

13. Ashley McBride, "Families Worried About Merging Sankofa and Kaiser. How Did the School Community Make It Work?" *The Oaklandside*, February 25, 2021, https://oaklandside.org/2021/02/25/sankofa-kaiser-merger-coronavirus-pandemic, retrieved February 28, 2023.

14. James Harris, "Oakland Proud: Do We Give Liberal Protests a Pass?" TownBiz, February 12, 2021, https://townbiz.substack.com/p/oakland-proud, retrieved February 28, 2023.

15. Kelsey Smoot, "White People Say They Want to Be an Ally to Black People. But Are They Ready for Sacrifice?" *The Guardian*, June 29, 2020, https://www.the guardian.com/commentisfree/2020/jun/29/white-people-ally-black-people -sacrifice, retrieved February 26, 2023.

16. Smoot, "White People Say They Want to Be an Ally to Black People. But Are They Ready for Sacrifice?"

FAREWELL

1. We want to acknowledge the far more positive interpretation of what it might mean for white educators to conspire that Jeff Embleton shares in this volume.